This book is to be returned on or before the
last date stamped below.
You may have this book renewed for a further
period if it it not required by another reader.

the spa
directory

THIS IS A CARLTON BOOK

Design copyright © 2002 Carlton Books Limited
Text copyright © 2002 Suzanne Duckett
This edition was published by Carlton Books Limited in 2002
20 Mortimer Street
London W1T 3JW

A CIP catalogue record for this book is available from the British Library.

ISBN 1 84222 522 7

The author and publisher have made every effort
to ensure that all the information in this book is correct
and up to date at the time of publication. Neither the
author nor the publisher can accept responsibility for
any accident, injury or damage that results from using
the ideas, information or advice offered.

Editorial Manager: Judith More

Art Director: Penny Stock

Executive Editor: Zia Mattocks

Editor: Lisa Dyer

Additional text: Alice Whately

Research Assistant: Cressida Seebalack

Picture Editor: Elena Goodinson

Design: DW Design, London

Production Manager: Alastair Gourlay

Printed and bound in Dubai

the spa

directory

suzanne duckett

CARLTON
BOOKS

contents

INTRODUCTION

For me, a good spa combines beauty and medicine, healing and prevention, using both ancient and modern techniques. A spa should provide unadulterated stress-busting pampering and look-better, feel-good beauty treatments. It should be a bolt hole, where you can spend well-deserved 'me' time, and leave feeling that your mind and body are more at one, no matter how short your stay.

Even after ten years working as a health and beauty journalist it's been a hard task to pick the best spas from around the world. By travelling widely, talking to fellow writers and industry experts, and by veering off the beaten track, I have discovered some slightly more unusual and uncharted spas in far-flung places to complement the traditional favourites.

The book is split into four zones around the world, each organized alphabetically by country and with a quick-reference chart, so you can easily find the spas that suit your needs, budget and dreams. The spas have been defined by five categories:

Destination – dedicated to wellbeing; every guest is there to spa.

Hotel/Resort – a spa hosted by a hotel; guests may or may not be there to use the spa facilities.

Day spas – for quick-fix pampering and grooming, you can spend any time from 30 minutes to all day there; usually found in cities.

Medical – more for health than beauty, and combining alternative therapeutic cures and remedies with conventional spa treatments.

Mineral Springs – a spa with its own on-site source of seawater or natural mineral or thermal water used in hydrotherapy treatments.

To help you make sense of the difference between shiatsu and watsu, there's a glossary of spa treatments and therapies, and essential advice on spa etiquette.

Finally, I'd love to hear about spas you have visited and your suggestions on spas you think I should consider adding to *The Spa Directory*. E-mail me at suzanneduckett@thespadirectory.co.uk.

In the meantime, kick back, relax and let me take you to a better place ... Happy spa-ing!

SPA ETIQUETTE

The nudity issue

Don't let bashfulness get in the way of a good treatment. It's the norm to disrobe for massage and body treatments, and your therapist is trained to protect your modesty by draping your body with towels, only exposing the part they are working on. If you prefer, you can leave on your own underwear, or ask for disposable.

Many full body treatments include your bottom and breast area. The French even pay attention to the breast area during facials as they see it simply as an extension of the face and neck. In Germany, France, Eastern Europe and Scandinavia, people tend to go *au naturel*, and you're much more likely to get a male therapist. Even the steam rooms are mixed, with everyone stark-naked, although retiring types can slip into a swimsuit.

If you feel uncomfortable about having a male therapist, ask who will be doing it when you book; if it's a man, tell them you'd prefer a woman. British and American spas tend to be more modest, while therapists in the Far East usually work only on the same sex (they make it very clear otherwise).

Dress (and undress) codes

The dress code outside treatment rooms varies from spa to spa. Destination spas are very informal with people drifting around in towelling robes all day, even for dinner. Check with individual spas about their dress code for evenings, as some do expect you to dress for dinner. In hotels and resort spas, where you're mixing with 'clothed' people, you need to dress for meals and 'out of spa' areas.

Spa manners

• Arrive early for your class or treatment. About 30 minutes in advance is recommended.

• Turn off your mobile (cell) phone. In any spa it's a cardinal sin to have your phone ring.

• Keep your voice down. Spas are places where people go for a bit of peace and quiet. Hot tubs, saunas and steam rooms are also places to unwind and relax, so keep conversations with your best friend down. Respect other people's needs. You may want to start talking to the person lounging next to you but if they're not being particularly responsive to your conversational gambits, let them be.

• Complaining about a treatment after it's finished is like moaning about a bad meal when the waiter comes to clear your plate. Therapists aren't telepathic, so it's up to you to communicate your needs. If you'd rather not listen to music, tell them; if you're uncomfortable with the pressure during a massage, say so.

• Always shower before a treatment/sauna/steam or Jacuzzi.

Tipping

There's no pressure to tip. You can add 10 per cent if you want to but a smile replacing a frown and verbal thanks is usually enough.

Booking

It's imperative to book treatments in advance, especially if you are going somewhere for a few days. Don't leave it until you arrive, as by that time your favourite therapies may well be booked up.

EUROPE

	PAGE	TYPE	PRICE	LUXURY	HEALTHY FOOD	GYM	POOL	OUTDOOR SPORTS	ALTERNATIVE TREATMENTS
Abano Grand Hotel, Italy	53	Hotel/Resort/Medical/Mineral Springs	*	✓	✓	✓	✓	✓	✓
Academy Spa, England	81	Day	**			✓	✓	✓	✓
Aqua Spa at the Sanderson Hotel, England	82	Hotel/Resort/Day	***	✓	✓	✓	✓	✓	✓
Anassa Thalassa Spa, Cyprus	26	Hotel/Resort	***	✓	✓	✓	✓	✓	✓
Bath House at the Royal Crescent Hotel, England	84	Hotel/Resort/Day	**	✓		✓	✓	✓	✓
Berkeley Health Club & Spa, England	86	Hotel/Resort/Day	***	✓	✓	✓	✓		
Bliss London, England	87	Day	***						
Blue Lagoon Geothermal Spa, Iceland	50	Day/Medical/Mineral Springs	*						
Brenner's Park Hotel & Spa, Germany	40	Hotel/Resort/Day/Medical	**	✓	✓	✓	✓	✓	✓
Capri Beauty Farm, Italy	54	Hotel/Resort	***	✓	✓	✓	✓	✓	
Champneys Health Resort, England	88	Destination/Day	**	✓	✓	✓	✓	✓	✓
Charles Worthington Day Spa, England	90	Day	***	✓	✓	✓	✓	✓	✓
Château de Limelette, Belgium	22	Hotel/Resort/Day	*	✓	✓	✓	✓	✓	✓

	PAGE	TYPE	PRICE	LUXURY	HEALTHY FOOD	GYM	POOL	OUTDOOR SPORTS	ALTERNATIVE TREATMENTS
Chewton Glen, England	91	Hotel/Resort/Day	**	✓	✓	✓	✓	✓	✓
Clinique La Prairie, Switzerland	74	Destination/Medical	***	✓	✓	✓	✓	✓	✓
Cowshed, England	92	Hotel/Resort	***	✓		✓	✓	✓	
Danubius Thermal & Grand Hotels Margitsziget, Hungary	46	Hotel/Resort/Day/Medical/Mineral Springs	*	✓	✓	✓	✓	✓	✓
Danubius Thermal Hotel Hévíz, Hungary	48	Hotel/Resort/Medical/Mineral Springs	*		✓	✓	✓		✓
Danubius Thermal & Sport Hotel Bük, Hungary	49	Hotel/Resort/Medical/Mineral Springs	*		✓	✓	✓	✓	✓
Domaine des Hautes Fagnes, Belgium	23	Destination/Hotel/Resort	*			✓	✓	✓	✓
Dorchester Spa, England	93	Hotel/Resort/Day	***	✓	✓	✓	✓	✓	✓
Las Dunas, Spain	69	Destination/Hotel/Resort/Medical	**	✓	✓	✓	✓	✓	✓
Elemis Day Spa, England	94	Day	**	✓		✓			✓
Escape Spa at the Scotsman Hotel, Scotland	111	Hotel/Day	**	✓	✓	✓	✓	✓	✓
La Ferme de Beauté, France	32	Hotel/Resort/Day	**	✓	✓	✓	✓	✓	✓
La Ferme Thermale d'Eugenie, France	33	Hotel/Resort/Mineral Springs	**	✓	✓	✓	✓	✓	✓

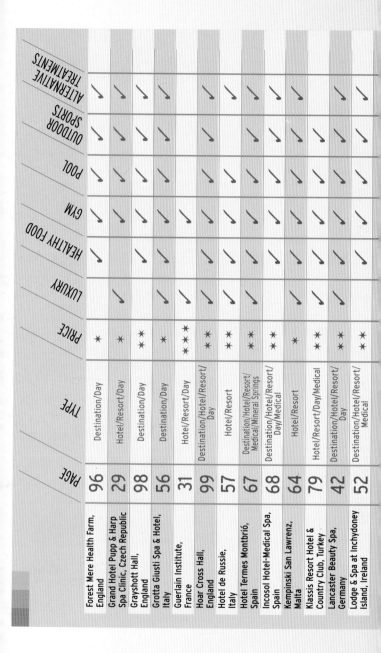

	PAGE	TYPE	PRICE	LUXURY	HEALTHY FOOD	GYM	POOL	OUTDOOR SPORTS	ALTERNATIVE TREATMENTS
Forest Mere Health Farm, England	96	Destination/Day	*			✓	✓	✓	✓
Grand Hotel Pupp & Harp Spa Clinic, Czech Republic	29	Hotel/Resort/Day	*	✓	✓	✓	✓	✓	✓
Grayshott Hall, England	98	Destination/Day	**			✓	✓	✓	✓
Grotta Giusti Spa & Hotel, Italy	56	Destination/Day	*		✓	✓	✓	✓	✓
Guerlain Institute, France	31	Hotel/Resort/Day	***	✓					
Hoar Cross Hall, England	99	Destination/Hotel/Resort/Day	**	✓	✓	✓	✓	✓	✓
Hotel de Russie, Italy	57	Hotel/Resort	**	✓	✓	✓	✓	✓	✓
Hotel Termes Montbrió, Spain	67	Destination/Hotel/Resort/Medical/Mineral Springs	**	✓	✓	✓	✓	✓	✓
Incosol Hotel-Medical Spa, Spain	68	Destination/Hotel/Resort/Day/Medical	**	✓	✓	✓	✓	✓	✓
Kempinski San Lawrenz, Malta	64	Hotel/Resort	*	✓	✓	✓	✓	✓	✓
Klassis Resort Hotel & Country Club, Turkey	79	Hotel/Resort/Day/Medical	**	✓	✓	✓	✓	✓	✓
Lancaster Beauty Spa, Germany	42	Destination/Hotel/Resort/Day	***	✓	✓				✓
Lodge & Spa at Inchydoney Island, Ireland	52	Destination/Hotel/Resort/Medical	**	✓	✓	✓	✓	✓	✓

	PAGE	TYPE	PRICE	LUXURY	HEALTHY FOOD	GYM	POOL	OUTDOOR SPORTS	ALTERNATIVE TREATMENTS
Louison Bobet Thalasso-therapy Centre, Spain	70	Hotel/Resort/Medical	**		✓	✓	✓	✓	✓
Lucknam Park Hotel & Spa, England	100	Hotel/Day	**	✓	✓	✓	✓	✓	✓
Marbert Beauty Farm, Austria	18	Hotel/Resort/Day	**	✓		✓	✓	✓	✓
Mayr Health Spa, Austria	19	Destination/Medical	**		✓	✓	✓	✓	✓
Le Meridien Limassol Spa, Cyprus	28	Hotel/Resort/Day	**	✓	✓	✓	✓	✓	✓
Le Mirador Resort & Spa, Switzerland	76	Destination/Hotel/Resort	***	✓	✓	✓	✓	✓	✓
Naantali Spa Hotel, Finland	30	Hotel/Resort/Day	*			✓	✓	✓	✓
Nirvana Spa, England	101	Day/Mineral Springs	**	✓	✓	✓	✓	✓	
One Spa, Scotland	112	Hotel/Day	**	✓	✓	✓	✓	✓	✓
Pavilion Spa at Cliveden, House, England	102	Hotel/Resort	***	✓	✓	✓	✓	✓	✓
Ragdale Hall Health Hydro, England	103	Destination/Day	**		✓	✓	✓	✓	✓
Rogner-Bad Blumau Hotel & Spa, Austria	20	Destination/Day/Medical	*		✓	✓	✓	✓	✓
Royal Parc Evian, France	36	Hotel/Resort/Day/	**	✓	✓	✓	✓	✓	✓

Quick-reference Charts

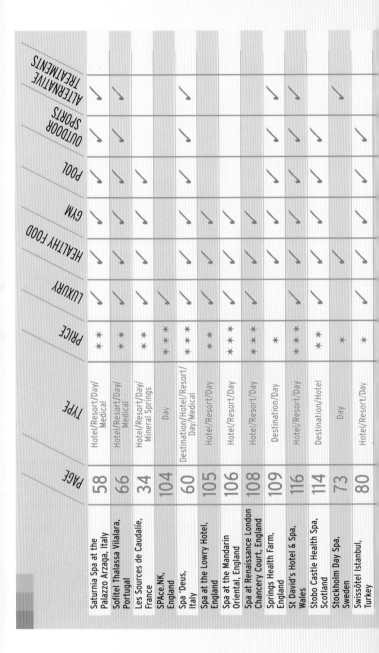

	PAGE	TYPE	PRICE	LUXURY	HEALTHY FOOD	GYM	POOL	OUTDOOR SPORTS	ALTERNATIVE TREATMENTS
Saturnia Spa at the Palazzo Arzaga, Italy	58	Hotel/Resort/Day/Medical	**	✓	✓	✓	✓	✓	✓
Sofitel Thalassa Vilalara, Portugal	66	Hotel/Resort/Day/Medical	**	✓	✓	✓	✓	✓	✓
Les Sources de Caudalie, France	34	Hotel/Resort/Day/Mineral Springs	**	✓	✓	✓	✓		
SPAce.NK, England	104	Day	***	✓	✓	✓	✓		
Spa 'Deus, Italy	60	Destination/Hotel/Resort/Day/Medical	***	✓	✓	✓	✓	✓	✓
Spa at the Lowry Hotel, England	105	Hotel/Resort/Day	**	✓	✓	✓	✓		
Spa at the Mandarin Oriental, England	106	Hotel/Resort/Day	***	✓	✓	✓	✓		
Spa at Renaissance London Chancery Court, England	108	Hotel/Resort/Day	***	✓	✓	✓	✓		
Springs Health Farm, England	109	Destination/Day	*	✓	✓	✓	✓		
St David's Hotel & Spa, Wales	116	Hotel/Resort/Day	***	✓	✓	✓	✓	✓	✓
Stobo Castle Health Spa, Scotland	114	Destination/Hotel	**	✓	✓	✓	✓	✓	✓
Stockholm Day Spa, Sweden	73	Day	*	✓	✓	✓	✓	✓	
Swissôtel Istanbul, Turkey	80	Hotel/Resort/Day	*	✓	✓	✓	✓	✓	✓

	PAGE	TYPE	PRICE	LUXURY	HEALTHY FOOD	GYM	POOL	OUTDOOR SPORTS	ALTERNATIVE TREATMENTS
Termas Marinas Castelar, Spain	72	Destination/Hotel/Resort/Day/Medical	★		✓	✓	✓	✓	✓
Thalassa & Beauty Centre at La Réserve, Belgium	24	Hotel/Resort/Day	★★			✓	✓	✓	
Thalassotherapy Institute, France	38	Hotel/Resort/Medical	★	✓	✓	✓	✓	✓	✓
Thalgo La Baule, France	39	Hotel/Resort/Medical	★	✓	✓	✓	✓	✓	✓
Thermae del Parco, Italy	61	Hotel/Resort/Medical	★★	✓	✓	✓	✓	✓	✓
Thermae Sylla Spa, Greece	44	Destination/Hotel/Resort/Day/Medical/Mineral Springs	★★★	✓		✓	✓	✓	✓
Les Thermes Marins de Monet-Carlo, Monaco	65	Destination/Hotel/Resort	★★★	✓		✓	✓	✓	
Therme Vals, Switzerland	78	Hotel/Resort/Mineral Springs	★★		✓	✓	✓		
Toskana Therme, Germany	43	Destination/Day/Mineral Springs	★		✓		✓		✓
Utopia Health & Leisure Spa, England	110	Day/Hotel	★★			✓	✓		
Villa d'Este, Italy	62	Hotel/Resort	★★★		✓	✓	✓	✓	

Marbert Beauty Farm

✳ ✳

Address: Grand Hotel Sauerhof, A-2500 Baden,
Weilburgstrasse 11-13, Austria
Telephone: (+43) 2252 412 510
Booking details: reservation-sauerhof@rtk.at
Website: www.sauerhof.at

Located at the Grand Hotel Sauerhof in a serene park setting
in the heart of the spa city of Baden, famous for its medicinal
springs, the efficient Marbert Beauty Farm specializes in sulphur
bath-based specialities, alongside the more usual and some not-
so-usual treatments, too. There is an impressive indoor swimming
pool with huge windows all down one side letting in plenty of
natural light, and a sauna, solarium, fitness room and tennis
courts, and bicycles that you can hire to ride around the hotel's
parkland. When you've experienced all the pampering the spa
has to offer, it's worth visiting one of the older, more authentic
Roman-style public thermal baths in the city.

The ambience: The hotel is a big, white, corporate-looking building
with the spa and wellbeing centre attached to it.

Regular guests: Cultural spa-goers at the weekends, and seminar-
and conference-goers during the week.

Treatment menu: An extensive list of treatments: facials, herbal
oil wraps, salt wraps, massage, anti-cellulite treatments, hand and
feet treatments, and waxing, as well as magnetic field therapy.

House speciality: Sulphur baths from the spa's in-house spring, and
Kniepp therapy (baths based on Father Sebastian Kniepp's methods).

Cuisine: Healthy food at the spa, or go to the hotel's gourmet
restaurant for Austrian and international dishes. Detoxers should
steer clear of the hotel's wine cellar and wine-tasting sessions.

Ideal for: A base for indulgence while spa-hopping around Baden.

What to pack: Your own bathrobe and slippers, as they aren't
provided, and a spa map of the area.

Mayr Health Spa

**

Address: A-9082 Maria Worth-Dellach, Kärnten, Austria
Telephone: (+43) 4273 25 110
Booking details: (+43) 4273 25 110
or ilana@360travel.co.uk
Website: N/A

Uniformed nurses, doctors, therapists - even the chefs - at the Mayr Health Spa implement an immaculately healthy (if somewhat lacklustre) lifestyle. An early-rising/early-to-bed regime, strict diets and the best in medical and general care ensure that even the most below-par guest will leave on a high. Although it is not big on beauty-based 'pampering', the spa does offer the glamorous Decléor brand of treatments, and more functional peels and masks, based on sea salt and algae, to enhance the detox process.

The ambience: A no-nonsense spa, like a comfy, health-focused boarding school for adults - there's even a lights-off rule at 9.30 pm.

Regular guests: People from all walks of life who suffer from stress, digestive problems and other medical ailments come here to find relief.

Treatment menu: Diverse medically related programmes, internal purification regimes, intensive diets, exercise therapy and healing treatments, and a few treats - a facial or foot reflex-zone massage.

House speciality: The FX Mayr Health-Cure is worked out to your individual needs. Based on the theory that most physical and emotional disorders result from a malfunctioning digestive system, it includes healing fasts, intestinal detoxes, sound and dance therapy, reflexology and appropriate exercise.

Cuisine: The restaurant caters mainly for restricted diets but the food is generally tasty, light but filling, and easy to digest.

Ideal for: Serious health-seekers willing to dedicate time (two to three weeks is recommended) and to apply themselves to a strict disciplinarian regime, foregoing luxuries and treats.

What to pack: Books or playing cards to while away the evenings.

Rogner-Bad Blumau Hotel & Spa

*

Address: A-8283 Bad Blumau 100, Austria
Telephone: (+43) 3383 5100 9449
Booking details: spa.blumau@rogner.com or
reservierung@blum.rogner.com
Website: www.blumau.com

The Rogner-Bad Blumau Hotel is so dedicated to the quest for health and wellbeing that just checking in gets you free, full use of the indoor and outdoor thermal pools, the freshwater wave pool, cold-water pools, whirlpools, indoor and outdoor sauna areas, the sanarium with colour-light stimulation, Roman and Turkish baths, the aromatherapy chamber, a relaxation area and access to the secluded nudist island. In between all that, you can indulge in the superior spa treatments or activate your mind and body with the huge choice of activities. Like the beauty and holistic wellbeing list, activities on offer span from the mild to the outrageous. There is a gym with personal- and cardiovascular-training experts, spinning and aerobics classes, tennis, biking and horse-riding, as well as aqua jogging (jogging in deep water), Masai walking (inspired by the African-Masais, this requires you to wear specially designed sports shoes that intensify fat-burning). All in all, Rogner-Bad is an all-round health-and-beauty amusement park for adults.

The ambience: The largest work-of-art hotel in the world, the Rogner-Bad Blumau, designed by architect and artist Friedensreich Hundertwasser, is made up of a handful of rainbow-coloured buildings nestling in unspoilt meadowland. Both a unique and unusual look, it's the spa equivalent of Disneyland.

Regular guests: The health-conscious, sporty and those seeking peace and quiet. Many guests return again and again.

Treatment menu: With its own hot springs and every kind of treatment you can think of, plus a lot more you would never dream of, the spa is one of Europe's leading holistic health centres. There is absolutely everything, from therapeutic water cures (to wallow in or swallow), traditional to unusual massages (aromatherapy to Tui

Na and lomi lomi), body cocoons, sound therapy and meditation. The packages are second to none and day passes are available.

House speciality: Any treatment involving the thermal waters is highly recommended. Alternatively, the Cleopatra Bath, in which you bathe in mare's milk and are doused with essential oils, is incredibly nourishing.

Cuisine: Nine restaurants and bars provide a wide choice of international and local cuisine, including à la carte dishes and buffets laden with healthy foods.

Ideal for: Anyone who wants to relax and recharge. If you need to be kept busy, but 'fun busy', to keep your mind off everyday pressures, this would be a good place to come. Children are welcome.

What to pack: The contents of a sports shop. You'll need a gym kit, hiking shoes, cycling shorts, horse-riding gear, a swimsuit (or not, if you're heading to the 'all-over tan' beach, in which case you'll need plenty of sunscreen for sensitive areas).

Château de Limelette

*

Address: Rue Charles Dubois 87, B-1342 Limelette, Belgium
Telephone: (+32) 10 42 19 99
Booking details: chateau-de-limelette@
chateau-de-limelette.be
Website: www.chateau-de-limelette.be

Hidden away in the Lauzelle woods, 30 minutes' drive from Brussels, Château de Limelette is a sumptuous nineteenth-century hotel built in Anglo-Norman style. A flower garden dotted with waterfalls and fountains surrounds the château, which also has an outdoor pool, gym and the largest marine balneotherapy centre in Belgium. The rooms are spacious and tastefully furnished, and the beds are big enough to spend an entire weekend in. Outdoor activities include golf, tennis, squash, mountain biking and clay pigeon shooting.

The ambience: A tranquil hideaway, this hotel blends rural charm with luxurious indulgence to create an escape-from-the-world feel.

Regular guests: Crème de la crème of Belgian society and corporate types milling about the business centre and conference rooms.

Treatment menu: At the light, bright Thalgo Limelette, a team of osteopaths, physiotherapists, hydrotherapists and beauty counsellors efficiently whisk about. Algae, seawater and hot and cold baths are briskly dispensed, in addition to Thai and Tao massages. Smokers tend to head for the respiratory cocoon, while those more interested in cosmetic treatments love the Beauty Centre.

House speciality: The Postnatal Package, which is guaranteed to kickstart your post-baby body beauty plan.

Cuisine: Gastronomes will savour the gourmet menu at the Saint-Jean-des-Bois, which is located in a pretty pavilion overlooking the woods. Low-fat food is served at the Thalgo Light restaurant.

Ideal for: Couples. The magical environs of the château are wonderfully romantic.

What to pack: Beach shoes for the spa.

Domaine des Hautes Fagnes

*

Address: Rue des Charmilles 67,
B-4950 Ovifat-Waimes, Belgium
Telephone: (+32) 80 44 69 87
Booking details: (+32) 80 44 69 87
Website: www.hotel2.be

Located in a protected parkland between the Ardennes and the Rhine valley, the hotel allows the jaded and burnt-out to unwind in the spa or let off steam through diverse activities. The conference halls and meeting rooms mean that the complex can get booked up for corporate events and team-building exercises, but the sports facilities are worth the trip, with nature walks, tennis, volleyball, basketball, badminton, boules, and many more from which to pick. To get a little downtime, visit the sauna, hammam, aqua gym and pool, or take a gymnastics course to help increase your suppleness.

The ambience: A health and sports retreat set in rustic wilderness, where overall wellbeing is achieved through exertion and pampering.

Regular guests: Executives on team-building schemes and fitness fanatics who want mentally and physically challenging pursuits.

Treatment menu: The list includes bust masks, facials, grooming treatments and massages, with marine therapies a speciality.

House speciality: The Anti-Stress Package includes a sauna, steam, water jets, body scrub and the Seaweed Pack – an energizing thalgo treatment – followed by massage and lymphatic drainage.

Cuisine: The Hot Stone Fagna is a customer-participation event; you choose the ingredients and have them cooked right before your eyes. The à la carte restaurant serves seasonal food with a focus on fish.

Ideal for: Families and outdoorsy nature-lovers.

What to pack: Cross-country skis in winter and climbing gear in summer so you can scale Signal de Botrange, Belgium's highest point.

Thalassa & Beauty Centre at La Réserve

✷✷

Address: Elizabetlaan 158-169,
B-8300 Knokke-Heist, Belgium
Telephone: (+32) 50 61 06 06
Booking details: info@la-reserve.be
Website: www.la-reserve.be

Located in Belgium's fashionable seaside resort of Knokke-Heist, the modern low-rise La Réserve hotel is perched on the edge of a shimmering blue lake, making it the ideal hostelrie for watersports enthusiasts. In addition to a 25 x 12 metre (80 x 40 foot) indoor swimming pool, which is filled with heated, purified seawater, and covered tennis and squash courts, guests can also partake in the numerous other sporting activities that are available in the local area, such as bowling, bicycling, golf, go-karting, horse-riding and fencing. The beach is just 300 metres (328 yards) away, and offers perfect conditions for sailing, windsurfing and volleyball. The hotel has a large terrace that stretches right to the water's edge and 110 spacious and elegant rooms (five of which are exclusive suites) – each with its own sunbathing deck.

For those seeking less strenuous activities, there is the spectacular Het Zwin nature reserve, where quiet waterways, salt marshes and silent forests play host to a variety of flora, fauna and bird life. The old town of Knokke-Heist has museums, cultural centres, Norman churches and shops galore. Guests can also visit the neighbouring medieval town of Bruges, with its stunning architecture, quaint streets and chocolate shops selling calorie-laden trays of rich, creamy confectionery.

The ambience: Cool white corridors with black-and-white chequerboard tiled flooring and vaulted ceilings combine with sumptuous European-style furnishings and the occasional dash of Flemish rustica to give a nicely eclectic feel.

Regular guests: Those wanting to combine business with pleasure. The town of Knokke-Heist is a well-known conference centre and international meetings are frequently held in the hotel's numerous boardrooms.

Treatment menu: The treatments at the Thalassa Centre focus on thalassotherapy (the use of seawater, which is rich in mineral salts and oligo-elements that are easily absorbed by the skin, for therapeutic purposes) and fango (mud) remedies. There's also a sauna, Turkish bath (hammam) and hydrojet tub with extra stomach stimulator. Complementary massages include reflexology, shiatsu and Ayurvedic varieties, and the beauty parlour places special emphasis on expert hair removal, stripping guests of every last unwanted strand.

House speciality: The Beauty Centre at La Réserve does not offer any exclusive treatments as such, preferring to concentrate all its energies on the myriad benefits of thalassotherapy.

Cuisine: Healthy European fare is available from La Sirene restaurant, while breakfast is eaten at the Victoria restaurant, which serves hot fresh coffee and warm croissants.

Ideal for: Families; couples; singletons. The beach, golf course, historic town and shopping opportunities provide enough variation to keep everyone happy.

What to pack: Your binoculars so that you can join the 'twitchers' and go bird-watching in the nature reserve.

Anassa Thalassa Spa

⋆⋆

Address: Latsi, 8840 Polis, Cyprus
Telephone: (+357) 26 888 000
Booking details: anassa@thanos-hotels.com
Website: www.thanoshotels.com

The five star Anassa hotel is situated right on the shore of the Asprokemnos Beach, which is considered to be one of the most beautiful stretches of coast off the island of Cyprus. According to local legend, Aphrodite, the Greek goddess of love and beauty, used to bathe nearby at the gateway to the Akamas Peninsula, which makes it a fitting location for the erection of a building dedicated to the serious business of beauty.

Today, spa-goers head to the Thalassa (the Greek word for 'queen') mainly in search of beauty, relaxation and indulgent pampering – love and romance is a given, hence the number of doe-eyed honeymooners. The hotel is built in classical style, with acres of cool marble, and guest villas have the quiet charm of a Byzantine village. All of the rooms are super-spacious and luxurious, and have balconies with panoramic sea views. Some of the suites have private sea-facing terraces, complete with plunge pools and whirlpools.

For those who want to work up a good sweat through aerobic activity – as opposed to watching beads of moisture form while lounging in the sauna – there is a small but adequately equipped gym. It is also possible to join organized rock-climbing and hill-trekking expeditions. Classes in holistic disciplines, such as yoga and tai chi, are also available.

The ambience: Luxurious, elegant and chic, with a clientele to match. The stunning spa is located in an out-of-the-way underground crypt.

Regular guests: Rich and stylish travellers, plus holiday-of-a-lifetime honeymooners.

Treatment menu: The spa specializes in thalassotherapy, hydrotherapy and E'Spa aromatherapy-based treatments. There's also an extensive range of other popular revitalizers, including marine-based algae wraps, massages, reflexology, shiatsu and aromatherapy. More unusual treatments include metamorphic foot massage, which is reputed to unblock the energy lifelines in the body. The hairdressing salon will guarantee to calm your follicles and make sure your crowning glory is restored to its sleek best following periods spent in the frizz-inducing atmosphere of the treatment rooms, saunas, steam baths, Roman-style indoor heated pool and exercise pool.

House speciality: The Seaweed Body Wrap is the best, though perhaps not most glamorous, way to detox (the seaweed is real and the smell is potent).

Cuisine: Four superb restaurants in the hotel offer a wide variety of local and international cuisine, using fresh produce from the spa's own organic farm and a daily supply of fresh, locally caught fish. You can be pretty healthy if you put your mind to it, especially at Pelagos, where there's plenty of Mediterranean-style grilled fish and a range of mouthwatering salads.

Ideal for: A luxurious spa holiday in the sun without too many restraints or deprivations.

What to pack: A designer swimsuit and something chic, simple and stylish for the evenings.

Le Meridien Limassol Spa

**

Address: PO Box 56560, CY 3308 Limassol, Cyprus
Telephone: (+357) 25 862 000
Booking details: enquiries@lemeridien-cyprus.com
Website: www.lemeridien-cyprus.com

Slick and vast, this spa is the only indoor/outdoor thalassotherapy complex in the eastern Mediterranean. There are four outdoor and three indoor seawater pools with specific salinity for various health and beauty benefits. There's also an Algaeotherapy Centre dedicated to detoxing and purifying, an enormous hammam, saunas, whirlpools, two plunge pools and four relaxation areas. Fitness plays a big part here, as does stress management and weight control. Outdoor sports facilities include a jogging route and tennis courts; there is an excellent gym with floor-to-ceiling windows.

The ambience: A calm oasis of water-focused health, beauty and wellbeing within a fun, upbeat holiday resort.

Regular guests: Couples of all ages and nationalities, French and Greek actors, a few ambassadors and the stray executive.

Treatment menu: Around 24 treatment rooms provide standard massages, facials, cellulite-busters and wraps. The sea plays a big part in the treatments and you will be showered (literally) with skin-glowing minerals and salts from the big blue.

House speciality: Plug your ears with earplugs and put on a special eye mask: the Underwater Water Therapeutic treatment gives you a seawater float while a therapist massages your pressure points.

Cuisine: Cypriot specialities are available from the rustic open-air Le Vieux Taverna and there are also French, Japanese and calorie-counted meal options. Poolside and terrace restaurants with lunch buffets offer healthy choices – just keep your eye off the desserts.

Ideal for: Young couples with small children and those who want to have plenty of treatments without breaking the bank.

What to pack: Changes of swimwear for the numerous 'wet areas'.

Grand Hotel Pupp
& Harp Spa Clinic

*

Address: Karlovy Vary, a.s, Mírové náme sti 2,
360 91 Karlovy Vary, Czech Republic
Telephone: (+420) 17 31 09 111
Booking details: rezervace1@pupp.cz or (+420) 17 31 09 630
Website: www.pupp.com

Grand Hotel Pupp is the centrepiece of this spa town. The oldest
building dates back to 1701, while recent additions include spas,
riverside hotels, a garden café and a golf club nearby. The spa
experience is split between the Harp Spa Clinic (linked to the hotel
by a corridor) and its nearby sister facility, the Castle Spa, both
catering for medical ailments, skincare and muscular problems,
both with Roman baths with solariums, steams and saunas.

The ambience: Picturesque, fairytale neo-Baroque grandeur.

Regular guests: Historically, Beethoven, Liszt, Wagner and Dvorak
spent time here; today, guests include Euro-kings, such as Juan
Carlos of Spain and Harald of Norway, and visiting film stars.

Treatment menu: The Harp Clinic list ranges from collagen
facials, lymphatic massages and mud wraps through acupuncture
and homeopathy to medical and preventative therapies, and
rehabilitation programmes for metabolic and muscular disorders.

House speciality: The Baths, filled from a local natural spring –
oxygenated, mineral-rich, sea salt or therapeutic – promise a lift.

Cuisine: No special menu or spa restaurant for spa-goers so select
carefully from the rich desserts and pastries at the Café Pupp. The
hotel's elegant Grand Restaurant Pupp offers an assorted Czech and
international menu for the evening.

Ideal for: Spa buffs polishing their skin ... culture buffs their history.

What to pack: An Eastern European history book – for a sense of
the cultural significance of the spa.

Naantali Spa Hotel

✳

Address: Matkailijantie 2, FIN-21100 Naantali, Finland
Telephone: (+358) 2 44 55 660
Booking details: rezervace1@pupp.cz or
info@naantalispa.fi
Website: www.naantalispa.fi

Overlooking the dramatic Baltic Sea, the Naantali Spa Hotel and
Sunborn Yacht Hotel are linked together by a shopping promenade.
Not surprisingly the theme of the spa is water (health-hunters
have been visiting the hot springs in the town for almost 300 years).
The complex contains four Finnish saunas, two Turkish baths, two
heated Roman pools, two indoor and one outdoor swimming pools,
and exercise pursuits from boxing to watersports. If you take sauna
life as seriously as the Finns, you can book a royal or presidential
suite with your own sauna and open-air terrace.

The ambience: The Naantali is the world's first spa 'ship', as it feels
as though you are on a deluxe cruise, except without the seasickness.

Regular guests: Healthy conventioneers and spa-going tourists.

Treatment menu: There are lots of water-, clay- and peat-based
treatments, including water-jet massage, herbal Jacuzzis and
aromatic baths. Massages, facials and body treats using the French
marine-based Phytomer line can be booked. Physical examinations
and fitness tests for all kinds of conditions are also available.

House speciality: The Polar Night Bath is designed to boost the
mind and body after the long period of winter darkness. A soothing
soak in herbal oils is followed by a dose of light therapy. The Natural
Clay Body Treatment with detoxifying blue clay is another favourite.

Cuisine: A handful of restaurants and bars offer a broad range of
cuisine, from gourmet à la carte to light, healthy buffets.

Ideal for: A cultural/spa trip to Finland, home of the sauna.

What to pack: Young children - the Moomin Valley, the world-
famous nature and fairytale park, is within walking distance.

Guerlain Institute

★★★

Address: Hôtel de Crillon, 10 Place de la Concorde,
75008 Paris, France
Telephone: (+33) 1 44 71 15 00
Booking details: reservations@crillon.com
Website: www.crillon.com

The Guerlain Institute at the Hôtel de Crillon is close to the prestigious boutiques of the Faubourg-St. Honoré, the Champs Elysées, the Louvre and many more of Paris's top cultural spots. Here, exercise is replaced with shopping and sightseeing, and the only weight lost will be from your purse. There are only three small treatment rooms, which are like the hotel bedrooms – fussy, cosy and inextricably French. The treatment list is short but beauty-full. In addition, there are separate saunas and hammans for men and women, and a stylish, wooden-floored gym on the sixth floor.

The ambience: A grand, boudoir-style seventeenth- and eighteenth-century Parisian hotel with a bijou, decadent spa to match.

Regular guests: Well-groomed locals and weekend visitors on a romantic break, who have booked in for some last-minute beautifying.

Treatment menu: As expected, all treatments feature Guerlain's products and consist mainly of ultra-relaxing face and body treats.

House speciality: The Zen Acupression, with the sought-after practitioner Sendi, is a 90-minute Japanese-based, Shiatsu-style massage that aims to rebalance vital energies. It consists of stretching movements and pressure applied to energy points.

Cuisine: It's more a case of eating wealthy than healthy here. Fattening French gastronomy rules, so forget calorie-counting. Eyebrows being in perfect shape are what counts here.

Ideal for: Girls who put self-indulgent, complexion-perfecting facials and pampering massages (that involve lying down) as a priority over anything that involves effort on their part.

What to pack: Your lover – it's hopelessly romantic here.

La Ferme de Beauté

✳ ✳

Address: Les Fermes de Marie, Chemin de Riante Colline,
74120 Megève, France
Telephone: (+33) 4 50 93 03 10
Booking details: contact@fermesdemarie.com
Website: www.c-h-m.com

The mountain retreat, Les Fermes de Marie, is 69 chalet-style rooms in eight lodges. Heart-shaped shutters and Ralph Lauren-style interiors create a stylish cosiness. The spa building is built from smooth, glaciated boulders, which are said to emit a healing energy and, judging by the contented expressions on the staff and guests, the theory's very plausible. The ten treatment rooms are decorated with wood beams, stone and terracotta tiling. To compensate for that fondue meal, there's a glass-walled pool, fitness and stretching classes, a small gym, plus skiing in winter and walking in summer.

The ambience: Homey and cosy. This mini alpine hamlet combines a spa holiday with a taste of mountain living.

Regular guests: The King and Queen of Sweden rent a private chalet here during ski season, but more down-to-earth families visit, too, with their raucous children and dogs.

Treatment menu: Facials, wraps and body treatments use Les Fermes de Marie's own line of products, Edelweiss, made from mountain herbs and flowers. In addition, there is hydrotherapy, whirlpools, massages, LaStone Therapy and reflexology.

House speciality: The Body Pack with Mountain Plant Oils involves being enveloped in a moisturizing body pack for 20 minutes.

Cuisine: A diet menu is available, although it's not pushed. Rôtisserie offers healthy-ish food and the Gastronomy serves French cuisine. As for the cheese-themed Fromagerie, dieters will have to resist.

Ideal for: A family who want laid-back luxury and extra-special treatment for the kids – who get to eat supper in their own den.

What to pack: Your dog, if you have one, and skiwear in winter.

La Ferme Thermale d'Eugenie

✶✶

Address: Les Pres d'Eugénie, 40320 Eugénie-les-Bains,
Landes, France
Telephone: (+33) 5 58 05 06 07
Booking details: guerard@relaischateaux.fr
Website: www.michelguerard.com

Four hotels, three restaurants and the spa are settled in 16 hectares (40 acres) of landscaped park. The experience here is a wonderful combination of spa life and the good life. The French don't believe in sacrificing pleasures to look good, but instead focus on give and take – giving in to lavish food and good wine, and taking away the results with a detoxifying body wrap. La Ferme Thermale d'Eugenie is styled like a half-timbered Landaise farmhouse and the baths date back to 1750. Serious curists stay at La Maison Rose, the simplest and least expensive of the hotels, where only *cuisine minceur* is on the menu.

The ambience: This spa/hotel/restaurant hamlet oozes exquisite French country charm and smacks of rustic luxury.

Regular guests: Tense, exhausted city-dwellers from all over the world looking for unabashed, honest pampering and relaxation.

Treatment menu: Treatments revolve around the waters from the spa's thermal spring: hydromassage, thermal mudbaths and steams.

House speciality: The Kaolin (white clay) Bath, invented in 1976 by co-owner Michel Guérard, is a soak in a sunken bath filled with a fine clay blend – recommended for rheumatism, digestive problems and stress.

Cuisine: Chef Michel Guérard developed *cuisine minceur* (basically, lean cuisine) in the 1970s; hence, the spa food is probably the best you'll find anywhere. Alternatively, Restaurant Michel Guérard boasts three Michelin stars and pays homage to classic Landes cuisine.

Ideal for: Spa-goers who believe in 'everything in moderation'.

What to pack: Stylish, understated clothes.

Les Sources de Caudalíe

**

Address: 33650 Martíllac, Bordeaux, France
Telephone: (+33) 5 57 83 82 82
Booking details: vino@caudalie.com
Website: www.caudalie.com

The luxurious Les Sources de Caudalíe in Bordeaux has just under 50 rooms and suites, and the food – whether light spa options or gourmet cuisine – is overseen by a two-Michelin-star chef. Here, the food philosophy is small, carefully monitored portions rather than heaps of tasteless non-fat chow that leaves you feeling empty. Plus, you're actually encouraged to drink red wine with your meals, as the staff preach that one, two at the most, glasses of wine a day are good for you.

Attached to the hotel, the Vinotherapie spa is set in the stunning Graves Vineyards of the Châteaux Smith Haut Lafitte Winery, making it the first grapevine spa in the world. Built in wood and marble, it's calming in a very non-clinical way and the treatments are as enjoyable as they are effective. French women aren't

famous for their enthusiasm for exercise, so working out isn't big here. However, there is a gym (usually empty), and bicycles can be hired for a ride through the vineyard's quiet, winding dirt tracks.

The ambience: Modern minimalism meets French country in the spa, while the cream-coloured stone hotel, filled with antiques, feels more like an old château.

Regular guests: Slim, stylish French women, along with trendy, young Europeans and wine-lovers touring Bordeaux.

Treatment menu: Massages, body wraps and baths combining the virtues of naturally hot water drawn from the spring – some 540 metres (1,800 feet) below the vineyard, and rich in minerals and trace elements – with Vinothérapie, the beautifying and anti-ageing benefits of grapes. The Crushed Cabernet Body Scrub, made from grapeseed oil, Bordeaux honey and organic essential oils, leaves skin clear and smooth. The Sauvignon Massage uses grapeseed oil from Sauvignon grapes, along with organic oils, and is intoxicatingly relaxing (if you like a firm massage, you'll need to tell your therapist). There are also familiar favourites: manicures, pedicures, facials and waxing. The two- to six-day packages, with focuses on relaxing, slimming and fitness, among others, are superb.

House speciality: The Wine Barrel Bath is a hydromassage jet experience that involves sitting in a wooden wine barrel full of exploded chilled grapes. It is said to improve circulation, help eliminate cellulite and either relax or rejuvenate, depending upon your preference.

Cuisine: The low-calorie, detoxification diet served in La Table du Lavoir is calorie-patrolled rather than -controlled. Lunches and dinners only contain 500 calories but still manage to be delicious. The food in the hotel restaurant, La Grand Vigne, is another matter – excess body matter! However, purists can embark on Caudalíe's detoxification diet, the medically supervised *cure de raisin* programme that involves eating grapes and grapes alone for seven days during the harvest months of September to October.

Ideal for: A spa-lover and a wine-lover. The latter can take a wine class while the other enjoys the spa, and both will be happy.

What to pack: A swimsuit for all the 'wet' treatments.

Royal Parc Evian

★★

Address: South Bank of Lake Geneva, BP8,
74501 Evian-les-Bains Cedex, France
Telephone: (+33) 4 50 26 85 00
Booking details: reservation@royalparcevian.com
Website: www.royalparcevian.com

The beautiful Royal Parc Evian is essentially a private park-holiday resort with two hotels, sports facilities, spa and outdoor activities spread over a spacious and tranquil 17 hectares (42 acres). All of the staff are friendly and take great pride in the Royal Parc's reputation for having a first-class spa and healthy, tasty, creative food. Grass tennis courts, an equestrian centre, a climbing wall, golf course and archery are among the activities you can try after you've been re-energized in the spa – skiing trips can also be arranged in winter. If you just want to finish off your book, there is ample summertime chill-out space by the pool, in the rose garden or on the banks of Lake Geneva.

Accommodation is divided between the Hotel Royal and the Hotel Ermitage, both within the Royal Parc complex. The most cost-effective way to enjoy the resort is to book the spa treatments and accommodation together.

The ambience: A stylish, health-orientated modern indoor – and a lush, green outdoor – playground for all ages, nestled between the mountains and idyllic Lake Geneva.

Regular guests: International and French holiday-makers who want a bit of everything in the leisure-and-pleasure department.

Treatment menu: The on-site Better Living Institute is a sizeable wellbeing facility with an à la carte choice of relaxation therapies, massages, aesthetic body and facial treatments, fangotherapy (mud therapy), reflexology and a broad range of re-energizing and detoxifying scrubs, rubs and wraps. Doctors and dieticians are available to advise on nutrition, assess your profile and work out a programme tailored to your specific needs. Highly trained staff work throughout the 13 treatment rooms, 12 hydrotherapy rooms and nine massage rooms, which facilitate top-quality treatments.

House speciality: The epic five-day Re-Energize Plan is a combination of indulgences to treat every inch of your outer body, including toning, moisturizing, massaging, and many more. Simultaneously, your inner body is reborn through such therapies as vital organs stimulation, flexibility training and lymphatic drainage. Each day has a theme: Purity, Deep Relaxation, Balance, Re-Energizing and Re-Vitalization.

Cuisine: The Parc has eight eateries. Notable are the Jardin des Lys, which serves Synergetic Cuisine, a specially developed style of cooking that combines the properties of each ingredient to produce a desired outcome, such as re-energizing, balancing or purity. The overall aim of Synergetics is to provide low-calorie, high-energy food. If required, a chef and dietician can work together on creating bespoke combinations for inspired low-calorie gastronomy. The more formal French Le Café Royal is not so health-conscious and serves rich, showy, modern, devil-may-care three-course meals.

Ideal for: A week-long holiday for an active family, a fit and healthy couple of any age, or two girlfriends looking to pamper themselves.

What to pack: Your lucky dress for evenings at the nearby casino - to win enough for your next visit.

Thalassotherapy Institute

*

Address: Atlanthal Hotel, 153 Boulevard des Plages,
64600 Anglet, Biarritz, France
Telephone: (+33) 5 59 52 75 75
Booking details: info@atlanthal.com
Website: www.atlanthal.com

Located just 45 metres (50 yards) from one of the most beautiful beaches on the Basque coast, the Atlanthal is a modern low-rise hotel which sprawls over three floors. The light, airy guest rooms have views overlooking either the Atlantic or the parkland. The hotel, close to the Chiberta golf course, offers guests the relaxing combination of rambling the fairways and wallowing in the spa's hydrotherapy pools. There's a gym and outdoor pool, while hiking, biking, horse-riding, watersports and tennis are also available.

The ambience: Friendly and relaxed. Because the hotel welcomes babies and young children, there's an easy-going atmosphere.

Regular guests: Families – the Txiki Club occupies children aged between 4 and 12 years old while you pamper yourself senseless.

Treatment menu: Hydrotherapy, mud treatments, anti-stress massages, shiatsu and programmes to combat 'heavy legs' are on offer. A six-day stop-smoking regime includes acupuncture, dietary consultation and effective ways to manage withdrawal, combined with aerosol treatments and a special smoker's facial.

House speciality: The Future Maman features hydrotherapy, algotherapy, massage, bust treatments, facial and nutritional consultation. The Jeune Maman includes slimming and firming rubs, vertebrae re-alignment, hydrotherapy and baby swimmer sessions.

Cuisine: In addition to serving traditional French food, the chefs also produce personalized eating plans.

Ideal for: Parents, keen golfers and ocean bathers: the bracing Atlantic water is guaranteed to boost vitality.

What to pack: Your own and your baby's health records.

Thalgo La Baule

✳

Address: Royal-Thalasso Barrière, 6 Avenue Pierre Loti,
44504 La Baule, France
Telephone: (+33) 2 40 11 48 48
Booking details: royalthalasso@lucienbarriere.com
Website: www.lucienbarriere.com

Located in a wooded park facing the Atlantic Ocean in Brittany,
the Royal-Thalasso Barrière hotel has an imposing neo-Norman
façade and evokes the *belle époque* spirit of Old World seaside
resorts. Rooms are fittingly traditional with boldly patterned
fabrics, a strong colour palette and wooden balconies overlooking
a sandy beach. There's a fully equipped gym at the spa, and guests
can tee off at the 45-hole Golf International Barrière course.

The ambience: Light, bright and very discreet. The serene spa
atmosphere enables guests to instantly relax.

Regular guests: The Parisian party set, families and golf obsessives.

Treatment menu: Organized on three levels to cater for seawater,
dry and beauty treatments, the Thalassotherapy Centre employs
a team of physicians, physiotherapists, hydrotherapists, osteopaths
and dieticians, who adopt a holistic approach to health, beauty and
fitness. In addition to the Thalgo Osteoarthritis Cure, Thalgo Diet
and Slimming Cure, and the MédiMer Anti-Ageing Cure, there's also
reflexology, aromatherapy, shiatsu, treatments for postnatal and
menopausal women, and an anti-tobacco programme.

House speciality: Thalasso New Look guarantees the makeover of
your life. Under the scrutiny of a make-up artist, hairdresser and style
consultant, this six-day course helps you to enhance your image.

Cuisine: Gourmet dishes are available at the hotel, while low-calorie
options are served in the spa.

Ideal for: Mothers with babies, and lovers of this part of the world –
Brittany has beautiful beaches, salt marshes and ancient pine forests.

What to pack: Your paints to capture the scenery on canvas.

Brenner's Park
Hotel & Spa

* *

Address: Schillerstrasse 4-6, D-76530 Baden-Baden, Germany
Telephone: (+49) 72 21 90 05 00
Booking details: reservations@brenners.com
Website: www.brenners.com

The spa, situated in the hotel building, offers an array of modern-day facilities, many inspired by the town's Roman origins. There is an ancient Rome-style swimming pool bordered with an impressive colonnade and heated benches to keep towels warm, two side-by-side whirlpools designed for one person in each, and a Frigidarium, an open-air cold-water plunge pool for serious chilling out.

The highlight is the Spa Suite, which comes complete with a butler to look after your every whim. The suite can be booked by individuals who want time on their own or by groups of up to four people. It contains a Laconicum (a heated room) with green quartzite mosaic benches that gently warm the body,

helping to sweat out toxins. It also has a Japanese flower blossom steam room, infused with the essences of jasmine and orchids, a sauna, a revitalizing shower with rain, mist, light and aroma effects, and a large whirlpool.

The physically active can try their hands at indoor and outdoor tennis, a fully equipped gym with in-house private trainers, a sprung-floor aerobics studio and separate meditation studio, plus spacious gardens for strolling, power walking or jogging. For nature-friendly fitness fans, there are also opportunities to go mountain biking and climbing.

The ambience: Brenner's Park Hotel, which dates back to 1872, has an old-time grandeur and is adorned with flamboyant flower displays, chandeliers and marble baths with gold taps (faucets). The modernized spa is just as showy.

Regular guests: Mature couples on healthy breaks and traditionalists wanting to 'take the waters' that Baden-Baden is famous for, as well as guests from the neighbouring Caracalla Baths – one of the grandest bathhouses in the world (bathing there is *au naturel*, so be prepared if you intend to visit).

Treatment menu: Facials and body treatments include massages, scrubs, body packs with essential oils, make-up advice, manicures and pedicures. The day- and week-long programmes are worth considering as they offer a good balance of treatments to tie in with the length of your stay.

House speciality: The Meridian Acupressure massage is designed to decrease stress, tension and lethargy, and to increase energy and enthusiasm.

Cuisine: Both gourmet and spa, international and regional, cuisine is available in the main dining room. There is also the more casual Black Forest Grill, or have your meal alfresco on the Summer Terrace. Fitness cocktails and vitamin drinks can be enjoyed in the Sports Bar.

Ideal for: Spa-goers who want first-class, old-world hotel charm coupled with modern spa facilities.

What to pack: Something glamorous for the casino.

Lancaster Beauty Spa

✳ ✳

Address: Schlosshotel Lerbach, Lerbacher Weg,
D-51465 Bergisch Gladbach, Germany
Telephone: (+49) 22 02 20 40
Booking details: info@schlosshotel-lerbach.com
Website: www.schlosshotel-lerbach.com

Just ten-minutes drive from Cologne, the Schlosshotel Lerbach is a fairytale castle situated in one of Germany's most beautiful parks. Surrounded by gentle rolling hills, the hotel, with its ivy-covered façade, has an indoor pool and 54 rooms and suites – all of which are decked out in English country-house style. The Lancaster Beauty Spa is low key but professional and is perfect for the more diffident spa-goer who is likely to want as much privacy as possible.

The ambience: Sybaritic, serene and seriously stylish.

Regular guests: Couples and business executives: the hotel has three conference salons where delegates can fuel corporate chat with delicious German food and wine.

Treatment menu: In addition to algae, mud and nine different water therapies, guests can indulge in a range of top-class treatments using products by La Prairie, Sisley and Lancaster. If you like serious pampering, try the caviar facial or the silk glove massage. There's also aromatherapy, light therapy and LaStone massage.

House speciality: The Thalasso Plus Cure is a 180-minute treatment, which includes algae body peeling, an algae bath, and personalized body treatment and facial. At the end of the cure, guests can repair to a relaxation room to sip a cup of mineral-packed algae tea.

Cuisine: The Dieter Müller restaurant serves gourmet food that is light as a feather, while the Castle restaurant offers regional cuisine.

Ideal for: The garden pavilion offers the perfect location for a wedding, followed by a reception in the rose garden or courtyard.

What to pack: Your walking shoes and a head for heights – hot-air ballooning is available nearby (as are tennis and cycling).

Toskana Therme

*

Address: Hotel an der Therme, Wunderwaldstr 2a,
D-99518 Bad Sulza, Germany
Telephone: (+49) 36 46 19 28 81
Booking details: hoteltherme@aol.com or
toskana@kbs.de
Website: www.liquid-sound.com

Funky, modern and minimalist, the Hotel an der Therme looks more like a luxury ocean liner than a guesthouse. Situated in the ancient spa town of Bad Sulza, the rooms are decorated with modern artworks and overlook the cultural region of Weimar, where bushy forests, vineyards and rolling hillsides are dotted with castles. Next door is Toskana Therme, the hotel's futuristic spa, housed beneath vast domed ceilings. Guests can wallow in a choice of four saltwater pools, or dive into the clear waters of the Liquid Sound Temple, which offers relaxing underwater light and sound projections.

The ambience: Hip and happening.

Regular guests: Journalists, photographers and TV producers.

Treatment menu: In addition to steams and saunas, guests can also enjoy light and colour therapies. A wellness programme offers treatments from reiki to Hawaiian healing massage. Skincare and cosmetic consultations are comprehensive, and holistic and medical treatments are available at Klinkzentrum Bad Sulza.

House speciality: Aqua Wellness is a deeply relaxing aquatic therapy, which takes place in a warm pool and invites you to re-experience the security of floating in the womb. Ideal for anyone suffering from joint or muscle pain, the programme combines soft stretching movements, deep tissue massage and breathwork.

Cuisine: Diet menus are available; otherwise, traditional German fare.

Ideal for: Anyone interested in experiencing a totally new multimedia phenomenon – and music buffs.

What to pack: Your goggles, so you can open your eyes underwater.

Thermae Sylla Spa

* *

Address: Wellness Hotel, Loutra Aedipsos, Evia, Greece
Telephone: (+30) 22 606 0100
Booking details: thermaesylla@thermaesylla.gr or
sales@thermalia.co.uk
Website: www.thermaesylla.gr

Perched on a promontory overlooking the crystal-clear sea of Evoikos, the 100-year-old Thermae Sylla Spa is an impressively neo-classical palace, which has recently been lavishly refurbished. Rooms are large and comfortable, the outdoor pool big enough to get some laps underway, and the gym has magnificent views over the sea and mountains. The hotel is also close enough to Athens for guests to take a day trip to Delphi, Olympia and the Acropolis.

The spa is famed for its restorative mineral waters, which have been spouting up from their earthy depths for 5,000 years. According to legend, Hercules was an early convert to their curative powers, using the waters to soothe his strapping limbs. In addition, both Aristotle and Plutarch regarded the thermal waters of Aedipsos as the most powerful known to man, while scientists today acknowledge them as packing a cocktail of minerals that can help ease all manner of ills, including arthritis, rheumatism, skin problems and even gynaecological disorders.

The ambience: The swankiest hotel in town, the Thermae Sylla Spa mixes expensive decor with a minimalist approach. Expanses of marble are embellished with crystal chandeliers and gilt-edged mirrors, but the all-white colour scheme is conducive to soothing the mind, body and soul. Exceptionally friendly staff is another feature – and special attention is lavished on singletons.

Regular guests: Well-heeled Athenians, who bill it as one of the best places to get 'up close and personal' with Greek actors and bouzouki singers. Greta Garbo, Sir Winston Churchill, Omar Sharif and Maria Callas have also dipped their toes in the waters here.

Treatment menu: All new guests have a medical consultation, following which a personal programme is drawn up. There are 35 hydrotherapy treatments to choose from, including a Volcano

Steam Bath, which mixes the steam from rocks with the therapeutic waters to ease aches and pains. Reflexology, inhalation therapy, for the prevention and cure of respiratory ailments, and Kraxenofen and Haybath, special therapies for back and neck pain, are also available. For pure indulgence, the Cream Cleopatra bath is highly recommended. Guests lie naked on a waterbed while their body is slathered in a deep moisturizing cream. They are then wrapped in tissue, covered with a heated blanket and left to emerge 30 minutes later. The grape-paste facial is another star treatment.

House speciality: The Oriental Rasul takes place in the hammam. Guests daub their bodies with Moroccan fango muds before sliding onto a heated turquoise-tiled throne and inhaling the herbal-infused steam. Meanwhile, soft music plays and tiny lights twinkle overhead. After 30 minutes, a soft rain descends to wash off the mud and you are ushered into a candle-lit relaxation room.

Cuisine: The hotel has two restaurants, both of which place great emphasis on organic ingredients. Lightly grilled meat and fish dishes, accompanied by steamed vegetables and salads drizzled with olive oil, are available at the Mediterranean restaurant, while the Edipsos serves traditional Greek dishes.

Ideal for: New mothers, who want to be pampered following childbirth, and single people on a touring holiday.

What to pack: Your sunglasses – the glare from the bright light bouncing off the white-painted buildings can be a little harsh.

Danubius Thermal & Grand Hotels Margitsziget

*

Address: H-1138 Budapest, Margitsziget, Hungary
Telephone: (+36) 1 452 6200
Booking details: margotel@hungary.net
Website: www.danubiusgroup.com

Situated on the beautiful island of Margitsziget in Budapest, and surrounded by the cool blue waters of the river Danube, the luxurious Danubius Thermal Hotel, adjacent to the older, more traditional Grand Hotel, is fast becoming known for the excellence of its newly renovated spa. A modern building, surrounded by thick forest, the hotel has indoor and outdoor swimming pools, as well as facilities for tennis and cycling. Rooms are modern and comfortable with views over the surrounding parkland or across the river.

The historical Grand Hotel, which was built in 1873 and restored in 1987, is linked to the Thermal Hotel by a heated underground

passageway. Elegantly furnished in a classical style (there are acres of marble floors), guest rooms have views either over the park or the river. The centre of Budapest is a short drive away, and offers a wealth of cultural sights for guests who want to explore one of Europe's most romantic cities.

The ambience: Clinical and comprehensive. In addition to the health and fitness centre, the first floor is devoted to medical services, including cardiology, laser eye treatments, dentistry and facial cosmetic surgery.

Regular guests: Wealthy Hungarians, couples and families with children old enough to appreciate the beauty of Budapest.

Treatment menu: The recently renovated Danubius Premier Fitness Club has stunning views over the island and features all the facilities of a first-rate spa. In addition to balneotherapy — there are three thermal springs on the island — there is also a fully equipped gym and spinning, step and stretch classes. Personal trainers are available on request and there are also classes in complementary disciplines such as yoga, tae-bo, tai chi, and qi-gong. The oxygen inhalation treatment is especially beneficial for smokers, while the Thai massage and underwater massage will benefit anyone suffering from muscle and joint pain. Guests looking for more superficial improvements should visit the Beauty Salon Anna, which uses Guinot and !QMS collagen products. Teeth whitening at the dental clinic is another option.

House speciality: The fresh fango (mud) baths, which are comprised of decomposed aquatic plants transported from nearby Lake Hévís, are excellent for easing rheumatic complaints. The mud is mixed with the thermal waters to create a potent and energizing body treatment.

Cuisine: Traditional Hungarian hot dishes — as well as lighter, less indulgent fare — are served at restaurants in both hotels.

Ideal for: Older people who will find the restorative natural thermal waters particularly beneficial for such geriatric complaints as rheumatism, arthritis and back pain.

What to pack: A guide book to make the most of Budapest, should you venture out.

Danubius Thermal Hotel Hévíz

*

Address: Kossuth Lajos u 9-11, Hévíz H-8380, Hungary
Telephone: (+36) 83 341 180
Booking details: dhtheviz@mail.matav.hu
Website: www.danubiusgroup.com/heviz/

Set close to the lake in Hévíz − a countryside town in one of Hungary's most beautiful regions − the Thermal Hotel is a modern seven-storey building surrounded by trees. A mecca for anyone suffering from joint or muscle pain, the thermal waters from the lake are the most abundant in Europe. There's an indoor pool at the spa, while guests who prefer to bathe alfresco can visit Lake Balaton. There's also a biocosmetic beauty salon.

The ambience: Rustic, friendly and low-key, the focus is on curative treatments to help guests return home free from pain.

Regular guests: The older generation, who are more likely to suffer from degenerative disorders.

Treatment menu: Following a diagnostic examination, guests are prescribed balneo-, electro- and mechanotherapies to help relieve rheumatic, arthritic and circulatory problems. Treatments using the lake's highly curative peat mud are also available, in addition to massages such as reflexology and lymphatic drainage. Exercise classes and a fasting programme are also available for those who need to shed some pounds.

House speciality: The Subaquale Traction Bath helps to free up movement of the spine. Weights are fastened around the waist and the client is then suspended in thermal waters for 15-20 minutes.

Cuisine: Hungarian cuisine, as well as vegetarian and diet dishes, are offered at the hotel's two restaurants.

Ideal for: Anyone suffering from a bad back or rheumatoid arthritis.

What to pack: Your medical notes.

Danubius Thermal &
Sport Hotel Bük

*

Address: Bük H9740, Hungary
Telephone: (+36) 94 558 500
Booking details: thermal.sales@savaria.hu
Website: www.danubiusgroup.com/buk

Close to the Austrian border, the Thermal & Sport Hotel Bük is a luxurious, modern hostelry with numerous sporting facilities. There's an 18-hole golf course, indoor and outdoor pools, tennis and squash, and the chance to enjoy cycling, volleyball, basketball, horse-riding, shooting and water polo. Rooms are modern, bright and cheerful, and the new Fun Bath in the landscaped gardens has whirlpools, power showers and underwater massages. Less sporty types will be relieved to find that there's plenty of culture, too. The medieval town of Sopron boasts more than 200 diverse historical buildings and guests can visit the open-air theatre at Fertörákos.

The ambience: Relaxed and informal. Although this hotel has all the luxury of a four-star establishment, it has none of the attitude.

Regular guests: Families or couples wanting to sightsee and work out.

Treatment menu: In addition to balneotherapy and mud treatments, there's also a traction bath guaranteed to bring relief to bad backs. Complementary therapies include massage, reflexology, acupuncture, aromatherapy, Ayurveda and yoga. Beauty offerings include anti-cellulite treatments, permanent make-up and teeth-bleaching.

House speciality: Osteoporosis Kinesitherapy. A new treatment that includes gentle massages using oil, underwater massage, balneotherapy and steam.

Cuisine: A choice of Hungarian, international and low calorie dishes is available at Nils Holgersson, the hotel's main restaurant.

Ideal for: Those who want to get fit in an unpressurized environment.

What to pack: Golf shoes.

Blue Lagoon Geothermal Spa

*

Address: PO Box 22, 240 Grindgavik, Blaa Ionio, Iceland
Telephone: (+354) 420 8800
Booking details: (+354) 420 8800
Website: www.bluelagoon.is

The Blue Lagoon is located on the Reykjanes peninsula in south-western Iceland, just 15 minutes from Keflavik International Airport and 40 minutes from the cultural capital, Reykjavik. The lagoon is bright turquoise in colour and surrounded by geothermal white beaches, broiling geysers, lava caves and silica mud flats. Wallowing in the steaming waters here makes you feel like you're on another planet. In fact, Iceland's lunar-type landscape is so out of this world that Neil Armstrong chose it to rehearse his moonwalk. The spa's state-of-the-art facilities include modern changing rooms and showers, an indoor lagoon pool, silica mud areas, a private geothermal beach and a geothermal sauna located inside a lava cave.

Dedicated converts can take home (or buy online through the website) Blue Lagoon geothermal skincare products, which are specially formulated with the active ingredients

unique to the thermal waters. As it is a day spa, guests usually stay at the nearby Hotel Blue Lagoon.

The ambience: Otherworldly and ethereal. The backdrop of lunar landscape and the imposing, futuristic, metal Swartsengi power station, which generates electricity from the geothermal seawater, makes this natural lagoon look like something out of *Star Wars*. And speaking of stars, the Northern lights are spectacular here.

Regular guests: Locals (businessmen to housewives, young to old), tourists and those looking for a natural cure for skin conditions, such as psoriasis and eczema. Francis Ford Coppola, Kevin Costner and Jerry Seinfeld have dipped in here, too.

Treatment menu: The Blue Lagoon's geothermal mineral-rich seawater is treatment in itself. Bursting with natural active ingredients, including gently cleansing and exfoliating white silica mud, nourishing and softening blue-green algae and balancing, relaxing salts, the water's been scientifically proven for its healing effect on skin diseases. There's also an outpatient clinic here with trained medical experts dedicated to the treatment of more serious cases of psoriasis.

House speciality: The shoulder massage is a gentle soothing treatment that takes place in the lagoon. Being massaged while enveloped in the warm healing waters is deeply relaxing and restorative. 'Land' massages include an energy treatment designed to enhance your energy flow, using oils based on Blue Lagoon silica mud, and eucalyptus and pine oils. The Luxury package, which consists of a ten-minute massage in the lagoon, followed by some extra time to wallow, before being slathered in a mud mask, is a good all-rounder.

Cuisine: The modern café, with stunning views over the lagoon, has a 'global' menu. It uses the best-available Icelandic ingredients, including fresh seafood from the local fishing village Grindavík. Unfussy, tasty dishes, such as Mediterranean bouillabaisse and poached salmon with lemon sauce, delight all visitors.

Ideal for: Anyone suffering from a skin disorder.

What to pack: A stylish, any-colour-but-turquoise, swimsuit to stand out from the crowd.

Lodge & Spa at Inchydoney Island

**

Address: Clonakilty, West Cork, Ireland
Telephone: (+353) 23 33143
Booking details: reservations@inchydoneyisland.com
Website: www.inchydoneyisland.com

Although close to Cork, the Lodge & Spa sits by the edge of two stunning beaches with powder-fine sand. The main feature is the impressive Thalassotherapy Centre – the only one outside Continental Europe – which pumps fresh ocean seawater, filtered and heated to body temperature, daily into a magnificent pool containing massage jets to soothe stressed-out muscles. You can come here to change your life, or simply take a pollution-free breather from it.

The ambience: Peaceful and remote; the sound of surf is healing in itself. Although not fabulously glamorous, it is very comfortable.

Regular guests: Popular with sports stars, including England footballers, as it specializes in sports injuries. Other regulars are spa-industry insiders, practising what they preach, and French guests wanting to combine a spa break with a pint of Guinness.

Treatment menu: With treatments based on oceans and lotions, you can try balneotherapy, brumisation (sea-mist steam), marine-based facials, cellulite-eliminators and all types of massage and wraps.

House speciality: Thalasso treatments in the dedicated pool.

Cuisine: Thanks to a gourmet dining room, you can still be a foodie and lose weight, but don't let the handmade chocolates left on your pillow each night catch you off guard. Calorie and fat contents are clearly marked on the menu. Specific requirements can be met under the supervision of the on-site medical consultant.

Ideal for: Those seeking regenerating sea-based treatments, along with lung-cleansing sea air and soul-cleansing sea views.

What to pack: A sweater and rainwear for walks on the beach.

Abano Grand Hotel

*

Address: via V. Flacco, 35031 Abano Terme, Padova, Italy
Telephone: (+39) 049 824 8100
Booking details: ghabano@gbhotels.it
Website: www.gbhotels.it

Situated in the gently rolling hills of Euganean Regional Park, and filled with Empire-style furnishings and oil paintings, the Abano Grand Hotel is grand without being stuffy and the attention to detail is clear from the moment you check in. Bedrooms have a traditional European feel with thick carpets, chandeliers and boldly patterned upholstery. Two floors are dedicated to health and wellbeing at the lavish Beauty & Fitness Centre, and there is a fantastic indoor pool. In the well-tended garden are two outdoor pools, one with massaging jets and a whirlpool. The pools are all filled with thermal water kept at different temperatures and can be used all year round. Guests can also tour the hills by bicycle or play tennis at the neighbouring Metropole hotel.

The ambience: Both hotel and spa are homey and inviting.

Regular guests: Rich Europeans suffering the after-effects of too many long lunches.

Treatment menu: A doctor prescribes the thermal treatments, which mix mud mined from a nearby lake with mineral water that flows from the Alps to the ground beneath Abano. Treatments include shiatsu, reflexology, reiki, Ayurveda, acupuncture, Bach flower remedies, aromatherapy, Kneipp therapy and facial fango.

House speciality: The anti-cellulite treatment uses Abano Thermal Cream and involves body peeling, lymph drainage, electro-stimulation, a slimming massage and a body wrap.

Cuisine: Italian dishes are available at the main restaurant. Guests on a nutrition plan, drawn up by a doctor in food science, can either follow the low-calorie diet or carry out a short controlled fast.

Ideal for: Couples and culture-vultures.

What to pack: Something chic to wear to the formal restaurant.

Capri Beauty Farm

✷✷

Address: Capri Palace Hotel & Spa, Via Capodimonte,
2b 80071 Anacapri, Italy
Telephone: (+39) 081 978 0111
Booking details: info@capri-palace.com
Website: www.capri-palace.com

Capri Palace Hotel & Spa is stunningly situated 300 metres
(1,000 feet) above the sea, commanding fantastic views of the
Mediterranean and Gulf of Naples. Offering more than just fluffy
bathrobes and wrinkle-busters (although there are plenty of
both), the aptly named beauty farm has a team of doctors and
physiotherapists to help arrange a programme that's right for
you. Following a medical check-up, a personalized regime and
treatment schedule will be drawn up. A typical stay here is a
week long, and thanks to the list of treatments, from the holistic
to the downright cosmetic, you're guaranteed to look good, as
well as feel good, by the time you leave.

For those interested in fitness as well as beauty, there's an
excellent gym with American equipment, a covered pool for
pounding out lengths and calories, and organized aqua-aerobic
classes and ecological walks, where you can discover some of
the most unspoilt parts of the Island while walking off lunch.

The ambience: A stunning haven of pale stone floors, white walls,
elegant columns, delicate furnishings, cream orchids, rich wood
materials and antique gold mirrors, chandeliers and ornaments.
The spa evokes Mediterranean charm and is like a contemporary
version of an ancient imperial palace.

Regular guests: Glamorous Euro-cash, especially Italians dropping
names and a few pounds. Celebrities, including Harrison Ford,
Donatella Versace, Mariah Carey and Liz Hurley, are fans, too.

Treatment menu: From detox to botox, there's a whole range
of massages, mud packs and thermal cures, a good selection of
thalassotherapy-based therapies, a handful of more cosmetic
treatments, plus treatments geared towards helping back and joint
pain. High-tech machines aid weight loss, improve breast tone, and

diminish stretchmarks and skin blemishes. There's even body peeling and botox to get rid of imperfections and wrinkles. For such a glamorous property, the treatments are surprisingly comprehensive.

House speciality: The legendary Leg School helps with problems ranging from cellulite to circulation. Apparently, Sophie Loren owes her still-great legs to the school's treatments.

Cuisine: Genuine Mediterranean food with lots of homemade bread, pasta and desserts can be found at the three hotel restaurants. Diet food comes part and parcel of all the superb, comprehensive packages that are available.

Ideal for: Luxury spa-seekers who refuse to forfeit glamour on their journey to looking and feeling like a million euros.

What to pack: Chic designer flat mules and the latest sunglasses to accessorize your plain robe during the day, and your most glamorous strappy dresses for pre-dinner cocktails. If you were to come down to dinner in your robe here, people would think you'd taken leave of your senses.

Grotta Giusti Spa & Hotel

*

Address: Via Grotta Giusti, 1411,
51015 Monsummano Terme, Toscana, Italy.
Telephone: (+39) 0572 90771
Booking details: info@grottagiustispa.com
Website: www.grottagiustispa.com

At the foot of the hills of Monsummano, surrounded by lush green parklands and olive trees, Grotto Giusti Terme boasts a natural grotto called the Inferno. Complete with dripping stalactites and stalagmites, this is the most authentic, organic steam bath you're ever likely to come across. Hot waters from an underground lake, 'bicarbonate-sulphate-calcium-magnesium' vapours and 98 per cent humidity create an eerie, unearthly, but naturally detoxifying environment. Guests don bathrobes and slippers, and head down to this hazy cave to sit on wooden deck chairs and breathe in a newfound sense of equilibrium and wellbeing. Afterwards they are led back up to the spa for a shower and massage.

The ambience: A fusty but friendly nineteenth-century private villa, previously home to the Italian poet Giuseppe Giusti; the thermal grotto creates an out-of-the-ordinary spa experience.

Regular guests: International travellers here for the grotto.

Treatment menu: In addition to steams, the spa offers ozonized baths, mud therapy, a thermal pool, massage, plus tailor-made packages, a dermatology clinic and medical consultations.

House speciality: The Grotta and Hydromassage Jet involves a sweat in the grotto followed by a burst from a revitalizing water jet.

Cuisine: You can indulge without guilt in the traditional, but lighter and lower-calorie, Tuscan cooking.

Ideal for: A romantic spa break in stunning Tuscan countryside.

What to pack: Credit cards for clothes' shopping in nearby Florence.

Hotel de Russie

✳✳

Address: Via del Babuino 9, 00187 Rome, Italy
Telephone: (+39) 0632 8881
Booking details: reservations@hotelderussie.it
Website: www.roccofortehotels.com

Location, location, location! Situated in the fashionable Via del Babulino facing the Piazza del Popolo, Hotel de Russie is a stylish hideaway made for chilling out in an otherwise bustling city. Top-notch facilities in and around the intimate spa include: five treatment rooms, all with state-of-the-art, electronically controlled, heated couches; a saline hydropool and circular seated area with water jets that pleasantly pummel your back, hips and thighs; Jacuzzi; sauna; aromatic steam room; and a gym.

The ambience: This millennium Roman hotel combines nineteenth-century elegance with clutter-free modernity. Pink- and white-washed walls and white canvas umbrellas shading picturesque gardens make you feel as though you're on a romantic Italian film set.

Regular guests: The jet-set/film-set. Tom Cruise, Penélope Cruz, Cameron Diaz, Leonardo DiCaprio and Russell Crowe frequent the hotel, alongside various princesses, dukes and duchesses.

Treatment menu: Hydrotherapy is a strong point here, but there are also the trendiest treatments, such as LaStone and Watsu (underwater shiatsu). You can even get your cellulite blasted with microtherapy and your wrinkles filled with collagen.

House speciality: Rebirthing, available on request, is designed to awaken and release emotions and tensions stored up since birth. If that sounds a bit too wacky, stick to the ever-popular Decléor facial.

Cuisine: Gourmet Mediterranean cuisine uses local produce, and the health menu, devised for dieters, doesn't dishearten.

Ideal for: A weekend in Rome combined with chilling out and stepping out (it's close to the famous Spanish Steps).

What to pack: A slouchy outfit for the alfresco relaxation area.

Saturnia Spa at the Palazzo Arzaga

**

Address: 25080 Carzago di Calvagese
della Riviera, Brescia, Italy
Telephone: (+39) 0306 80600
Booking details: info@palazzoarzarga.it
Website: www.palazzoarzaga.com

The stunning spiritual fifteenth century Palazzo Arzaga (previously used as a monastery until the 1800s) is enclosed by the beautiful countryside and hills of Lake Garda, and is probably northern Italy's most exclusive spa and golf resort. Careful modernization has created an impressive five-star hotel with frescoed suites, golf courses, swimming pools, fine-dining restaurants, a conference centre and the stylish Saturnia Spa, named after the famous thermal waters of Tuscany.

Ideal for weight loss and rejuvenation, the thermalized Slim & Tonic pool is one of the highlights of the spa. A prolonged dip in the pool – which is rich in natural mineral salts, including magnesium, potassium, bromine, sodium and iodine – helps to stimulate the metabolism and induce the weight-loss process. Because the water is maintained at a warm 30-32°C (90-94°F), it promotes relaxation, intensifies physical exercise and boosts blood circulation.

As for light exercise and workouts, there's plenty of outdoor space for long walks, two superb 18- and 9-hole golf courses, an open-air gym, swimming pool, low-impact aerobics, stretching and toning classes, plus yoga and tai chi.

The ambience: Old Italian elegance with a few modern twists sums up the feeling here. Bedrooms are furnished with antiques, the bathrooms have floor-to-ceiling Italian marble, and even the spa has a sophisticated grace.

Regular guests: Wealthy holiday-makers spending lots of time and money on themselves in and around the spa, and high-powered businessmen taking a short break to improve their game plan on the golf course as well as at the negotiating table.

Treatment menu: The major aims of the Saturnia Spa are wellness, relaxation and massage, anti-ageing, weight loss, fitness and beauty. Scientific cosmetology and thermal medicine adds weight to the treatment list (but takes it off you). Made-to-measure programmes, from one-day to two-week packages, include accommodation, meals and private consultations. For example, with the Ideal Weight Programme, your calorie intake is controlled with a delicious personalized Arzaga Light menu and you're up early, walking, jogging, doing tai chi and special aquatic hydrogymnastics in the thermal pool before enjoying slimming treatments in the spa. With the Total Relax programme, the goal is to relax, recharge and purify your body through personalized massages, essential oils, body wraps with detoxifying muds and healthy, nutritious, well-balanced eating.

House speciality: The Anti-cellulite treatment with Saturnia mud brings you the health and detoxifying benefits of natural mud with Biolega extracts, which help reduce the appearance of cellulite and leave your skin as soft as silk.

Cuisine: The hotel's gourmet restaurants – Sala Moretto and La Taverna – offer Italian and international cuisine, plus the low-calorie Arzaga Light house menu, or 'light haute-cuisine,' as it's known.

Ideal for: Sophisticated spa-goers.

What to pack: A light, loose, comfortable outfit for the Stretching massage, which is based on methods used for preparing Olympic athletes for their arduous challenges.

Spa 'Deus

✳ ✳ ✳

Address: Via le Piane 35, 53042 Chiancano Terme, Italy
Telephone: (+39) 0578 63232
Booking details: info@spadeus.it
Website: www.spadeus.it

Close to the medieval villages of Pienza, Chiusi and Montichiello, the Californian-style Spa 'Deus means 'spa of the gods,' and there is certainly something otherworldly about this restful resort. Old-world elegance is mixed with New-Age Zen to create a soothing sanctuary, where the philosophy is a holistic one. Although many people come here to lose weight, the emphasis is on teaching guests how to optimize their mental and physical energy using the natural healing powers of water, diet and exercise. The benefits of walking are stressed, with early morning hikes a prominent feature.

The ambience: Friendly, enthusiastic and enlightened. On arrival, guests are ushered into a cool, dark interior, where classical music and a scented atmosphere immediately soothes jangled nerves.

Regular guests: Film stars, fashion designers, models, singers and politicians; Franco Zeffirelli and Ray Charles are both big fans.

Treatment menu: The list includes Pilates, spiritual dance, tai chi, yoga, rebirthing and hydrotherapy. Massages on offer are hot stone, shiatsu, Ayurveda, aromatherapy and reflexology. The Olympic-size pool features an underwater gymnasium and climbing wall. The High Colonic treatment, which rids the colon of accumulated toxins, is recommended, as is the firming Biolift facial.

House speciality: The Biological Immunity Analysis, imported from the USA, measures the efficiency of the immune system and the functioning of the organs. It also indicates mineral deficiencies.

Cuisine: Diet meals include zesty juice drinks, vegetable soups and foil-baked salmon. Guests can also enrol in a diet cooking course.

Ideal for: Couples who want to shape up in a romantic setting.

What to pack: Your hiking boots.

Thermae del Parco

✶✶

Address: Forte Village Resort, SS 195–km 39.600,
0910 Santa Margherita di Pulu (CA), Sardinia, Italy
Telephone: (+39) 070 92171
Booking details: forte.village@forte-hotels.com
Website: www.fortevillageresort.com

This huge 'village'-style resort offers a big choice of accommodation, from swanky private villas through modern hotel rooms to lower-budget family bungalows. The luxurious, tranquil and intimate spa is sectioned off in an enclave, tucked away from the bustle of the resort and protected by trees, bright-coloured plants and flowers. Other facilities include an enormous sauna, mosaic steam room and Turkish bath, plus plunge pools. The energetic can use the resort's gym, 17 tennis courts, bikes or windsurfing school.

The ambience: Informal, tropical and resembling a laid-back traditional Italian village.

Regular guests: Italian society in big Versace shades and Italian footballers in small Versace trunks.

Treatment menu: Aside from some massages and beauty staples, all treatments are influenced by thalasso-therapeutic methods: marine mud wraps, mineral-rich sea-salt scrubs and thalassotherapy pools, including a cellulite-busting saline bath and dense black 'sea oil' solution pool. There's also a medical centre for serious ailments.

House speciality: The 90-minute bathing package uses all five thalassotherapy pools, which vary in temperature and saline density.

Cuisine: Over 20 restaurants offer everything from local Sardinian fare to steaks. A doctor and dietician are on hand to help with weight loss, and although there is low-calorie cuisine and menus are peppered with healthy dishes, this is not the place to be on a diet.

Ideal for: A week-long holiday for couples and families (there are excellent facilities for children) who want a beach/spa holiday.

What to pack: Sunglasses for the day and sequins for night.

Villa d'Este

✳ ✳ ✳

Address: 22012 Cernabbio, Lake Como, Italy
Telephone: (+39) 031 3481
Booking details: reservations@villadeste.it
Website: www.villadeste.it

This historical residence, built by architect Pellegrino Pellegrini in 1568, is opulent and majestic, with landscaped formal gardens, and rooms are available in either the Queen's pavilion or the Cardinal's building. In the spa, the striking Zen-like interior, with its dark slate-coloured walls, rich woods and minimalist flower displays, creates a real sense of serenity and seclusion, enhanced by the fact that the spa and sports club can only be reached via an underground passageway. Forget New-Age ocean wave music, the spa at Villa d'Este is far too sophisticated for that. Instead, opera music is piped through the sound system, making you feel majestically uplifted before you've even had a treatment.

If you don't feel like being pummelled in the spa, you can pump iron in the small but high-tech gym, try out the golf simulator, or play squash or tennis in one of the eight courts. You can go sailing, windsurfing or canoeing at the Sporting Club before relaxing in the sauna or hammam. Swimming in the huge rectangular pool that floats on the lake feels just as though you are swimming on the deck of a cruise liner.

The ambience: Manmade glamour meets manicured Mother Nature. This elegant, grand hotel is set in acres of magnificent private gardens on the banks of the romantic Lake Como.

Regular guests: As a former residence of European aristocrats, this hotel has warmly welcomed more rich-and-famous than a chat-show host – from Winston Churchill, Elizabeth Taylor, Madonna and Bruce Springsteen, to David Bowie and Iman, who took it over for their wedding.

Treatment menu: The treatments here are more traditional than experimental, but are carried out with the utmost professionalism. There's a strong accent on hydrotherapy, and six private cabins are furnished with special hydrotherapeutic equipment for hydromassage and slimming baths. There is also a fairly good selection of face and body treatments, from the deep-tissue massage, through breast firming to anti-ageing facials.

House speciality: Try one of the many beauty packages on offer. They all offer two or three days of intensive beautifying and will leave you uplifted on the outside as well as the inside. Choose from the Intensive Beauty Programme, Beauty and Relax Programme or the Wellbeing and Beauty Programme. All come inclusive of low-calorie menu options and deluxe accommodation.

Cuisine: A diet menu can be organized, but shrewd selections on the regular menus can be just as healthy. Choose from Kisho, for Japanese food, the Verandah, overlooking the lake and gardens, the informal Grill, or the poolside bar that's open during the summer for lunch and only serves light meals, salads and snacks.

Ideal for: A special-occasion weekend away for a couple who enjoy the finer things in life.

What to pack: Your most sparkly rocks and frocks for the evenings.

Kempinski San Lawrenz

*

Address: Triq ir-Rokon, San Lawrenz, GRB 104 Gozo, Malta
Telephone: (+356) 21 558 640
Booking details: info@sanlawrenz.com
Website: www.bodyandsoulholidays.com

Situated on the pretty island of Gozo, just south of Sicily in the Mediterranean, the Kempinski San Lawrenz has been built to resemble a typical Maltese villa. Guests are transferred by helicopter from the neighbouring island of Malta to the 106-room resort, which has two floodlit tennis courts, squash courts, a fitness centre, and an outdoor pool. The majority of rooms are light, airy junior suites, with cool stone walls and a chill-out zone. The Wellness Centre is similarly chic and boasts an atmosphere of complete peace and privacy. Guests wishing to explore can take a jeep safari around the island and visit Gozo's inland sea.

The ambience: Grand without being intimidating.

Regular guests: Families. The resort has a children's pool and there are beaches nearby where you can sail, waterski, canoe and dive.

Treatment menu: The Wellness Centre has an indoor pool and thalgo centre, with Vichy showers for water massage and a Blitz shower to help decongest fatty deposits. Ayurvedic treatments – administered following a consultation with a doctor – include massages, supplemented by herbal medicines. An aphrodisiac treatment increases virility, improves libido and counters impotence.

House speciality: Pick one of the Kerala oil therapies. In *dhara*, a steady stream of medicated buttermilk is poured onto the head; during *chavitti thirummu*, a practitioner hangs from a rope and corrects body alignment by massaging the client with his feet.

Cuisine: Mediterranean dishes, using fresh fish and vegetables, are available in L'Ortalan. For more casual fare, visit the It-Terz eaterie.

Ideal for: Families and couples.

What to pack: Your driving licence, so you can explore by car.

Les Thermes Marins de Monte-Carlo

✳ ✳ ✳

Address: 2, Avenue de Monte-Carlo,
MC 98000 Principaute de Monaco
Telephone: (+377) 92 16 49 46
Booking details: thermes@sbm.mc
Website: www.montecarloresort.com

Overlooking the Mediterranean, where elegant yachts ply the sea's azure depths, this luxury resort reflects the expensive lifestyle of Monaco's richest residents. As a result, Les Thermes Marins de Monte-Carlo concentrates on returning guests to maximum attractiveness with minimum effort: toxins are much more likely to be released via a seaweed wrap than sweated out on a Stairmaster. An entire floor is devoted to seawater therapies, and rooms are plush but unfussy, featuring a Zen-like decor of natural furnishings.

The ambience: Chi-chi, glamorous and exclusive. The sunlight in the spa washes through the floor-to-ceiling windows and helps to stimulate vitamin D and boost endorphins.

Regular guests: Monaco's glitzy party set and affluent Europeans wanting to indulge in some serious pampering.

Treatment menu: Massages include shiatsu, plantar reflexology, fasciatherapy and aromatherapy, while beauty treatments at the Salon Bleu use Lancaster products and include dermabrasion and non-surgical face-lifts. There are six-day Complete Cure packages, too.

House speciality: The four-handed Effusion massage uses warm seawater, essential oils and dynamic synchronized manipulation.

Cuisine: Tuck into low-calorie food that doesn't compromise on taste at L'Hirondelle. Guests can also visit l'Atlantide bar for delicious, vitamin cocktails and other high-energy thirst-quenchers.

Ideal for: The seriously narcissistic.

What to pack: Designer-wear is essential for seeing and being seen.

Sofitel Thalassa Vilalara

✳✳

Address: Praia das Gaivotas, Alporchinhos-Porches,
Algarve, Portugal
Telephone: (+351) 282 320 000
Booking details: www.accorhotels.com
Website: www.accorhotels.com

Sofitel Thalassa Vilalara is positioned on a stunning brick-red cliff overlooking a secluded bay and white sandy beach in a part of the world where the sun shines 300 days of the year. Add the fact that it also has one of the best thalassotherapy centres in Europe with a full-blown spa, and you've got the perfect place to rest, recoup and bring your body, mind and soul back into balance. In addition, there are saunas, Turkish baths, all the fitness motivation you need, plus excellent sailing and watersports for water babes. On land, there's a fitness centre, yoga, tai chi, golf and tennis for those who want to burn calories but have an aversion to 'exercise'.

The ambience: The place has a fun, summer holiday resort vibe. Those fascinated, rather than fanatical, about their spa breaks help create the easy-going and relaxed atmosphere.

Regular guests: Successful professionals with young children and small groups of females on girly breaks.

Treatment menu: Thalassotherapies, individual hydromassages, seaweed exfoliation treatments, detoxifying algae massages, mud wraps and cellulite treatments are all performed under medical supervision following a check-up. And that's not forgetting the array of jet-stream baths, showers and pools designed to relax and renew.

House speciality: The Bride-to-be Programme will help you lose a little weight and gain a healthy glow for the big day.

Cuisine: There is a gourmet restaurant, a poolside bar and a dietetic restaurant serving mouthwatering low-calorie meals.

Ideal for: Sun, sea, sand and spa-seekers, and brides-to-be.

What to pack: Sexy swimwear. You'll be ready for it after a week here.

Hotel Termes Montbrió

✷✷

Address: Carrer Nou 38, 43340 Montbrió
del Camp, Costa Daurada, Tarragona, Spain
Telephone: (+34) 977 81 4000
Booking details: hoteltermes@gruprocblanc.com
Website: www.gruprocblanc.com

Situated in the seaside town of Tarragona, Hotel Termes Montbrio is a grand resort, which seamlessly combines 1900s architecture with a more modern approach. Rooms are regally decorated and five of the eight suites have a different cultural theme – British, Tuscan, Colonial, Arabic and Japanese. The hotel is surrounded by luxuriant gardens, complete with a sprawling pool, lake and numerous fountains and courtyards. Activities include golf, tennis, horse-riding, diving, sailing and trekking through the Delta del Ebro Nature Reserve.

The ambience: Although this luxurious resort is big, bustling and efficient, it still manages to retain its Continental charm.

Regular guests: Business groups and families. The hotel has two convention centres and Port Aventura amusement park is nearby.

Treatment menu: The well-equipped spa and leisure centre has a hot-spring pool, giant jacuzzi and gym. In addition to numerous rejuvenation treatments – including hydrotherapy, anti-cellulite regimes, reiki, reflexology, aromatherapy and watsu – guests can also check in to the Surgical Clinic for botox, liposuction, rhinoplasty, face-lifts, breast augmentation and permanent make-up.

House speciality: The seven-day anti-tobacco programme helps guests kick their dependency through breathing techniques, steams, acupuncture, facial shiatsu and oxygen remedies.

Cuisine: Le Sequoia and l'Horta Florida both serve healthy Mediterranean fare. Low-calorie menus are also available.

Ideal for: Anyone wanting to slip in a sneaky nip-and-tuck.

What to pack: Sunglasses and a large, brimmed hat to hide evidence of facial 'enhancements'.

Incosol Hotel-Medical Spa

✶✶

Address: Urbanización Golf Río Real, s/n,
29600 Marbella, Spain
Telephone: (+34) 952 666 4000
Booking details: (+34) 952 86 0909 or comercial@incosol.com
Website: www.incosol.com

In the Río Real valley, amid subtropical gardens, lies the modern nine-storey Incosol. Only a short walk from the coast and enjoying nearly year-round sunshine, the resort makes an ideal relaxation destination. There are a plethora of activities on offer, as well as pools, Jacuzzi, saunas, a gym and an aqua-gym, but these are all adjuncts to the real focus. The spa and treatment centre takes a serious approach to improving the appearance and health of clients. The units offer intensive supervised programmes for diabetes, weight loss, nutrition, sleep disorders, psychology, physiotherapy and skin, endocrine and heart problems.

The ambience: A professional, private medical clinic within a bright, spacious and luxurious resort.

Regular guests: Rich and famous Europeans who are worried about their longevity and appearance.

Treatment menu: Plastic surgery options, such as face-lifts, peels and transdermal therapies, are available alongside massages, body wraps, reflexology, Kniepp showers, lymphatic drainage and facials.

House speciality: Any one of the tailored programmes: choose from Juventa Anti-Ageing, Weight Loss/Anti-Cellulite or a beauty package.

Cuisine: La Pergola and El Mirador serve local seafood and their diet-controlled menus contain calorie and fat breakdowns. There is also a poolside buffet and grill, and Beach Club restaurant.

Ideal for: Jetting in for a face-lift on the quiet, anyone with serious health issues, or those inclined towards the best medical science and technology have to offer.

What to pack: Your medical records.

Las Dunas

✶✶

Address: La Boladilla Baja Ctra. de Cadiz, Km 163.5,
29689 Estepona, Málaga, Spain
Telephone: (+34) 952 79 4345
Booking details: reservas@las-dunas.com
Website: www.las-dunas.com

Constructed in Andulacian style with Moorish influences to reflect
the area's cultural heritage, the low-rise, flamingo-coloured Las Dunas
is surrounded by fountain-filled gardens, reminiscent of a Spanish
hacienda. Rooms are large and luxurious, and each has a sundeck
with views across the Mediterranean. Watersports are available at
the beach nearby, and activities on dry land include horse-riding,
golf and mountain-biking. Touring excursions can also be arranged.

The ambience: Sleek and sophisticated, this place is run like
a well-oiled machine.

Regular guests: European jet-setters and families.

Treatment menu: Built to resemble a Roman sanatorium, the
Serenity Spa has frescoed walls and a marble jacuzzi. At the Regina
Sol Kur-Clinic within the spa, therapies are prescribed to create
a symbiotic rejuvenation programme. There are extensive health
check-ups, oxygen and colonic therapies, thalassotherapy and a
week-long zap-that-cellulite programme. Complementary treatments
include reiki, aromatherapy, reflexology and yoga.

House speciality: The !!QMS facials include specific treatments for
different age groups. Those on the wrong side of 40 will be delighted
to discover that the fruit acid content in the facials is higher than
the usual five per cent, delivering spectacular – but safe – results.

Cuisine: Healthy cuisine is served at the Lido, while Bistro Felix offers
Asian dishes. Ingredients are organically grown at the hotel's farm.

Ideal for: Keen golfers. The hotel has an in-house golf pro and
there are more than 40 greens stretching along the coast.

What to pack: Your golf clubs.

Louison Bobet
Thalassotherapy Centre

✴ ✴

Address: Hotel Byblos Andaluz, Mijas Golf,
29650 Mijas Costa, Málaga, Spain
Telephone: (+34) 952 47 3050
Booking details: comerical@byblos-andaluz.com
Website: www.byblos-andaluz.com

A sprawling Andalusian palace, the Hotel Byblos Andaluz overlooks the beautiful Mijas mountain range. Surrounded by two 18-hole golf courses, the decor at this luxurious hotel combines classical Roman and Greek elements with brilliant splashes of Moorish mosaics and traditional Spanish fountain-filled courtyards. The interior is decorated mostly in soothing sandstone and peaceful white, and guest rooms are themed around four styles: Arabian, Andalusian, Roman and Rustic. Expect king-size four-poster beds, marble bathrooms, tasteful European furnishings and panoramic views across the golf course to the blue-tinged mountains beyond.

In addition to golf, outdoor activities include swimming in the freshwater pool, tennis and French *boules*. There are also two aquaparks nearby, which children will love, while parents can enjoy day trips to numerous historical sites, including Rhonda, the Alhambra in Granada, Seville and Cordoba. Also within driving

distance is Marbella, where there are fabulous opportunities for shopping and hanging out at poseur's paradise, Puerto Banus. Guests can visit Sierra Nevada for a spot of skiing from December to May.

Connected to the hotel, the all-white Thalassotherapy Centre is a haven of rest and relaxation. Named after the three-times winner of the Tour de France, who discovered the benefits of seawater cures while recovering from a serious car accident, the institute bases its recuperative regime on hydrotherapy, using seawater piped directly from the Mediterranean.

The ambience: Relaxed and informal. Guests are free to take their health and fitness concerns as lightly or as seriously as they want without feeling pressurized to clock up miles on the treadmill.

Regular guests: This is where high-powered businessmen come to enjoy the golfing, while their wives take advantage of the spa.

Treatment menu: Following a medical check-up with the spa's doctor, guests can consult a hydrotherapist who will draw up a personalized programme to help alleviate specific complaints. A physiotherapist is also on hand to ease aches and pains. The thalassotherapy treatments include algotherapy, which contains almost as much iodine as 10,000 litres (2,200 gallons) of seawater. Programmes that combine homeopathic remedies and nutrition with thalassotherapy are available for weight-loss, detoxifying, metabolism, circulation and boosting the immune system.

House speciality: La Prairie products, renowned for their efficacy in rejuvenating skins that are tired, stressed or simply 'past a certain age,' are available at the neo-classical beauty centre. The Caviar Treatment is particularly spoiling and the results are so pleasing that you'll wonder how you lived without this face-saver.

Cuisine: In addition to special diet menus, guests can tuck into deliciously light Andalusian dishes at La Fuente, with its mosaic courtyard. Healthy drinks, made from a refreshing mix of fruit, vegetable and plant juices, are available at the Tisaneria.

Ideal for: Families, as there's something for everyone here.

What to pack: A flashy outfit is essential if you plan to do some promenading in Puerto Banus.

Termas Marinas Castelar

*

Address: Hotel Castelar, Castelar, 25,
39004 Santander, Cantabria, Spain
Telephone: (+34) 942 225 2000
Booking details: grupocastelar@mundivia.es
Website: www.grupocastelar.com

The Castelar is a townhouse hotel which occupies a privileged position on the bustling marina of Santander. It is also bang in the centre of town, where the Festival Palace hosts concerts, theatre and ballet during the summer months. The hotel is small – there are just 35 rooms decorated in a bold palette of blue and ruby red – while bayside rooms have a glass wall overlooking the marina. The spa is also small and intimate, with a little pool and a team of dedicated staff.

The ambience: Chic and sleek. Because the hotel is central, guests can combine pampering treatments with shopping and sightseeing.

Regular guests: Business people and families. The hotel has a meeting room, and kids love the beach.

Treatment menu: Thalassotherapy remedies, using the region's mineral-rich thermal waters, are carried out under strict medical supervision, and there's also an osteopath on hand to help relieve back pain. Complementary therapies include reflexology and aromatherapy, and the spa also offers slimming treatments, such as lymph drainage and anti-cellulite, in addition to age-defying facials.

House speciality: The flower petal bath, a superbly sybaritic treatment, requires little more than sinking back into a tub of fabulously fragranced water.

Cuisine: Although there are no special diet menus at the rooftop restaurant, the food is healthy and includes fresh fish and produce.

Ideal for: Spa-goers who love the invigorating effect of the sea.

What to pack: Your deck shoes. Thanks to the quayside location, sailing enthusiasts can charter a yacht at a moment's notice.

Stockholm Day Spa

*

Address: Åhlens City, Master Samuelsgatan 57,
plan 4, Stockholm, Sweden
Telephone: (+46) 8 676 64 50
Booking details: stockholmdayspa@ahlens.se
Website: www.stockholmdayspa.com

Located on the top floor of the Åhlens City department store, the day spa provides a welcome oasis of peace away from the hectic city below. Designed by the Spaus group, the interior is light, calming and merges function with beauty. The naturally and neutrally toned decor helps to create an environment that is monastically quiet yet allows for areas of activity. The spa's ethos is to provide a haven in which busy urbanites can slow right down.

The ambience: Fresh, clean and very Scandinavian, with lots of blond wood, ceramic tiled floors and white towels.

Regular guests: Professional city-dwellers looking for a combined retail and spa therapy break from work.

Treatment menu: The usual range of grooming treatments, facials, body wraps and skincare treatments is available, along with hydrotherapies and many massage options. As expected, saunas are an important focus of the spa, with aromatherapy essences enhancing the experience. Pick from a variety of packages, such as the six-hour package that includes facial, pedicure, aroma sauna, two Mindzone classes, a spa lunch and a tea buffet.

House speciality: Mindzone exercise classes blend Eastern and Western disciplines to promote an inner and outer workout. They include qi gong, hatha yoga, Doln (a self-massage), meditation, breathing techniques, Zen Energy (dynamic movements mixed with slow ones), Sotai (body realignment/balancing), and more.

Cuisine: The tea and water bar serves healthy drinks and snacks.

Ideal for: A refreshment on a whirlwind shopping/touring holiday.

What to pack: Your gym kit for the not-to-be-missed Mindzone.

Clinique La Prairie

✶✶✶

Address: CH-1815 Clarens-Montreux, Switzerland
Telephone: (+41) 21 989 3311
Booking details: info@laprairie.ch
Website: www.laprairie.ch

Clinique La Prairie is set against the idyllic backdrop of Lake Geneva and the Alps. Here, you can check in for a couple of days of pampering and subtle fine-tuning in the beauty department, or add a couple of weeks (not to mention 00s on your bill) and totally reinvent yourself.

The spa's aim is to enhance your lifestyle and feel-good factor, whatever it takes – whether it's a new diet or a new nose. Top experts from every walk of health, beauty and medical professional life are on hand for specialist advice, from diet and nutrition through fitness and exercise, to cosmetic and plastic surgery. The full-week programme is a popular choice and from the moment you're met by the clinic's private limousine at the airport to the moment you leave, your every health and beauty need is taken care of. You barely need to even think for yourself. What's more, with only 23 guest rooms and a handful of luxury suites, the spa is not swarming with people, so you won't feel as though you're being rushed through on a production line.

The ambience: This exclusive health and medical spa feels like a cross between a private hospital and a luxury hotel. Uniformed nurses, doctors in white coats, adjustable beds in the bedroom and blood tests before breakfast give it the hospital feel, but comfortable rooms with Bang & Olufsen TVs and mini-bars (minus the alcohol) provide the hotel vibe.

Regular guests: Glamorous ladies-of-leisure, high-flying executives and the odd celebrity wearing dark designer sunglasses, all trying to turn back the clock.

Treatment menu: An extensive range of up-to-the-minute medical and aesthetic treatments, all under one roof, includes everything from general surgery, gynaecology and urology, collagen injections and dental surgery to stress-busting, pampering massages and face and body peels that instantly leave you renewed and glowing – minus needles, stitches or pain.

House speciality: Cellular rejuvenation therapy for the over-40s, from CLP's ground-breaking on-site research lab, involves life-boosting injections containing bioactive substances that allegedly counteract and even reverse age-associated processes. Another high-tech option is Beauty-Med, a muscle-toning programme originally designed by NASA to keep astronauts' muscles maintained in space.

Cuisine: The hotel's gourmet restaurant serves a selection of healthy, nutritious and, where necessary, interesting calorie-controlled dishes.

Ideal for: A solo spa break for a serious health and beauty overhaul. Most people who come here are in pursuit of the post-break 'Oooh you look well!' compliment from friends, family and work colleagues that lasts for more than a mere week.

What to pack: An empty vanity case to stock up on products from the clinic's own pricey, but effective, skincare range, Swiss Perfection, and the better-known, luxurious La Prairie line.

Le Mirador Resort & Spa

★ ★ ★

Address: CH-1801 Mont-Pélerin,
Montreux/Vevey, Switzerland
Telephone: (+41) 21 925 1111
Booking details: mirador@attglobal.net
Website: www.mirador.ch

If you've always fantasized about the lush green meadows and mountain peaks of *Heidi* fame, Le Mirador Resort & Spa is the place for you. Personifying all the good things about Switzerland – bar the chocolate – this five-star complex is situated on the slopes of Mont-Pèlerin in the heart of the Swiss Riviera with panoramic views of Lake Geneva, the Rhône Valley and the snow-capped French Alps. This is also the Levaux wine region, so acres of vineyards mix with lush meadows and charming trails, which thread in and out of peaceful woods.

Inside this elegant, country-manor-style hotel the decor is luxurious and traditional, with oil paintings, period furnishings and stained-glass windows a-plenty. There are 12 suites and 93 sumptuous guest rooms, decked out with swagged curtains, chintz bedspreads and large marble bathrooms. Most of the rooms also have their own balconies and all have air-conditioning, cable TV and VCRs.

The spa, which adjoins the hotel, is totally tranquil, and has a swim-through indoor/outdoor pool with spectacular views, saunas, steam rooms, multijet showers and whirlpools, and a fitness centre with state-of-the-art cardiovascular equipment. There are

also three tennis courts, volleyball, table tennis and a computer-simulated golf course, where guests can practise their putting.

The ambience: Seriously grown-up and luxurious, Le Mirador is an oasis of calm. The rarefied atmosphere here means that the kids are best left at home.

Regular guests: Gallic glitterati regularly go into hiding here to shed a few kilos. Other regulars are de-stressing executives and chic French women, who wear lipstick in the pool and insist on carrying their pet shitzhus around like precious purses.

Treatment menu: The Mirador describes itself as a *'sans regimen'* spa, which basically translates as a self-indulgent fat farm where guests are free to spend more time in the beauty salon than on the treadmill. Predictably, there are myriad different kinds of massages available (40 at the last count, including a jet-lag massage, reiki, reflexology and Ayurveda). There's also a wide variety of bodycare including a stretchmark treatment and bust-shaper, hydrotherapy and facials. The spa uses Pevonia products – made from a wholly natural fruit and flower mix – and the Phytomer range, which bases its lotions on marine ingredients.

House speciality: The weight-loss programme at the on-site Cambuzat Centre is a 9- to 15-day treatment (depending on how much you've overindulged in the past six months). Based on a method that has its origins in behaviourism, the aim is to encourage people to undergo a long-lasting 'essential inner change', which will help them to perceive healthy eating and fitness in a way that is less boot-campish than many other regimes.

Cuisine: For light fare, there's the glass-sided Le Patio, which has a large terrace and serves low-fat, three-course 400-calorie lunches, which look and taste as though they are 1,000-plus. For gourmet food (foie gras, fresh figs, truffle salad), visit Le Trianon, a top-flight French restaurant, where the crystal-teardrop chandeliers and blue-and-gold colour scheme match the sophistication of the cuisine.

Ideal for: Rich Europeans who habitually spend vast sums of money maintaining their shape.

What to pack: Euro resort-wear, such as sports shirts, loafers, a chiffon scarf and granny's pearls.

Therme Vals

✳ ✳

Address: Hotel Therme Vals, CH-7132 Vals, Switzerland
Telephone: (+41) 81 926 8080
Booking details: hotel@therme-vals.ch
Website: www.therme-vals.ch

Vals is a beautiful village in the Swiss Alps and the valley is famous for its therapeutic springs and pure mountain air. The ultra-modern spa has been constructed into the mountain slope and has the look and feel of a new-millennium bathhouse. A covered bridge or foot-path (depending on room location) leads you to the spa, situated at cellar level, where a labyrinth of stone pools, filled with thermal waters, awaits. There's a 42ºC (107ºF) Fire Pool, a chilled 14ºC (57ºF) plunge pool and a scented flower pool. Reclining on one of the leather sofas by the large window, après treatment, watching skiers skimming over the fresh snow, is a truly magical way to chill out.

The ambience: A contemporary, masculine and Spartan feel gives this spa a trendy but serene, and very still, atmosphere.

Regular guests: Cool locals and stylish spa-trekkers.

Treatment menu: Effective water-based thalasso treatments, massages, body packs, exfoliations, and jet massages and baths are geared towards relaxation rather than the curative, and carried out behind smooth concrete walls and translucent blue-glass doors.

House speciality: Try any of the fantastic packages, from Stress-Busting (four nights half-board, an all-over exfoliation, massage, facial and Jacuzzi jet) to the Valser Slimming Cure (13 days and nights of detoxing weight-loss treatments with a low-calorie diet).

Cuisine: Meals in the Chessi (Swiss for 'cauldron') have a regional flair. The calorie-aware can devour tasty light offerings, whereas the calorie-don't-care can opt for epic six-coursers.

Ideal for: An exhilarating winter spa-cum-ski break.

What to pack: A waterproof camera to take some pictures of this architecturally stunning spa.

Klassis Resort Hotel & Country Club

✶✶

Address: Altıntepe Mevkii Seymen,
Silivri, 34930 Istanbul, Turkey
Telephone: (+90) 212 727 4050
Booking details: info@klassis.com.tr
Website: www.klassis.com.tr

Located in woodland along the coast, this luxury resort features an 18-hole championship golf course, equestrian centre, Olympic-size pool, tennis courts, gym and a kids' club. Other sporting facilities include watersports, table tennis, bowling, basketball and billiards. The spa offers a less strenuous approach to healthy living, with four programmes for Beautification, Weight Loss, Relaxation and Recovery. Rooms at the colonial-style country club are sumptuously furnished and all have views across the verdant golf course.

The ambience: Lively and social at the hotel; calm, efficient and scientific in the spa.

Regular guests: People who are truly committed to improving their health, parents with young children and businessmen.

Treatment menu: All treatments use Thalgo products and include Hoffa massage (a German method of manipulation), underwater massage, frigithalgo (a cold wrap applied to the legs to eliminate water retention), and the Breast Care treatment, which will give you the cleavage of your dreams.

House speciality: The Collagen Velvet Skincare facial is particularly good for older clients. A serum is mixed with a large dose of collagen to moisturize and smooth out wrinkles.

Cuisine: Chefs specialize in diet meals using precise cooking methods to ensure they are rich in vitamins and minerals.

Ideal for: Athletic types and families.

What to pack: Sports gear to enjoy all the facilities on offer.

Swissôtel Istanbul

*

Address: Bayildim Cad. No. 2 Maçka, Besiktas,
80680 Istanbul, Turkey
Telephone: (+90) 212 326 1100
Booking details: emailus@swissotel.com
Website: www.swissotel.com

Located on the European side of Istanbul, this modern hotel is set amid 26 hectares (65 acres) of lush gardens leading to the cobalt-blue waters of the Bosphorus. Although the city is steeped in a history rich in Roman, Byzantine and Ottoman empires, it has long since discarded its image of bad-tempered camels and Aladdin-style slippers, and the modernity at Swissôtel reflects this. Rooms are equipped with all modern conveniences and have windows overlooking the spires and minarets of the city's mosques. At the spa, there are indoor and outdoor pools, a gym with state-of-the-art equipment, floodlit tennis courts, a Turkish bath and golf simulator.

The ambience: Cool and calm, in stark contrast to the city outside.

Regular guests: Corporate types, holidaying families and locals.

Treatment menu: The Bosphorus Spa & Wellness Centre offers two types of massage, while guests at the Beauty Centre can enjoy a variety of facials, anti-ageing treatments, bust rejuvenation, aromatherapy, paraffin hand massage and Ayurvedic massage.

House speciality: The hammam takes place in an all-white marble treatment room and includes a massage and salt-glow scrub.

Cuisine: The 15 restaurants cater for every taste – from Japanese and Chinese at the Miyako and Ku-Kong restaurants, to Swiss at the cosy Swiss Chalet and Turkish at the Taslik Turkish Restaurant. Lavish French cuisine is served at La Corne D'Or, while low-fat menus are available at the Jacuzzi Health Restaurant.

Ideal for: Families with young children and culture vultures.

What to pack: Your binoculars to get a closer view of Istanbul's exotic skyline from the comfort of your room.

Academy Spa
✴✴

Address: Oakdale Place, Harrogate,
North Yorkshire HG1 2LA, England, UK
Telephone: (+44) (0)1423 524 060
Booking details: (+44) (0)1423 524 060
Website: www.academyspa.com

The Academy Spa in the pretty, and pretty quiet, town of Harrogate is on the top-floor of a suburban health club (which you have full use of as part and parcel of the full-day packages). Eastern-style design with dark wood, bamboo, tropical orchids and lit candles, coupled with an extensive pampering and pruning list, ensures that you will leave looking like the composed goddess you really are.

The ambience: Non-pretentious, with welcoming, professional staff. The Japanese-style interior has an instantly calming effect.

Regular guests: Local professionals, local TV celebrities and members of the adjoining health club.

Treatment menu: East-meets-West up north to stop your body going south! Take your pick from a handful of aromatherapy-based Elemis facials and body treatments, different types of massage, slimming and detoxing body specials, and all of the usual beauty groomers such as waxing, make-up lessons, manicures and pedicures. They do some fantastic half- and full-day packages, too.

House speciality: The Exotic Frangipani Body Nourish Float is a mind-altering Thai foot ritual using hot lime, reiki and chakra-cleansing. Warm frangipani oils are drizzled over the front and back of your body, then you are wrapped in foil and left to snooze on the wonderfully supportive flotation bed. A nourishing milk bath and face-and-scalp massage follow.

Cuisine: Light snacks are served overlooking the tennis courts.

Ideal for: A day of out-and-out pampering.

What to pack: An overnight bag if you're not a local; you won't want to travel far afterwards.

Agua Spa at the Sanderson Hotel

★ ★ ★

Address: 50 Berners Street,
London W1P 3AD, England
Telephone: (+44) (0)207 300 1414
Booking details: (+44) (0)207 300 1414
Website: www.ianschragerhotels.com

Just minutes from the burger joints and clothes stores of Oxford Street, London's busiest shopping strip, the Agua Spa couldn't be more of a tranquil retreat. Greeted by bellboys who probably moonlight as male models, you are welcomed into a blue holographic space-age lift and taken up into what feels like another world.

Forget any ideas of hackneyed dark wood, corporate-looking granite and vacant-eyed therapists in stiff cotton overalls. This two-storey bathhouse in Ian Schrager's Sanderson oozes originality and stylish serenity. From the marble mosaic floors, diaphanous white curtains, glamorous Louis XV chairs and Venetian mirrors in the boudoir-style changing room to the pretty therapists wearing white linen trousers and T-shirts, you'll feel like you've died and gone to heaven.

The treatments are fabulous, and the relaxation areas are the best you'll find anywhere. Instead of a communal lounge, you have your own separate cosy booth, surrounded by flowing white curtains. The room contains a comfy lounge chair, your own mini TV and a radio and headphones so you can tune in and switch off. Yoga classes are held during the week in the relaxation area or in the courtyard when the sun is shining.

The ambience: If heaven had a spa, this is what it would be like: high ceilings, sounds of bubbling water, white billowing curtains and therapists who massage like angels.

Regular guests: London's most stylish spa-goers – magazine beauty editors, affluent tourists and corporate spa-trippers enjoying a work freebie. The Sanderson Hotel also attracts a number of London's showbiz set including film stars Ewan McGregor and Jude Law.

Treatment menu: The menu runs from indulgent body treats, wraps and massages to cutting-edge facials and grooming necessities, such as waxing, eyelash tints and manicures. Agua beautifully fuses Eastern philosophies with modern-day Western techniques in treatments that nurture from the outside in. They've also got a great selection of therapies for men, from the Agua Total De-stresser to a chest or back wax.

House speciality: The Aromatherapy Rose Facial is a deeply relaxing, 60-minute facial to calm, soothe and revitalize city-fried or jet-lagged complexions. Massage techniques are used to release tension in the back, neck, scalp and arms, as well as in the face.

Cuisine: Dieticians and nutritionists offer private advice. The restaurant, Spoon+, designed by Philippe Starck, is overseen by French chef Alain Ducasse. There are a couple of set menus, which offer delicious but healthy meals and light bites. The lobster sandwich is a must-have.

Ideal for: City-dwellers needing an emergency respite from the big smoke and fashionistas who like to dress up even when they dress down – even in the pre-massage relaxation area, image is everything.

What to pack: A large credit facility and a baseball cap and shades to fool the paparazzi on your way out.

Bath House at the Royal Crescent Hotel

✶✶

Address: 16 Royal Crescent,
Bath BA1 2LS, England
Telephone: (+44) (0)1225 823 333
Booking details: reservations@royalcrescent.co.uk
Website: www.royalcrescent.co.uk

People have been flocking to Bath for centuries, seeking pleasure or cure from its world-famous hot mineral springs, and the Bath House at the Royal Crescent is probably the most gracious, most civilized, way of enjoying the modern-day spa experience. A tranquil oasis set within the hotel's grounds, it features a 12-metre (39-foot)-long warm relaxation pool with soundproofing to ensure silent swims. There are also cool and tepid plunge tubs, steam, sauna, and a range of beauty treatments and complementary therapies. Exercise-wise, the gym is well-equipped and personal trainers are available upon request. There's also a studio where weekly yoga, tai chi and Pilates sessions take place. For those who want to forget everything and put their head in the clouds, the hotel has its very own hot-air balloon. The city is also home to an exhilarating mix of international festivals, music, sport, and individual shops and antique centres, not to mention numerous museums and architectural sites, and the Theatre Royal.

The ambience: Quiet grandeur in the hotel and just plain quiet in the spa. The church-like arched windows and creative use of natural woods, stone, bamboo and slate make time spent in this holistic haven almost a religious experience.

Regular guests: Film stars used to five-stars – Johnny Depp, for instance – and moneyed tourists visiting Bath.

Treatment menu: Although the focus is on ancient practices of bathing and cleansing, the spa offers wraps, exfoliation, facials, manicures and pedicures, as well as acupressure, reflexology and Indian scalp massage. Most treatments are based on the Bath House's own bespoke collection of 16 pre-blended essential oils, which you can buy to carry on the good work at home.

House speciality: The Bath House Treatment is a two-hour sequence of bathing, cleansing, exfoliating and massaging that will leave you feeling refreshed with your skin velvety smooth.

Cuisine: Pimpernel's, the hotel's impressive restaurant, is open to both house guests and non-residents. It has a contemporary British menu, which draws on Mediterranean and Far-Eastern influences. The traditional English afternoon tea is not to be missed (unless you're on a diet) and attracts posh locals, so book in advance to ensure that you get a table with a comfy sofa.

Ideal for: Those wanting to be pampered in style and luxury. At the Bath House, it's more about self-indulgent relaxation and unadulterated beautifying, rather than losing weight and getting rid of cellulite.

What to pack: Smart attire for dinner and a book on the history of Bath so you can learn about the city's rich cultural heritage.

Berkeley Health Club & Spa

✳ ✳ ✳

Address: The Berkeley Hotel, Wilton Place,
London SW1X 7RL, England
Telephone: (+44) (0)207 235 6000
Booking details: info@the-berkeley.co.uk
Website: www.savoy-group.co.uk

The beauty of the Berkeley Spa is that it's situated on the top floor of the hotel, which gives you a bird's-eye view of Knightsbridge and Hyde Park, and makes you feel like the queen of the castle. The Romanesque rooftop pool has a glass roof that slides back when the sun is out, turning it into the finest sunbathing hotspot in town.

The ambience: An oasis of relaxation and pampering up high in the sky (except when the occasional alpha-male is pounding out lengths in the pool!)

Regular guests: Well-heeled Knightsbridge ladies and club members.

Treatment menu: Being a Christian Dior spa, there are a handful of very French, very decadent treatments for the face and body using Dior products. More soul-nourishing treats include LaStone, plus a collection of traditional Balinese treatments that have been created for the Berkeley with help and expertise from the Source at the Begawan Giri Estate in Bali (see pages 208–9).

House speciality: The LaStone Body Therapy uses penetrating heated stones, alternated with cool marble, to give a unique healing, relaxing and energizing effect. Considering that one stroke of a massage stone is the equivalent to ten massage strokes, it's no wonder you're left feeling uplifted.

Cuisine: Light sandwiches and snacks (some healthier than others), fresh fruit and smoothies are served by the pool.

Ideal for: Stressed-out Londoners and shopped-out tourists.

What to pack: Binoculars, to make the most of the spectacular view.

Bliss London

✶✶✶

Address: 60 Sloane Avenue, London SW3 3DD, England
Telephone: (+44) (0)207 584 3888
Booking details: (+44) (0)207 584 3888
Website: www.blissworld.com

Bliss London is the younger sister spa of Bliss Soho in New York and is basically a service station for a bevy of working, partying, and dating city females. In true New York style, the service is slick, treatments are ultra-modern and staff are all trained to the max. Prepare to be blissed out ...

The ambience: Stark, minimal and London Cool with a capital 'C'.

Regular guests: Jet-setting models, high-flying businesswomen and down-to-earth London girls paying for the name and location.

Treatment menu: Extensive (and expensive), the treatments at Bliss have latest skincare, massage, body therapies, nail- and footcare and waxing services, from indulgent booked-ahead massages to straight-in off-the-street manicures and emergency back rubs. The great thing about Bliss is that it also specializes in treatments for party girls with hangovers – in fact there's even the Hangover Herbie, an all-over pick-me-up for post-revellers.

House speciality: With the Ginger Rub, you are rubbed with freshly grated, detoxifying ginger and then foil-wrapped for 20 minutes before being given an incredible 100-minute massage. Prepare to be as mushy as the ginger by the end of this 135-minute treat.

Cuisine: Although there is no café, a tray is laden with healthy and unhealthy goodies, such as fruit, cheese and chocolate brownies.

Ideal for: Londoners wanting to escape but stay on the scene, be regularly relaxed and frequently waxed, and who want to keep stocked up on the latest Bliss beauty products.

What to pack: Your best friend. Start a night out with a drink and manicure at the nail bar before hitting London's bars – just make sure you've booked your Hangover Herbie for the next day.

Champneys Health Resort

** ** **

Address: Wigginton, Tring,
Hertfordshire HP23 6HY, England
Telephone: (+44) (0)1442 291 000
Booking details: reservations@champneys.co.uk
Website: www.champneys.com

One of the most famous health farms/spas in the world, and rightly so, Champneys is situated in a private mansion in the midst of 70 hectares (170 acres) of quintessentially English parkland. With the most extensive treatment menu in the country, the resort specializes in every field of health and beauty, not just pampering facials and beautifying body treats. There's diet and nutritional advice (including weight-loss programmes and regimes for food cravings and intolerances), and every type of fitness programme and class imaginable (the timetable is astonishing and ranges from spinning to ballet). Expert guidance on more internal issues is available within the LifeSpace programme, which is designed to

tackle stress-related illnesses and symptoms. Even though it was founded more than 60 years ago by a naturopath, Champneys has moved with the times and is still at the forefront of wellbeing breaks.

The ambience: Traditional and professional while exuding a friendly and unhurried atmosphere. Although known for its original Victorian wing, furnished with elegant antiques, the newly extended Garden wing imbues a more modern hotel feel.

Regular guests: Mainly women lolling around on their own or with a handful of friends. Champneys attracts a lot of health- and beauty-seekers from abroad, especially the Middle East and the USA. They've been host to their fair share of celebrities, too.

Treatment menu: From traditional no-nonsense Clarins facials, and manicures, pedicures and every type of massage and body wrap known to womankind, to the more unusual treatments such as watsu (a water shiatsu that is designed to relax and soothe the body, mind and soul in one go). Ayurveda and reiki healing are also available, plus a great range of more serious medically related treatments and services, including osteopathy and chiropody.

House speciality: Shirodhara is an Ayurvedic favourite involving warm oil being slowly drizzled over the third eye (the middle of your forehead). The therapy aims to induce a deep sense of relaxation, clear emotional blockages and improve intuition.

Cuisine: Dieting at Champneys is a glamorous affair. The food is healthy, delicious and satisfying, just lacking in calories. There are plenty of salads, vegetables, grilled fish and chicken dishes using only organic or naturally produced ingredients. Although your plate won't be overflowing (portions are carefully controlled and balanced), you won't go hungry. A light diet is available for those on more strict diets. There's also a good wine and champagne list, proving you're not expected to give up all your weaknesses overnight.

Ideal for: A weekend of wellbeing for stressed-out Londoners (it's just 60 minutes away by car), or a longer, more serious overhaul for those flying long-haul (it's 45 minutes from Heathrow).

What to pack: The dress-down code means you can float around most of the day in your robe and only need to pack 'real' casual clothes to wear for dinner.

Charles Worthington Day Spa

✳ ✳

Address: Percy Street, London, W1P 9FB, UK
Telephone: (+44) (0)207 7631 1370
Booking details: (+44) (0)207 631 1370
Website: www.cwlondon.com

Situated in a five-storey Georgian building, Charles Worthington's flagship concept salon and day spa is home to hairdressing, beauty therapy, relaxation and out-and-out pampering. The spa area, known as the Beauty Zone, is downstairs, tucked away from the noisy hairdryers and constant chatter in the hair salon. Super-soft robes and comfy slippers, a soothing water feature, fragrant burning oils, a minimalist stone fireplace and cheerful staff provide the perfect environment to help you forget why you got so stressed in the first place. Lottery winners should try the VIP evening party: six guests get pampered and beautified like royalty in the salon and spa, which are closed to the public on your arrival.

The ambience: An oasis of calm in the middle of the concrete jungle.

Regular guests: Media moguls, working girls on their day off and regulars to Charles's famous hairdressing salon upstairs.

Treatment menu: Fabulous facials, blissfull body treats and city-stress relievers, including LaStone therapy and reiki, are on the list.

House speciality: The hydrotherm massage takes place on a warm water-filled mini mattress that sits on top of the beauty couch. This technique makes the treatment more relaxing and effective because the therapist can work underneath your body.

Cuisine: No food is served, but the juniors will nip out and pick up whatever you want from the neighbouring cafés and eateries.

Ideal for: A pampering facial, massage and blow-dry before heading out for a night in the West End.

What to pack: Make-up and party dress so you can get ready there.

Chewton Glen

✶✶

Address: New Milton, Hampshire BH25 6QS, England
Telephone: (+44) (0)1425 275 341
Booking details: reservations@chewtonglen.com
Website: www.chewtonglen.com

Chewton Glen is a privately owned five-star hotel with a location that gives it the best of both worlds – it's on the edge of the magical New Forest and only a 15-minute walk from the sea. The spa offers up-to-date treatments carried out in the ten treatment rooms. There's a whirlpool, two saunas, a steam room infused with eucalyptus, and a relaxation room. You can work off the traditional English cream teas that Chewton Glen is famous for in the gym, during a game of tennis, or by swimming a few lengths in the 'ozone-treated' indoor pool. There's croquet on the manicured lawn and golf for more laid-back athletes, or keep-fit classes and a jogging trail that leads to the nearby beach for the enthusiastic.

The ambience: Chewton Glen is a smart but informal, chintzy but cosy, country-house hotel with an add-on spa that is geared around total self-absorbed indulgence, just like the hotel.

Regular guests: The rich and famous (the helicopter pad isn't just for show), country club members and international holiday-makers.

Treatment menu: Over 40 treatments, using Clarins, Guinot and E'Spa, ensure something for everyone. Choose from regular massages to Thai Yoga, or from luxury facials to algae wraps.

House speciality: Samadhi Synergy Synchronized Massage is a 50-minute treatment with two therapists. Self-absorbing enough?

Cuisine: Widely acclaimed for its food (it has a Michelin star), Chewton Glen does tip its hat to those watching their weight. The modern French-inspired menu in the one-and-only restaurant offers a variety of delicious dishes using local ingredients.

Ideal for: A restful weekend away with a few indulgences thrown in.

What to pack: Appropriate shoes and clothes for walking.

Cowshed

★★★

Address: Babington House, Babington near Frome,
Somerset BA11 3RW, England
Telephone: (+44) (0)1373 812 266
Booking details: cowshed@babingtonhouse.co.uk
Website: www.babingtonhouse.co.uk

Babington House is the sister club to the members-only Soho House in London, known for its following among the media, art and film world. It's the archetypal modern-day country house, full of the most stylish home comforts you wish you could afford. The historic Main House is early Georgian with a distinctly contemporary decor. The bedrooms have solid oak floors, modern furniture, large bathrooms and walk-in showers. The Cowshed, the spa named after its previous occupants, has a sauna, steam, mini gym, and indoor and outdoor pools, as well as treatment rooms.

The ambience: With an understated, down-to-earth luxury, it is like staying at a very wealthy, stylish, friend's country house.

Regular guests: London's media crowd and local executives.

Treatment menu: A whole range of pampering facials and pummelling massages designed to make you feel good about the here and now, rather than guilty about yesterday, are available in the Cowshed or the Mongolian *yurt* (tent) overlooking the lake.

House speciality: Until the Cows Come Home is a day package that includes a relaxing treatment (massage or facial), a couple of grooming treatments, plus something a little more alternative (holistic massage, reflexology or a luxury facial with essential oils). Lunch, drinks and full use of the facilities are included.

Cuisine: The food is Italian-inspired, country-style and absolutely delicious, but not spa-orientated. (You can't have everything.)

Ideal for: A romantic, indulgent clean or dirty weekend away.

What to pack: Leave all beauty lotions and potions at home as the fabulous Cowshed products are in the bathroom.

Dorchester Spa

✳ ✳ ✳

Address: Dorchester Hotel, Park Lane,
London W1A 2HJ, England
Telephone: (+44) (0)207 629 8888
Booking details: spa@dorchesterhotel.com
Website: www.dorchesterhotel.com

Steeped in elegance and tradition, the Dorchester is one of the oldest hotels in London. After being greeted at the revolving brass doors by an immaculate doorman in top hat and tails, you head down to the small but stylish spa located in the basement. Opulent Art Deco surroundings, walnut-and-marble changing rooms, saunas, steam rooms, spa baths and the best treatments money can buy contribute to an all-round glamorous hotel-spa experience.

The ambience: Private and exclusive. Although the spa is located next to London's busy Park Lane, it feels off the beaten track.

Regular guests: Celebrities looking for a sanctuary from waiting paparazzi, Hollywood stars sneaking in for treatments during press junkets, and manicured executives taking time out between deals.

Treatment menu: Top-notch therapists carry out top-notch treatments using products and techniques from Eve Lom, E'Spa, Jurlique and Thalgo. You can be slimmed, invigorated, detoxed, relaxed and groomed to perfection, thanks to the extensive list of fairly cosmetically orientated treatments.

House speciality: The infamous Eve Lom facial uses a combination of deep-cleansing putty, hot muslin cloths and lymphatic drainage massage to cleanse, unclog and rejuvenate the complexion.

Cuisine: Two main restaurants and a casual café in the hotel serve delicious but mostly calorific dishes, so choose carefully.

Ideal for: A short, swanky spa-and-shopping break. Although it is not the kind of spa for losing weight and kickstarting a fitness regime, it is the kind for getting pampered in the lap of luxury.

What to pack: *Vogue* magazine and an autograph book, just in case.

Elemis Day Spa

✷ ✷

Address: 2-3 Lancashire Court, Mayfair,
London W1S 1EX, England
Telephone: (+44) (0)208 909 5060
Booking details: elemisdayspa@elemis.com
Website: www.elemis.com

If there's one place where you can buy relaxation, it's at the Elemis Day Spa. Although geographically just around the corner from the thronging masses in London's West End, it's discreetly located at the end of a cute mews and mentally feels far from the madding crowd.

Individual sensory suites with private closets and showers ensure total seclusion, while decadence is guaranteed in the exotically themed suites, the Sensory Slipper Bath Garden – built into a Balinese garden, with pebbled walls and bamboo – and the ornate Moroccan herbal steam room. The suites include the dark, womb-like Moroccan suite, the Balinese suite and the Thai suite with its own relaxation area.

Whether you've got an hour or a whole day, the exotic, sensual treatments at this spa will transport your mind, massage your ego and soothe your soul. Sensuality, simplicity and vibrancy were the buzzwords used to inspire the treatments here, which have been taken from ancient exotic beauty rituals and therapies from all over the world. Hands-on therapy has been taken to another level with the aim of bringing physical and emotional balance even to the most frazzled Londoner.

The ambience: Far East meets the West End. A private bell at the front door gives an exclusive ring to this special spa. The wood interior, candles floating in water and immaculately groomed therapists wearing chic navy blue Chinese-style uniforms, who float around communicating in hushed whispers, create a sanctuary that makes guests feel as though they are a million miles from the outside world.

Regular guests: Harassed office workers looking for solace, loitering tourists looking for a rest, and pampered beauty editors looking for a story.

Treatment menu: Just reading through the menu brings about a sense of relaxation. An exotic blend of therapies from Bali, Tibet, Polynesia, Japan, Morocco and Thailand are on offer. You'll be spoiled for choice with the enticingly named Tahitian Bloom, Tropical Milk Treat, Japanese Silk Booster Facial and Cleopatra's Ritual, to name but a few.

House speciality: The Absolute Spa Ritual is a no-nonsense, 60-minute wellbeing massage. The package is tailored to each individual's requirements, so, whether you want to reduce stress, revive the spirit, relax aching muscles or balance the chakras, it's the perfect pampering treatment. It is coupled with the renewing, nurturing Japanese Silk Booster Facial, which is also tailored to your own personal needs.

Cuisine: Day packages include light lunches, fresh fruit and juice ordered in from Hush, the upmarket restaurant next door.

Ideal for: A birthday present for her, a Christmas present for him or a wedding present for both of them. (There's a wonderful Rasul treatment here, the traditional Arabian cleansing ritual that is perfectly designed for two.)

What to pack: An *A to Z of London* so you can find your way there, and more importantly, post-hedonistic treatment, find your way back home.

Forest Mere Health Farm

*

Address: Liphook, Hampshire GU30 7JQ, England
Telephone: (+44) (0)1428 726 000
Booking details: (+44) (0)8703 300 300
Website: www.healthfarms.co.uk

Whether you want to take the weight off your mind with stress-busting techniques and pampering, or some weight off your body with healthy eating and overdue exercise, Forest Mere is a good place to start. Set among velvety green lawns, thick woodland and facing a lake, Forest Mere has a prime location as well as all the trimmings of an exclusive health farm (thanks to a £14m refurbishment). That said, this place also has a reputation for being down to earth and unpretentious. It attracts people from all walks of life, and is a good place for spa virgins who won't be made to feel like an idiot if their spa etiquette isn't up to scratch.

There are two aerobic studios with unlimited group classes and workouts, a fully equipped gym with a good variety of weight-training and cardiovascular equipment, and a fleet of qualified instructors and personal trainers. The 24-metre (80-foot) indoor swimming pool and smaller outdoor pool, plus cycling, tennis, golf

and organized hiking in the surrounding countryside, will aid your campaign for better fitness. As for the mind, and more outer-body experiences, the list includes flotation tank treatments, Eastern-style scalp massage and life dance classes.

The ambience: In the middle of beautiful, rolling English countryside overlooking a tranquil lake, Forest Mere is like a friendly, buzzy private house.

Regular guests: British soap-opera stars and female guests of all ages. As the health farm is very male-friendly, don't be surprised to see a man or two padding around in a robe and slippers.

Treatment menu: Extensive. There's everything here from facials, massages, body scrubs and detoxifying, water-retention-reducing wraps – the standards of every spa menu – to the more eclectic Dry Flotation and Steamed Turkish Mud treatments. Alternative therapies are well represented, too, including acupuncture, hypnotherapy, Bach flower therapy and stress reduction, plus a handful of more quirky services on a slightly different level, including palmistry and astrology, perhaps to help point you in the right direction if you're at an emotional crossroads.

House speciality: Forest Mere has a fantastic thalassotherapy pool, the first of its kind in the UK. You can either dip into the warm mineral-rich pool with massaging hydrojets for a stand-alone, or rather float-alone, treatment or book one in for a relaxing prelude to another treatment. The bath is excellent for temporarily remedying cellulite and easing arthritis and general muscular and joint aches.

Cuisine: Excellently presented à la carte health food is on offer, with organic options. For serious dieters, there's a separate 'light-diet room' to prevent any drooling at the non-'light' plates.

Ideal for: Taking advantage of one of the specially designed mother-and-daughter packages and going on a pampering overnight stay. It's also great for a hen weekend or corporate event, as large groups are well catered for.

What to pack: Not a lot. Everything is laid on, and the well-stocked boutique has any item you might have forgotten. However, walking shoes are recommended for exploring the extensive grounds.

Grayshott Hall

✷✷

Address: Headley Road, Grayshott near Hindhead,
Surrey GU26 6JJ, England
Telephone: (+44) (0)1428 602 000
Booking details: reservations@grayshott-hall.co.uk or
(+44) (0)1428 602 020
Website: N/A

Like most of the well-established destination health farm/spas in
the UK, Grayshott is situated in acres of nature, even though it is
just a 60-minute drive from London. Gardens, woods and sweeping
lawns set the serene scene beautifully, immediately melting tension.
There's a real personal approach here, and the team of beauty
therapists, nurses, lifestyle counsellors and relaxation therapists
are dedicated to all aspects of health, beauty and wellbeing.

The ambience: Very, very quiet, to the point of feeling as though
you have to talk in a hushed voice. Ideal if you're longing for peace.

Regular guests: Locals on a frivolous pampering day, and dedicated
health-followers, here for a quick kickstart to a new lease of life.

Treatment menu: Facials for men and women, a small selection
of massages, a wide choice of body treats designed to pamper or
reduce inches, hydrotherapy baths, diet and fitness programmes,
and hypnotherapy are some of the options offered on this long list.

House speciality: The deeply relaxing LaStone massage, which is
carried out using hot and cold stones, is a popular one to try.

Cuisine: Food is not served in abundance, which is perfect if you
want to lose weight, and there's no alcohol – making a temptation-
free detox the most logical solution. Breakfast is served in your
room or the light diet room, and buffet lunches and dinner are
served in the dining room.

Ideal for: A first-time spa-goer. The intimacy and everything-
under-one-roof style of Grayshott makes it very unintimidating.

What to pack: Your own robe for the day (they don't supply them).

Hoar Cross Hall

**

Address: Hoar Cross, near Yoxall,
Staffordshire DE13 8QS, England
Telephone: (+44) (0)1283 575 748
Booking details: (+44) (0)1283 575 671
info@hoarcross.co.uk
Website: www.hoarcross.co.uk

Hoar Cross Hall is geared towards a more grown-up spa-goer, who likes traditional, oak-panelled, Persian-rugged, country-estate comfort rather than ultra-modern, simplistic surroundings. You can come here to lose weight, check out the state of your cholesterol and kickstart a new healthy-living regime or simply chill out in relaxed luxury, enjoying the occasional massage and yoga class.

The ambience: A relaxed atmosphere in a traditional stately home setting in the middle of the countryside.

Regular guests: Grown-up married couples and locals.

Treatment menu: An extensive menu offering something for every mind (and body), from G5 cellulite treatments and international facials and massages to flotation tanks and Ayurvedic therapies.

House speciality: Vishesh and Swedana. First, you have Vishesh, a firm Ayurvedic massage carried out by two therapists, which is designed to stimulate the release of toxins from the cells. Next up is Swedana, a herbal steam treatment which makes you mildly perspire, encouraging the release of more rogue toxins. The unique Water Grotto with massage area is a fun way to relax, too.

Cuisine: Excellent well-presented dishes are graded on how much fat and calories they contain. Weight-watchers' food is clearly marked.

Ideal for: Partners and friends in need of a pampering, healthy break. A good place for those who like to dress up a bit for dinner, as the restaurant is open to non-residents.

What to pack: A robe for the day (otherwise, you will have to pay a hire charge) and smarter clothes for dinner.

Lucknam Park Hotel & Spa

**

Address: Lucknam Park, Colerne, Chippenham,
Wiltshire SN14 8AZ, England
Telephone: (+44) (0)1225 742 777
Booking details: reservations@lucknampark.co.uk
Website: www.lucknampark.co.uk

Entered via an impressive mile-long, tree-lined driveway, Lucknam Park's 200 hectares (500 acres) of countryside are home to horse stables, tennis courts and an outdoor fitness course. Aside from the newly built stone spa, you can relax next to Lucknam's country-house fireplace or visit the beautiful nearby city of Bath.

The ambience: An elegant 300-year-old English stately home. Although slightly chintzy, it's friendly and touched with class.

Regular guests: Wealthy Japanese and American tourists, and local spa members over the age of 50.

Treatment menu: All the favourite beauty boosters are available: fake tan, a hair and nail salon, massages, and facials and body toners using marine derivatives in algae wraps, seaweed anti-ageing masks and O^2 marine facials. The scrubs and rubs for the face, neck and back are designed to cleanse, firm and refine the skin.

House speciality: A true back-to-basics treatment, the Luxury Aromatherapy Massage uses an oil of your choice to thoroughly and systematically massage every muscle in your body.

Cuisine: The Spa has a wide lunchtime and snack menu, including salads, light grills, open sandwiches and a good wine list. The first-class hotel restaurant serves gourmet dinners of roasted game and fowl, but the less carnivorous are also well catered for.

Ideal for: Lovers of traditional English hospitality, older in-laws for a day out, or an anniversary weekend playing Lord and Lady.

What to pack: Hardy outdoor shoes and all your airs and graces.

Nirvana Spa

✳✳

Address: Mole Road, Wokingham,
Berkshire RG41 5DJ, England
Telephone: (+44) (0)118 989 7555
Booking details: info@nirvanaspa.co.uk
Website: www.nirvanaspa.co.uk

Nirvana Day Spa has its own source of pure well water, so treatments are centred around water therapy. There's a superb collection of pools with varying benefits, from tranquil bathing in the Relaxation Pool, swimming in the 25-metre (80-foot) Fitness Pool to drifting away in the state-of-the-art Flotation Pools (the only pools with salt imported straight from the Dead Sea in the UK). It also offers up to 90 aerobic classes a week at the adjacent health club, a variety of fitness programmes and training for all levels, and an extensive choice of self-indulgent treatments.

The ambience: Very quiet and chilled-out, even down to the calming classical music piped into the changing rooms.

Regular guests: Local members, countywide members (you can take out a 12-visits-per-year membership) and day spa guests.

Treatment menu: All the usual suspects, such as massages, facials, body wraps, manicures, and even laser hair removal for those planning on spending a lot of time wandering around in swimsuits.

House speciality: Flotation Therapy. Allegedly a 60-minute float in one of the pools is as refreshing as a whole night's sleep. By removing gravity and depriving your body of external stimuli as you float, your body really relaxes, your mind switches off and you achieve your own nirvana. Plus the salts and minerals have an excellent soothing, restorative effect on the skin.

Cuisine: Light, healthy spa cuisine is served in the Garden Café.

Ideal for: Escaping the English climate and experiencing a healthier respite with a friend.

What to pack: A couple of swimsuits and a pair of flip-flops.

Pavilion Spa at Cliveden House

★ ★ ★

Address: Taplow, Berkshire SL6 0JF, England
Telephone: (+44) (0)1628 668 561
Booking details: (+44) (0)800 454 063
Website: www.clivedenhouse.co.uk

Cliveden is a stately home situated on the River Thames in 122 hectares (over 300 acres) of parkland and gardens. After sweeping up the gravel driveway, you are greeted by uniformed footmen and your suitcases are unpacked by maids. Suites are bigger than most city apartments, and you can arrange to go horse-riding, shooting or fishing. With a four-to-one staff/guest ratio and a quaint spa that offers indulgent, no-nonsense treatments, you'll feel spoilt rotten.

The ambience: Understated luxury in a traditional English house with attentive but unobtrusive staff.

Regular guests: As the former home of three dukes, the Astor family and a Prince of Wales, Cliveden has been host to President Roosevelt, George Bernard Shaw, Winston Churchill and Charlie Chaplin. Today it attracts mainly corporate guests during the week and those in the pursuit of leisure and pleasure at weekends.

Treatment menu: Your archetypal beauty treatments for spa-goers who want to be pampered in a way they know and like.

House speciality: The Evening Primrose Oil Bath is not as it sounds. The 60-minute treatment encompasses a full-body exfoliation and a massage using a super-moisturizing concoction of goat's butter, almond oil and evening primrose oil, followed by a body wrap and 20 minutes on a warm flotation bed.

Cuisine: Gourmet food is available in the hotel's two restaurants and fat-controlled lunches and snacks are served in the Conservatory.

Ideal for: A couple who want to feel like VIPs for the weekend.

What to pack: Evening clothes – you'll feel like dressing up.

Ragdale Hall Health Hydro

✷ ✷

Address: Ragdale Village, near Melton Mowbray,
Leicestershire LE14 3PB, England
Telephone: (+44) (0)1664 434 831
Booking details: enquiries@ragdalehall.co.uk
Website: www.ragdalehall.co.uk

Easy-going Ragdale Hall isn't about hanging out with the glamour
set in designer loungewear; it's about letting it all hang out with
the down-to-earth crowd in fluffy robes. The 89 bedrooms, nearly
40 treatment rooms and a fleet of about 50 therapists mean that
Ragdale buzzes with activity. This is the perfect place for spa virgins
wanting to kickstart a new and more beautiful life, without feeling
like they have to have a facial, pedicure and their hair done before
they even get there. Although Ragdale have started to veer towards
the more spiritual therapies, they excel at the traditional ones.

The ambience: Ragdale has a reputation for friendliness and
it is full of chatty females.

Regular guests: Mothers and daughters spending quality time
with each other, groups of women visitors and loyal regulars.

Treatment menu: The extensive list of treatments uses well-known
products from Decléor, Clarins, Kanebo, Guinot and Elemis.

House speciality: You'll either love or hate the slightly left-field
Chakra Journey. While you lie on a Wave Translator (a couch/bed
with speakers located underneath), sounds and vibrations induce
a sense of relaxation and emotional clearing. The therapist gives
you a head- and sinus-clearing head, face and scalp massage.

Cuisine: Ragdale serves delicious healthy snacks and meals, and you
are allowed to buy a bottle of wine to accompany your evening meal.

Ideal for: Hen (bachelorette) parties and girly weekends.

What to pack: Robe and slippers.

SPAce.NK

✳ ✳ ✳

Address: 127-131 Westbourne Grove, Notting Hill,
London W2 4UP, England
Telephone: (+44) (0)207 727 8002
Booking details: (+44) (0)207 727 8002
Website: www.spacenk.com

SPAce.NK is one of those places that makes you go aaaaah! as soon as you walk through the heavy glass doors. Your mind stops racing, your heart stops pumping furiously, and your problems suddenly don't seem so all encompassing. The stylish unisex interior makes it a comfortable place for both men and women, who all pad around in matching robes and rubber flip-flops. The therapists drift about with enviable serenity in white trousers and tops, and make it their duty to get you ready to face the outside world again.

The ambience: Nicknamed Spank, SPAce.NK is a modern, pampering haven in fashionable Notting Hill that attracts a young, hip crowd.

Regular guests: Daddy's girls swanking in for a Rose Body Cocoon, funky mothers-to-be waddling in for a Pregnancy Massage, and body-beautiful cover girls strutting in for a post-workout sports massage.

Treatment menu: Edited versions of popular mind-and-body therapies mean that gimmicks have been left out. Effective facials, relaxing and detoxifying body wraps, and soothing massages ensure that you'll leave looking and feeling better than when you arrived.

House speciality: Body Balancing is an incredible top-to-toe treatment that combines energy massage and essential oils to rejuvenate the physical being and 'create a space for inner quiet'.

Cuisine: There's no food here, so don't arrive hungry. Plenty of herbal teas and water are on hand, though.

Ideal for: Beauty addicts, mothers and birthday girls being pampered before brunch at nearby eateries, Tom's Deli or Lucky Seven.

What to pack: A long list of your beauty must-haves – they're all sold in the adjacent beauty shop, Space NK.

Spa at the Lowry Hotel

**

Address: 50 Dearmans Place, Chapel Wharf,
Salford, Manchester M3 5LH, England
Telephone: (+44) (0)161 827 4000
Booking details: thespa@thelowryhotel.com
Website: www.rfhotels.com

A five-star hotel with a five-star spa, the Lowry makes a good
north-of-England city break, combining retox in the bar with detox
in the spa. It is situated in the heart of Manchester on the banks of
the River Irwell in part of the trendy Chapel Wharf development,
which means you can get out and explore the nearby shopping and
entertainment when you're not wrapped up in the spa (literally).

The ambience: The glass, steel and concrete design gives the
building an almost industrial, but stylish, vibe.

Regular guests: Working businessmen and frolicking couples.

Treatment menu: The spa is an E'Spa salon, so most of the
treatments revolve around the brand's aromatherapy products.
Everything is available here, from a Golfer's Tonic (a tension-
busting pre-tee-off treat) to the Detoxifying Spa Tonic (a 150-
minute session that spring-cleans your system). The day
programmes and leisure breaks are worth looking into, as
they take the confusion out of choosing treatments.

House speciality: Choose from the hot stone massage, which
incorporates deep tissue massage, shiatsu and lymphatic drainage,
or the personalized Total Holistic Body Care treatment.

Cuisine: The River Room, overseen by legendary chef Marco Pierre
White, serves up terrific, though usually calorific, French cuisine. No
low-calorie options except the obvious ones, like salads and grilled fish.

Ideal for: A romantic break with your partner or a fun weekend
with the girls or guys, where the spa and bar go hand in hand.

What to pack: Tracksuits for the gym, party clothes for the nightclub
and a hairdryer, as there isn't one in the room.

Spa at the Mandarin Oriental

★ ★ ★

Address: 66 Knightsbridge, Hyde Park,
London SW1X 7LA, England
Telephone: (+44) (0)207 235 2000
Booking details: (+44) (0)207 838 9888
Website: www.mandarin-oriental.com

The Spa at the Mandarin Oriental has managed to fuse Western luxury and expectation with Eastern spirituality and serenity. From the moment you arrive, you are encouraged to leave your outside necessities – along with your worries – at the door by exchanging your outdoor shoes for soft, rubber flip-flops. You are then led down dark grey granite steps to the peaceful Zen relaxation area, which has stunning works of art dotted around the walls. Here, the light is subdued and the only sounds are of running water and soft music coming from behind the closed doors of the lavish treatment rooms.

For those who are so stressed that they don't know whether they are coming or going, Treatment Rituals have been created. With this unique arrangement, you simply book the amount of hours you want beforehand and decide, with the help of your therapist, what treatments to have on the actual day. The Spa at the Mandarin Oriental is pricey, but it's worth every single penny.

The ambience: Incredibly peaceful, decadent but low-key glamour.

Regular guests: Females that fall into one, or all, of the following: highly paid; highly stressed; high-flyers; high maintenance. According to the spa spies, pop idols Britney Spears and Madonna are regular pre-premiere visitors.

Treatment menu: Incredibly advanced E'Spa beauty treatments mix East and West philosophies and techniques in such therapies as Optimal Release, a joint-easing treatment that includes a salt scrub, Balinese Synchronized Massage, a two-therapists session, and a selection of luxury body treatments and facials. Be sure to spend some time in the spectacular, meditative Amethyst Crystal

Steam Room, which is designed to induce mental peace and tranquillity. Try out the water therapies, too. There is a state-of-the-art Vitality Pool – a 36ºC (97ºF) mineral-water plunge pool with underwater massaging and soothing hydrotherapy jets.

House speciality: The Balinese Synchronized Massage is a comprehensive treatment involving a foot ritual and face, body and scalp treatment. One therapist is later joined by another therapist who, working in synchronized harmony, massage you into an intoxicating stupor. Be warned, though. It is so relaxing, that you are likely to dribble like a baby.

Cuisine: Fresh fruit and juices are served in the relaxation room, or you can head upstairs to the Park restaurant where the extensive menu also includes lighter, healthier choices.

Ideal for: A birthday present, anniversary present or 'just because I can' present. Also excellent for pop idols who just want to be idle.

What to pack: A swimsuit for those who shy away from public nudity (although some areas, such as the water therapy pools, steam and saunas are designated as female-only or male-only), and a pair of running shoes for jogging through Hyde Park.

Spa at Renaissance London Chancery Court Hotel

★ ★ ★

Address: The Renaissance London Chancery Court Hotel,
252 High Holborn, London WC1V 7EN, England
Telephone: (+44) (0)207 829 7058
Booking details: rhi.loncc.thespa@renaissancehotels.com
Website: www.renaissancehotels.com/loncc

The Spa is cosseting luxury from the moment you place your bare feet on the warm slate floors in the roomy changing rooms. The crystal steam room has heated marble seats, the circular relaxation room has a gold-leaf ceiling and tropical fruits on a platter, and the spacious Asian-influenced treatment rooms have the most comfortable therapeutic-designed couches you'll find anywhere.

The ambience: Teak and slate furnishings give a unisex feel.

Regular guests: Hotel guests, high-flyers and E'Spa fans.

Treatment menu: Being an E'Spa concept spa, all the treatments are the latest in holistic relaxation. Choose from indulgent massages, cocooning body wraps and soothing facials.

House speciality: The E'Spa Stress Buster starts with a foot ritual that involves you taking the weight off your feet and the therapist taking the weight off your mind (you are asked how you feel mentally and physically to ensure the treatment is beneficial). An exfoliation, body brushing and massage with hot stones follows. The spa also specializes in Shirodhara, a hot oil treatment.

Cuisine: A spa menu containing light, fresh, tasty dishes is included in the day package or as an extra with the half-day package, and is served upstairs in the hotel restaurant.

Ideal for: Tourists wanting a luxury hotel-spa near major London attractions and Londoners looking for a luxurious urban retreat.

What to pack: A tracksuit if you're coming for the day package as robes are not allowed to be worn in the restaurant.

Springs Health Farm

*

Address: Ashby de la Zouch,
Leicestershire LE65 1TG, England
Telephone: (+44) (0)1530 273 873
Booking details: (+44) (0)1530 273 873
Website: www.springshealthfarm.co.uk

There are over 60 treatment rooms at Springs, and with the amount of people going through them, it's not unusual to feel like a number rather than number one. However, you've got every treatment known to womankind going on behind closed doors, plus some excellent health and fitness facilities, and experts on hand for help with losing weight, kicking bad habits and learning to relax.

The ambience: Busy and buzzy, friendly and unpretentious, with lots of women napping on loungers.

Regular guests: UK football players and soap-stars having treatments to improve their performance on and off the screen.

Treatment menu: A standard treatment menu in keeping with the Health Farm groups offers massages, facials, body wraps and flotation. They also have a wonderful thalassotherapy pool.

House speciality: The Mud Wrap Float begins with an application of detoxifying mud. You are then wrapped in foil and lowered into the water in a dry flotation bed – a bed-cum-bodysling that gives your body the full support of floating in water without getting wet.

Cuisine: The food has been specifically created with healthy eating in mind. The main restaurant menu has symbols marked clearly against each dish, indicating its calorie content (or not, as the case may be). You can even go back for seconds.

Ideal for: A mother-and-daughter or girlfriends' break. More girly and gossipy than romantic, so leave him at home.

What to pack: Smart-casual clothes for the evening. Although you are encouraged to stay in your robe during the day, they request 'normal' attire after 6 pm.

Utopia Health & Leisure Spa

* *

Address: Rowhill Grange Hotel & Spa, Wilmington,
Kent DA2 7QH, England
Telephone: (+44) (0)1322 615 136
Booking details: spa@rowhillgrange.com
Website: www.rowhillgrange.com

This rural retreat is set in a lush, traditional English country garden. The attention to detail in both the surroundings and the spa make it a great place for visitors to England to taste the real flavour of the country. The spa doesn't try to be too soulful or pretentious; instead, they excel at focused and nourishing spa treatments and feel-good pleasures.

The ambience: Faux-Roman mosaic baths are set deep in the gardens and lawns. Stately but not stuffy, the hotel is a cosy mix of corporate and comfort.

Regular guests: Tired, overworked mothers escaping from 'the kids', and corporate motivational groups.

Treatment menu: Lots of anti-ageing, cellulite-busting and skin-lifting programmes to tighten, tone, firm and help you battle against gravity. With over a dozen facials, underwater massage beds and a hair and nail salon, you can look as good as you feel.

House speciality: The Javanese Hot Oil and Mint Wrap is designed to relax and purify your mind and skin. Warm oil is massaged onto your body, then hot mint towels are firmly pressed into the skin. A brief scalp massage follows, while the minty aroma clears your head.

Cuisine: A brasserie menu is available to spa visitors, but self-indulgence is encouraged more than abstinence.

Ideal for: A special weekend treat for mothers, who deserve all the pampering they can get.

What to pack: A modest swimsuit.

Escape Spa at the Scotsman Hotel

**

Address: 20 North Bridge,
Edinburgh EH1 1YT, Scotland
Telephone: (+44) (0)131 556 5565
Booking details: (+44) (0)131 622 3800
Website: www.escapehealthclubs.co.uk

Escape Spa is a den of liquidity with a low-lit platinum 16-metre (52-foot) pool, spa pool, aroma-steam rooms, sauna, sanarium and arctic and tropical showers, which can all be used by day visitors. Most of the high-tech workout machines have personal TV screens, making exercise as pleasurable as possible. Be warned, however. What the spa giveth, the whisky bar taketh away. Their famous 'Room 399' bar stocks 399 single-malts, and when in Scotland ...

The ambience: The ultra-modern, masculine design uses slate tiles and steel mezzanine platforms, which overlook glass corridors.

Regular guests: Young couples on a city break, Edinburgh locals with gym and spa memberships, businessmen and tourists.

Treatment menu: E'Spa aromatherapy treatments including purifying and refining mud and algae body wraps, facials, and holistic massages.

House speciality: The Holistic Total Body Care is a rejuvenating journey for your skin and soul. Skin-brushing and an E'Spa body polish is followed by an express facial and a full-body massage, which includes a hot stone massage using aromatherapy oils.

Cuisine: The spa serves toasted sandwiches and simple salads, along with juices and healthy nibbles. North Bridge, the hotel's brasserie, is a stunning old room with a 360-degree indoor balcony, but serves an erratic mix of appetizers, grills and desserts.

Ideal for: The young at heart and upmarket stag weekends.

What to pack: Your man and your favourite CDs and DVDs – the hotel rooms have high-tech TV and audio systems.

One Spa

* *

Address: The Sheraton Grand Hotel & Spa,
8 Conference Square, Edinburgh EH3 8AN, Scotland
Telephone: (+44) (0)131 221 7777
Booking details: (+44) (0)131 221 7777
info@one-spa.com
Website: www.one-spa.com

Only a year old, it is apparent that expert time and money have been invested in this adjoining health club and spa. The Thermal Suite at One Spa is what makes this Scotland's leading spa and hydrotherapy facility. A designated floor hosts a range of hot and cooling therapies to cleanse and aid relaxation. The wet area includes a hammam, rock sauna, tepidarium, scented mist showers and a rooftop outdoor Jacuzzi-pool that fits about 35 people. The pair of essential oil-infused Cleopatra baths next to the swimming pool are fun if there are two of you. Unlike many other health clubs-cum-spas, the spa area is on a separate floor from the throbbing gym, creating a serene world of its own.

Being situated alongside one of Edinburgh's leading hotels means that you'll never be short of things to do when you're not indulging yourself in the spa. The concierge will point you in the right direction for local sights, recommended bars and restaurants, not to mention the city's stunning castle. A nearby gem of a rustic French restaurant, The Corner Bistro, is worth a visit and makes every minute spent working out in One Spa's superb gym or sweating out those toxins in the steam room worthwhile. A perfect city spa for indulgence, relaxation and feel-good pampering.

The ambience: Holistic spa meets bionic gym. A multilevelled labyrinth of modern, stylish and water-based facilities cater for every whim. Even though it's connected to a big corporate hotel, One Spa really does speak for itself.

Regular guests: Edinburgh's rich and body-conscious, and international business travellers who want to get lost for a self-pampering afternoon.

Treatment menu: Using Ayurvedic philosophies, E'Spa aromatherapy products and many Eastern rituals, One Spa has a comprehensive range of facials, massages, scrubs, rubs, wraps and soaks to complement its celebrated multiroomed thermal suite.

House speciality: The Serail Mud Chamber is a softening, detoxifying and purifying ritual. After applying a mudpack of chalk and healing earth to yourself, you'll dry out in a warm chamber to eliminate toxins before a herb vapour fills the air, letting the mud soften so that it can be showered off easily.

Cuisine: The spa bistro serves a simplified version of the hotel's Santini restaurant, including Tuscan salad, bruschetta and energy shakes. The Sheraton Grand has the usual corporate food choices of bar, brasserie or ballroom.

Ideal for: Tourists and day visitors who need a peaceful break from the bagpipes and steep hills around Edinburgh.

What to pack: A little confidence. The gym equipment and lockers are so high-tech that they need a James Bond-type watch to open them – you will need to ask how to use them.

Stobo Castle
Health Spa

✷✷

Address: Stobo Castle, Stobo, Peebleshire
EH 45 8NY, Scotland
Telephone: (+44) (0)1721 760 249
Booking details: (+44) (0)1721 760 600
Website: www.stobocastle.co.uk

A remote property on the River Tweed, Stobo Castle, with only 29 rooms, is the single destination spa in Scotland. The original stone building is from 1805, but the more recently added spa has greatly benefited from extensive and on-going modernization and recently won a prestigious UK spa award. The spa also has a unique glass-roofed relaxation and reception area, where you can let your thoughts wander and contemplate the world with renewed openness and clarity after a deeply satisfying massage. The emphasis is on sociable relaxation, rather than exertion, and Stobo offers free activities for all guests who want to improve their creative skills, including art and flower arranging, salsa dancing and a 'Chef's' demonstration. More rugged pastimes like fishing, shooting and horse-riding can also be arranged.

For those wishing to retreat even further from the outside world, Park Lodge is a private and more secluded self-contained building next to the castle which accommodates up to 12 people, ideal if you go with a group of friends.

The ambience: The discreet luxury of relaxed Scottish baronial grandeur set in majestic green hills and fresh, fresh air. You can't help but be inspired by the dramatic landscape, the only thing missing is film star Mel Gibson riding by dressed as Braveheart.

Regular guests: A vast majority of the guests here are Scottish, perhaps attempting to keep beautiful Stobo a secret from the rest of the world. Nice try!

Treatment menu: There are over 30 treatments for the body, including hydrotherapy, aromatherapy and G5 vibratory massages. For the face, there are deep-cleansing and detoxing facials, which are great for boosting the skin's vitality. Lastly, for your mind, there is a Dead Sea mineral flotation tank, where you can de-stress in peace.

House speciality: A super Collagen Facial stimulates cell renewal and reduces fine lines, replenishing and firming your face, and knocking years off in the process.

Cuisine: Famed for local salmon and trout, Stobo Castle uses local produce for rustic meals containing beef, game, lamb, venison and vegetables. Low-fat, healthy eating is promoted – fresh fruit is always on hand – and Stobo tradition means big, sociable, shared tables for all the meals.

Ideal for: Anyone wishing to switch off their mobile telephone (cell phone) – and the stresses of modern living – and recharge their batteries in a place of perfect peace. It's also great for hard-working urbanites looking for a genuine antidote to the oppressive concrete of their home city.

What to pack: Good books, walking shoes and a couple of entertaining old stories for around the fireplace. It's also worth bringing a track suit or loose clothes for hanging out during the day - kilts are not *de rigueur*.

St David's Hotel & Spa

✱ ✱ ✱

Address: Havannah Street,
Cardiff Bay, Cardiff CF10 5SD, Wales
Telephone: (+44) (0)2920 454 045
Booking details: reservations@fivestar-htl-wales.com
Website: www.roccofortehotels.com

Famous for having a TV set thrown out of the window into the sea by British pop star Robbie Williams, you really can do anything you want at this spectacularly modern hotel and spa, which looks like a streamlined ocean-liner (although taking it to the limits that Robbie did will almost certainly incur a hefty replacement charge).

St David's will organize anything from caving and potholing, gorge-walking to canoeing, pony trekking and paintballing to paragliding. Its location in Cardiff, now so cosmopolitan that it buzzes with day- and nightlife, means that you can get the most from your stay here, in and out of the impressive hydrotherapy-geared spa. The rooms are modern, minimal and easy on the eye, and all have views and sundecks overlooking the bay.

The spa is tucked away in its own corner of the hotel and even has its own café, where deliciously light and healthy five-star quality spa meals are served. The hotel provides big white fluffy dressing gowns for you to wear padding about in your room and in the spa, but you might want to take something a little more glamorous if you plan to spend plenty of time in the hotel as well as in the spa.

The ambience: Even though it is Wales's smartest hotel, St David's is very relaxed and casual – except in the spectacular atrium foyer, which has a high galleried airy structure that looks like the fizzy-lifting drink room in the movie based on Roald Dahl's story, *Willy Wonka & the Chocolate Factory*. And if any place can make you feel like you're floating, it's here.

Regular guests: Rugby fans in touch with their feminine side come here to enjoy pampering as well as rugger (the Millennium stadium is nearby). Small groups of couples and lone business executives seeking after-hours escapism in the spa, rather than the bar, are also frequent visitors.

Treatment menu: The spa specializes in hydrotherapy and detoxing treatments, and has an excellent saltwater hydropool with a corridor of underwater massage jets, water beds and swan-neck pummelling fountains, all of which help to obliterate tension and boost circulation. Treatments and products are from the divine E'Spa aromatherapy line. Packages, ranging from a day to a week, are superb, great value for money and well thought-out.

House speciality: The E'Spa Detoxifying Algae Wrap, just over 60 minutes of body brushing, exfoliating, buffing, polishing and wrapping, helps to speed up the elimination of your own personal toxic waste.

Cuisine: Delicious light dishes and juices are available in the spa, where you can wear your robe. There are yummy full-calorie meals and fabulous cocktails in Tides, the hotel restaurant where, whatever else, you will be wearing a post-spa smile.

Ideal for: A weekend of shopping, eating, drinking and spaa-ing.

What to pack: A rugby fan who's willing to try out a bit of beautifying and pampering.

THE AMERICAS

	PAGE	TYPE	PRICE	LUXURY	HEALTHY FOOD	GYM	POOL	OUTDOOR SPORTS	ALTERNATIVE TREATMENTS
Agua Spa at the Delano Hotel, USA	170	Hotel/Resort/Day	✶✶✶	✔			✔		✔
Arizona Biltmore Resort & Spa, USA	148	Hotel/Resort	✶✶✶	✔		✔	✔	✔	✔
Aveda Concept Spa at Strawberry Hill, Caribbean	136	Hotel/Resort	✶✶				✔	✔	✔
The Away Spa & Gym, USA	180	Hotel/Resort/Day	✶✶			✔			✔
Bacara Resort & Spa, USA	158	Hotel/Resort/Day	✶✶✶	✔	✔	✔	✔	✔	✔
Cal-a-Vie Spa, USA	160	Destination	✶✶✶		✔	✔	✔	✔	✔
Camelback Inn Resort, Golf Club & Spa, USA	150	Hotel/Resort/Day	✶✶		✔	✔	✔	✔	✔
Canyon Ranch, USA	152	Destination/medical	✶✶✶		✔	✔	✔	✔	✔
Canyon Ranch Spa Club, USA	175	Hotel/Resort/Day	✶		✔	✔	✔	✔	✔
Cap Juluca, Caribbean	128	Hotel/Resort	✶✶✶				✔	✔	✔
Cotton House, Caribbean	138	Hotel/Resort	✶✶✶	✔			✔	✔	✔

	PAGE	TYPE	PRICE	LUXURY	HEALTHY FOOD	GYM	POOL	OUTDOOR SPORTS	ALTERNATIVE TREATMENTS
CuisinArt Resort & Spa, Caribbean	130	Hotel/Resort	✶✶	✓	✓	✓	✓	✓	✓
Elemis Spa at the Aladdin Hotel Casino, USA	176	Hotel/Resort	✶✶✶	✓	✓	✓	✓		✓
Elysée Spa at La Samanna, Caribbean	140	Hotel/Resort	✶✶✶	✓	✓	✓	✓	✓	✓
Four Seasons Resort Scottsdale, USA	153	Hotel/Resort	✶✶	✓	✓	✓	✓	✓	✓
Givenchy Spa at the Merv Griffin Resort Hotel, USA	161	Hotel/Resort	✶✶	✓	✓	✓	✓	✓	✓
Golden Door Spa at the Boulders, USA	154	Hotel/Resort	✶✶✶	✓	✓	✓	✓	✓	✓
Golden Door Spa at Wyndham Peaks Resort, USA	168	Hotel/Resort/Day	✶✶✶	✓	✓	✓	✓	✓	✓
Grand Wailea Resort, USA	174	Hotel/Resort/Day	✶✶✶	✓	✓	✓	✓	✓	✓
The Greenbrier, USA	188	Hotel/Resort/Mineral Springs	✶✶✶	✓	✓	✓	✓	✓	✓
Green Valley Spa, USA	184	Destination/Medical	✶✶	✓	✓	✓	✓		✓
Grove Park Inn, USA	183	Hotel/Resort/Day	✶✶	✓	✓	✓	✓	✓	✓

	PAGE	TYPE	PRICE	LUXURY	HEALTHY FOOD	GYM	POOL	OUTDOOR SPORTS	ALTERNATIVE TREATMENTS
Helena Rubinstein Beauty Gallery, USA	181	Day	**						
Ikal del Mar, Mexico	144	Hotel/Resort	**	✓	✓	✓	✓	✓	✓
Las Ventanas al Paraiso, Mexico	146	Hotel/Resort	***	✓	✓	✓	✓	✓	✓
LeSport, Caribbean	139	Destination	**	✓	✓	✓	✓	✓	✓
Mandara Spa at the Ocean Club Resort, Caribbean	131	Hotel/Resort	***	✓	✓	✓	✓	✓	
Mezzanine Spa at Soho Integrative Health, USA	182	Day/Medical	**		✓	✓	✓		
Mii amo Spa, USA	156	Destination/Day	***	✓	✓	✓	✓	✓	✓
Miraval Life in Balance Resort, USA	157	Destination	***	✓	✓	✓	✓	✓	✓
Oasis Spa at LaSource, Caribbean	134	Destination	**	✓	✓	✓	✓	✓	✓
Ojai Valley Inn & Spa, USA	162	Hotel/Resort	**	✓	✓	✓	✓	✓	✓
Post Ranch Inn, USA	164	Destination	***	✓	✓	✓	✓	✓	✓

	PAGE	TYPE	PRICE	LUXURY	HEALTHY FOOD	GYM	POOL	OUTDOOR SPORTS	ALTERNATIVE TREATMENTS
Red Mountain Adventure Spa, USA	186	Destination/Medical/Hotel/Resort	**				✓	✓	
Ritz-Carlton Rose Hall, Caribbean	137	Hotel/Resort	***		✓	✓	✓	✓	✓
Sandy Lane, Caribbean	132	Hotel/Resort	***	✓	✓	✓	✓		✓
Shambhala Spa at Parrot Cay, Caribbean	142	Hotel/Resort	***	✓	✓	✓	✓	✓	✓
Spa at the Mandarin Oriental, USA	172	Hotel/Resort/Day	***	✓		✓	✓		✓
Spa Palazzo at the Boca Raton Resort & Club, USA	173	Hotel/Resort	***	✓	✓	✓	✓		✓
St Anne's Country Inn & Spa, Canada	124	Destination/Hotel/Resort	*		✓				✓
Tea Garden Springs, USA	166	Day	**						✓
Ten Thousand Waves, USA	178	Day	*		✓				✓
Two Bunch Palms, USA	167	Destination/Mineral Springs	**	✓	✓	✓	✓	✓	✓
Willow Stream Spa at the Fairmont Banff Springs, Canada	126	Hotel/Resort/Mineral Springs	**		✓	✓	✓	✓	✓

St Anne's Country Inn & Spa

*

Address: Haldimand Hills Spa Village,
RR1 Grafton, Ontario KOK 2GO Canada
Telephone: (+1) 905 349 2493
Booking details: (+1) 888 346 6772
Website: www.haldimandhills.com

St Anne's Country Inn & Spa is located 75 minutes east of Toronto,
just to the east of Cobourg. A charming stone inn at the heart of
a spa village, it sprawls across the Haldimand Hills and looks out
across a limitless view of Lake Ontario. The ten bedrooms have
names like Dolls House, Parlour Room and Flower Room and, as
their names suggest, are enchanting and chintzy. It's like staying
at a rich grandmother's house; although not necessarily in the
style in which you would decorate your own home, the rooms
are homey and comfy.

St Anne's has a year-round Fieldstone Grotto hydrotherapy facility,
which includes a large stone hot tub, a cold plunge pool and a
cedar-lined steam room, which emits so much eucalyptus scent

that your sinuses get a detox, too. Maison Sante, the fitness and wellness facility, is located 1 km (²⁄₃ mile) from the main inn. It has an indoor pool, class studio, private rooms for personal-training sessions, and a gym which includes Universal equipment, a treadmill, an elliptical trainer, and free weights and a bench. However, you may find the bike trips, hikes and walks on the estate's trails to nearby villages a more preferable, and natural, exercise alternative.

The ambience: Old-worldy country charm pervades St Anne's. Guests lounge around in robes and slippers, or soak in outdoor hot tubs almost everywhere you look.

Regular guests: Very relaxing but not overly expensive, the inn is a safe haven for Toronto's overworked and underpaid.

Treatment menu: Being an Aveda Lifestyle Salon, the treatments on offer at the spa have a gentle, natural approach, and are high-performing. All the classics, such as massages, mud packs, herbal wraps, facials, aromatherapy and reflexology, are on the menu, along with a few 'alternative' favourites such as reiki and Hawaiian lomi lomi massage.

House speciality: The innovative Milk and Sesame Stone Wrap is a 90-minute 'moisturizing ritual' in which a customized selection of smooth, warmed stones are placed on your body to support your spine and muscles. Additional hot basalt stones are used to massage a signature blend of buttermilk and sesame seeds onto the skin and the client is then wrapped in thermal linens to help them to sweat out toxins. The wrap is followed by wonderful face, scalp and foot massages, finishing with an invigorating shower.

Cuisine: The combination of country cooking and spa cuisine features local produce and herbs from the inn's own organic garden. Meals are simple and fresh, imaginative but recognizable, and while calories aren't discussed, the chef can accommodate most diets. Bring your own wine, as there's no alcohol licence at St Anne's.

Ideal for: A few girly days of detoxing and gossiping.

What to pack: You don't have to bring a bathrobe but as you are in it so much of the time, you may want to bring your own.

Willow Stream Spa at the Fairmont Banff Springs

✱✱

Address: PO Box 960, Banff, Alberta,
Canada TOL OCO
Telephone: (+1) 403 762 2211
Booking details: banffsprings@fairmont.com
Website: www.fairmont.com

Originally built in 1888, Banff Springs has benefited from several makeovers and developments, including a $100-million face-lift in March 2001. When you see the grandeur of this castle in the mountains, your mood will lift. A historical site, the attention to authentic design detail (replicated from European castles and manor houses) is excellent, even if the decor is a little stuffy, and service is impeccable. Outdoor activities vary according to the season, with skiing, hiking, fishing and golf on request. Although the spa treatments are on the unadventurous, traditional side, the resort has plenty of space and facilities to encourage you to relax for a comfortable day or two.

The ambience: A charming Canadian interpretation of a traditional Scottish castle – if slightly corporate – 'Scotland in the Rockies'.

Regular guests: Business travellers and young, adventurous, rich couples and Canadians who love European history but prefer not to cross the Atlantic.

Treatment menu: Willow Stream is a spacious, European-style spa with a broad collection of modern body and beauty treatments. Facials include a deep-cleansing Hungarian Organic Black Mud treatment, and a range of body wraps, scrubs and hydrotherapies give you a chance to rejuvenate your skin and lose any aches and pains. Local mountain spring water is put to good use in herbal baths, saunas and outdoor mineral whirlpools.

House speciality: Therapeutic minerals and botanicals, indigenous to the Rocky Mountains, make up the ingredients for the unique Mineral Body Scrub. The treatment involves a gentle exfoliation with the scrub, followed by an application of camomile lotion.

Cuisine: The spa bar has a nutritional, low-fat, light menu, while more substantial dining – a rotisserie-grilled lunch buffet with a mountain view – is served in the hotel's Bow Valley Grill. Castello Ristorante is a formal Italian, while Castle Pantry offers snacks and picnic food. The bistro-style Grapes Wine Bar is perfect for an intimate Canadian fondue – a calorific nightmare, but worth it.

Ideal for: A group of middle-aged friends who want to ski and relax in style.

What to pack: Binoculars for a closer inspection of the views of the surrounding mountain ranges, canyons, rock formations and the bountiful waterfalls.

Cap Juluca

★ ★ ★

Address: PO Box 240, Maunday's Bay,
Anguilla, British West Indies
Telephone: (+1) 264 497 6666
Booking details: capjuluca@anguillanet.com
Website: www.capjuluca.com

With one of the hottest reputations for luxury and glamour in the Caribbean, the exclusive Cap Juluca is set on the south-west coast of the coral island of Anguilla, in just under 80 hectares (200 acres) of tropical landscape on 3.3 km (2 miles) of white beaches. The resort's unusual Moroccan-style hotel with its Moorish architecture was inspired by North African souks and blends in perfectly with the flat terrain and panoramic shoreline. There are 72 whitewashed rooms, suites and villas with domed roofs, set along the coast, all of which are cleverly designed for privacy and have their own path to the beach. The rooms have lavish marble baths and French doors that open onto the ocean, along with a patio and balcony. The more upmarket villas have their own private pools.

Forget any ideas of a typical spa; here, the massage and spa rituals are carried out in your own villa, on a secluded spot on the beach, in a gazebo located on a sand dune at West Bay or in one of the two treatment rooms located at the main house. The amenities on offer are extensive, and include a fully equipped fitness centre

with personal trainers, private or couples yoga classes, bicycles for hire, the Golf Aqua driving range, a croquet lawn, tennis courts with a resident professional, and a variety of watersports, such as snorkelling, diving, windsurfing, waterskiing and sailing. This is more of a luxurious resort hotel with wonderful treatments than a traditional health spa.

The ambience: Simple, stylish, romantic and very peaceful. The owners have managed to create an Arabic minimalist decor that is still unashamedly decadent.

Regular guests: Cap Juluca attracts lookers, such as Tyra Banks and Claudia Schiffer, and onlookers who aren't phased about sunbathing alongside a celebrity.

Treatment menu: The small number of fabulous, carefully selected treatments are a combination of Anguilla- and Balinese-inspired rituals. The products incorporate local ingredients from the land and sea, such as flowers, herbs and sea minerals. Massages vary from therapeutic deep-tissue massage to sensual couple's massage (you can even do a course in massage techniques so you can take the benefits home) to the more spiritual hands-on art of healing, reiki.

House speciality: The exotic Juluca Ritual for Two, inspired by the scents and sensations of the island, is a 120-minute ritual of healing, rejuvenation and romance. It begins with a basil-and-mint clay body scrub to soothe and refresh you all over, followed by an aromatic shower, luxurious massage and is completed with a candlelit soak in tropical sea salts, strewn with petals, while you sip mint tea.

Cuisine: Cap Juluca has three restaurants from which to choose. The more formal Pimms serves an array of Euro-Caribbean and Asian specialities, and excellent local seafood. George is a casual bistro-style beachside eatery, which has a raw bar, barbecues and live entertainment. The intimate Kemia serves Moroccan hors-d'oeuvres and light snacks all day.

Ideal for: A honeymoon.

What to pack: Dark, dark, dark sunglasses, so if you do want to take a prolonged peek at a famous person you can do so subtly.

CuisinArt Resort & Spa

✷✷

Address: PO Box 2000, Rendezvous Bay,
Anguilla, British West Indies
Telephone: (+1) 264 498 2000
Booking details: reservations@cuisinartresort.com
Website: www.cuisinartresort.com

Inspired by the architecture of the Greek island of Mykonos, CuisinArt Resort has a particular, eccentric atmosphere which, though friendly, might not suit traditional tastes. There's a small, eclectic art gallery, a modern gym, a herb garden and hydroponic farm, all in close proximity. All 93 rooms, each with a private patio and marble bathroom, overlook Rendezvous Bay. The gardens are striking, with an impressive array of rich greenery and flowers.

The ambience: Whitewashed buildings are set in lush, tropical vegetation, creating a romantic and non-intimidating atmosphere.

Regular guests: New-age honeymooners looking for a slightly more soulful break, and fans of Greek architecture who can't bring themselves to stray from the Caribbean.

Treatment menu: The menu is organized into programmes, called 'escapes'. Fairly standard facials, scrubs and massages will not stretch a spa veteran's imagination, but some of the climate-sensitive skincare treatments are great – a simultaneous seaweed body mask and scalp massage will help your stress and impurities, well, escape.

House speciality: The Cucumber and Lavender Wrap, using home-grown ingredients, helps restore moisture to dry skin. Impurities are drawn out by the cucumber while aloe and lavender heal and soothe.

Cuisine: Pesticide-free fresh vegetables and fruit from the hydroponic farm are served at the three eateries: the gourmet Santorini, the poolside Mediterraneo and the Hydroponic Café.

Ideal for: Fashionable but easy-going spa fans who prefer the personal and flexible style of a boutique hotel.

What to pack: Tennis shoes – there are three all-weather courts.

Mandara Spa at the Ocean Club Resort

★ ★ ★

Address: PO Box 4-777 Nassau, Paradise Island,
Bahamas, British West Indies
Telephone: (+1) 242 363 2501
Booking details: www.sunint.com
Website: www.oceanclub.com

The resort is modern and luxurious, with considerate staff and top-notch service. If you are bringing a golf bore with you, though, be warned: the course, surrounded on three sides by turquoise sea, is one of the most talked-about in the Caribbean. Activities can be arranged beyond the tennis courts, gym and cycling trips on offer, but they are expensive. If this is not a worry, then yachting, helicopter trips or swimming with dolphins will be memorable.

The ambience: A modern, stylish resort, set against twelfth-century-style arches and garden statues hanging with bougainvillea.

Regular guests: Hollywood 'A' listers, global sports legends, sun-loving gamblers and the odd lottery winner.

Treatment menu: Billed as 'a sanctuary for one; a paradise for two', the Mandara Spa features eight private treatment suites, including four designed to accommodate couples. All treatments are influenced by Balinese or Caribbean traditions and begin with a ritual foot wash. The emphasis is on purification and looking good.

House speciality: A two-person four-hour spa marathon, the Bahamian Pathway to Radiance, features a foot treatment, lime-and-ginger salt glow, massage, aromapure facial and exotic hand ritual.

Cuisine: Daytime eating revolves around the Clubhouse and Beach Bar for grills, salads and sandwiches. For evenings, dine on the sand at Dune, which serves dishes inspired by hip New York restaurants.

Ideal for: A lavish wedding, or a Royal Highness wanting to lie low.

What to pack: Sports clothes and elegant eveningwear.

Sandy Lane

✳ ✳ ✳

Address: St James, Barbados, British West Indies
Telephone: (+1) 246 444 2000
Booking details: mail@sandylane.com
Website: www.sandylane.com

Sapphire-blue sea, pure white sand and incredible orange, pink and yellow sunsets, which give you a daily dose of free colour therapy, are the backdrop to this swanky hotel and world-class spa. From the moment you swish into the driveway in your chauffeured limousine, you know this isn't just another upmarket hotel. On arrival, you are immediately greeted with freshly chilled facecloths and iced glasses of tropical fruit punch, giving you your first taste of the luxurious world that is Sandy Lane.

A coral-stone crescent building with two grand staircases, which you can imagine Scarlett O'Hara sweeping down, is at the heart of the property. The stunning Greco-Romanesque spa stands separately from the hotel and is fronted by a spectacular waterfall, which cascades into a large cobalt-blue swimming pool, complete with water-spraying, coral-coloured stone dolphins. The spa's treatment rooms are bigger than most city-dwellers' apartments and the VIP suites could host a house party. If all the pampering leaves you a bit fuzzy-headed on the inside and frizzy-haired on the outside, expert blow-drys can be booked at the world-renowned John Frieda hair salon.

As you would expect, the gym is fully equipped with personal-training programmes and you can dabble in yoga, tai chi, Pilates and group exercise classes. All in all, this is the fast track to relaxation, and looking and feeling like a superstar, but it will cost you a wonderfully massaged arm and newly toned leg to get there.

The ambience: Elegant and stylishly relaxed. This beautiful, though slightly 'old colonial', froufrou hotel shouts decadence, money and extravagance.

Regular guests: The ice and two-slice, polo-playing brigade, the very rich and a succession of honeymoon couples splashing out on the holiday of a lifetime.

Treatment menu: With over 4,000 square metres (45,000 square feet) to play with, this spa isn't short of space or treatments. The combination of lavish, traditional therapies and modern, state-of-the-art treatments is inspired by a mêlée of different cultures from Barbados, the Far East and Europe. There are hydrotherapy suites with their own gardens, a Blitz-Jet room containing high-pressure jets to help boost circulation, break down cellulite and tone up slacking skin, and a Chakra Therapy room for carrying out more involved treatments such as the Ritual (see House Speciality below), Shirodhara and envelopments (exotic wraps and mind-and-body detoxifying treatments). Here, the practitioners work holistically, from head to foot (Ayurvedic foot therapy to Bajan head massage), as well as on the surface (with prerequisite beauty must-haves such as waxing and eyelash tints).

House speciality: The Ritual is a full day of unbelievable pampering. It includes a Rebalancing Aromatherapy Facial, a Purifying Herbal Linen Wrap with Hot Stones, a Detoxifying Sea of Senses and either the Essence of Earth or Oshadi Envelopment, followed by a choice of an Ayurvedic Holistic Massage or a Joint Massage.

Cuisine: Fine, fine-dining, fine, fine wine and an extensive cocktail list will give you the perfect excuse to treat yourself to a detoxing, skin-brushing, algae-wrapped recovery session the morning after.

Ideal for: A romantic retreat for couples seeking seclusion and for families with little ones of all ages who want a holiday with the best of everything.

What to pack: Far too much of everything in an ultra-expensive Louis Vuitton trunk.

Oasis Spa at LaSource

**

Address: Pink Gin Beach, PO Box 852, St George's,
Grenada, British West Indies
Telephone: (+1) 473 444 2556
Booking details: lasource@caribsurf.com
Website: www.lasourcegnd.com

Looking for a holiday where you return home in better shape than
when you left (with an all-over tan to boot)? You've just found it.
The luxury, all-inclusive LaSource, situated on the Pink Gin Beach,
is set in an oasis of white sand and crystal-clear sea. The resort

has about 100 rooms, which blend into the hillside and valley. The spa is very relaxed and down to earth; fitness-wise you are spoilt for choice. There are two or three classes or activities – including kickboxing and tai chi, aqua aerobics and scuba diving – every hour during the day, and you have world-class experts and sports coaches on hand for your every exercise need. It may sound pricey, but if you take advantage of all the facilities and experts here, it's amazing value for money. Tipping is strictly forbidden. As for the AOK (All-Over Knockout) tan, a short walk over a hill leads you to a very pretty, secluded little beach between the cliffs. LaSource apparently thinks of everything.

The ambience: Relaxed but buzzy. Dedicated to pleasure – for the body and the mind – there are lots of activities to occupy you, which creates an enthusiastic atmosphere.

Regular guests: Couples and groups of friends who get bored lying on a beach, yet want all the benefits of a beach-based holiday.

Treatment menu: Like its sister property in St Lucia, LeSport, the treatment range isn't revolutionary, but it's got everything a spa virgin could want (aromatherapy, Swedish massage, loofah rubs, seaweed wraps, facials, and so on), plus enough alternative pursuits and therapies for the more experienced spa-goer (such as yoga, reflexology, tai chi and stress management).

House speciality: The Aromatherapy Massage not only leaves you relaxed, but also improves circulation, encourages the elimination of toxins and helps to release long-term emotional tension.

Cuisine: Two restaurants offer buffet-style breakfasts and lunches and à la carte dinners, and the Terrace Bar located on the beach serves delicious barbecues. You will get fed and watered morning, noon and night. It doesn't matter how long you spend in the gym beforehand – if you want to lose a few pounds, you'll have to restrain yourself, especially where the free-flowing alcohol is concerned.

Ideal for: Singletons who don't want to be surrounded entirely by cooing couples. There's no single supplement, and the optional group dining and group activities make it easy to meet new people.

What to pack: Sportswear for every scenario – yoga and tai chi, gym or swimming – and smart-casual clothes for the evening.

Aveda Concept Spa at Strawberry Hill

✳✳

Address: New Castle Road, Irish Town,
Jamaica, British West Indies
Telephone: (+1) 876 944 8400
Booking details: reservations@islandoutpost.com
Website: www.islandoutpost.com/StrawberryHill

Strawberry Hill lies in the Blue Mountains, just outside Kingston. Once the site of a working plantation, its 10.5 hectares (26 acres) now provide spectacular 360-degree vistas of the city and valleys below. Rustic wooden villas feature mahogany four-posters with muslin canopies and crisp, white linens, simple tiled bathrooms, and spacious private verandahs. With the spa, pools, sauna, gym, delicious food, exotic gardens and must-do walks through nearby coffee plantations, it's a great place to make way for a new you.

The ambience: Small, low-key, luxurious and personal, the resort is traditionally colonial but without any old-money stuffiness.

Regular guests: Dressed-down dot-com millionaires and famous beauties Kate Moss, Naomi Campbell and singer Lauryn Hill.

Treatment menu: The Aveda Concept spa uses own-brand products to nurture the outside as well as the 'in'. Because there's not too much choice, you won't get stressed deciding what to have.

House speciality: The sensual Body Elixir takes place in a stone hut beside an open window. After an exfoliating massage, you lie under water jets, which are strategically placed onto pressure points to give you a stimulating but rhythmical massage.

Cuisine: The Strawberry Hill restaurant serves modern Jamaican cuisine. Light salads, pastas, soups and specials are served at lunch.

Ideal for: Solo spa-goers who want to spend time with themselves, and lovebirds who want to spend time with each other.

What to pack: A cardigan, pashmina or shawl for the evening.

Ritz-Carlton Rose Hall

✳ ✳ ✳

Address: 1 Ritz-Carlton Drive, Rose Hall, St James,
Jamaica, British West Indies
Telephone: (+1) 876 953 2800
Booking details: reservations@ritzcarlton.com
Website: www.ritzcarlton.com

Framed by the white beaches of the Caribbean and the mountains of Montego Bay, the resort oozes 'old plantation' charm. Plush bedrooms in the hotel and luxurious treatments in the spa ensure pampering every step of the way. Enjoy the Blue Mountains Sunrise Yoga or Cayman Sunset Stretch on the beach as a prelude or finale to a spa treatment, or try out the championship golf course. There are meeting and banqueting facilities, so expect to see lots of males in suits and loafers one minute, and Pringle sweaters and golf shoes the next.

The ambience: Lavish, fussy and grand, but friendly. The spa is decked out in earthy mahogany wood and restful leafy greens.

Regular guests: Couples getting married, newlyweds getting pregnant, and mothers and fathers getting harangued by their kids.

Treatment menu: From bride-to-be (Matrimony Fruit Bath) to mother-to-be (Maternity Massage), the treatments cater for every stage of life. They all have a tropical flair and make full use of local ingredients, such as sugar cane and wild-growing hibiscus.

House speciality: Jamaican sugar cane and grains of the finest white sand are mixed together to make the Sugar Cane Body Scrub, which is used to gently buff the entire body. A moisturizing concoction of papaya, mango, wild yams and exotic oils follows.

Cuisine: The handful of restaurants serve international, traditional American and local Caribbean dishes. There are one or two surprises, like Jasian (Jamaican ingredients cooked with Asian techniques) at Jasmine's restaurant. Healthy options are available at Horizons.

Ideal for: Wedding, parties, anniversaries and family holidays.

What to pack: Confetti!

Cotton House

★★★

Address: PO Box 349, Mustique, St Vincent, British West Indies
Telephone: (+1) 784 456 4777
Booking details: cottonhouse@caribsurf.com
Website: www.cottonhouse.net

The island of Mustique has rolling green hills, clusters of lush wood, spectacular cliffs plunging into deep-blue waters and white sandy beaches. Charming plantation-style houses are located amid beautifully landscaped gardens. It's the perfect setting for an intimate, 'private house' type of resort. Here, you can even choose your pillow from their 'pillow menu' (goosedown, feather and hypoallergenic to be precise). After being pampered in the mini, but newly expanded, spa tucked under a canopy of trees, you can take in watersports, tennis, motorboating or horse-riding.

The ambience: A discreet, personal and tranquil retreat.

Regular guests: Mustique is renowned as a hideaway for celebrities and royalty because of its natural beauty and seclusion. Cotton House is no exception.

Treatment menu: More of a pampering beauty oasis than a serious place to change your lifestyle, the spa was developed by E'Spa, so treatments include the company's favourites. Top-to-toe massages, body therapies, wraps, facials, manicures and pedicures are on offer.

House speciality: The cleansing and detoxifying Body Wraps come with the option of warm seaweed gel or marine and mud paste, and include body-brushing and exfoliation.

Cuisine: The resort offers signature Caribbean recipes, using the freshest ingredients, coupled with fine wines.

Ideal for: An elegant, relaxed destination for those seeking to get away from it all. You will not have to put a 'do not disturb' sign on the door to get some peace and quiet.

What to pack: An audio book. You'll be so relaxed that even reading will seem too strenuous.

LeSport

✶✶

Address: PO Box 437, Cariblue Beach, Castries,
St Lucia, British West Indies
Telephone: (+1) 758 450 8551
Booking details: info@advantage-leisure.plc.uk
Website: www.thebodyholiday.com

LeSport is a medium-sized resort but feels small and intimate; although it caters for quite a number of people, you don't feel like you're on a conveyor belt. Accommodation, meals, afternoon tea, refreshments and bar drinks, two treatments a day and full use of the superb sports facilities are part of the all-inclusive package. While the resort offers everything from aerobic classes, tai chi and yoga to windsurfing and waterskiing, the spa itself sticks to tried-and-tested treatments, with the odd more up-to-date remedy.

The ambience: Very relaxed and down to earth. LeSport didn't jump on the spa/wellbeing bandwagon, they were driving it.

Regular guests: Mainly couples (children under 16 are banned), but lots of single people on their own, too.

Treatment menu: The menu includes a comprehensive choice of beautifying treatments for men and women. Not as spiritually minded as some spas in this neck of the woods, it is nevertheless great for those wanting to dip their manicured toes in the spa holiday pool. The resort sells itself as a body holiday, and a holiday your body will have.

House speciality: Choose between Shirodhara, an Ayurvedic hot-oil treatment, and the Two-Hand Massage. Both should have warnings about not driving machinery like golf buggies afterwards.

Cuisine: You'll find buffets laden with fruit, salads and cooked delights, barbecues, a deli, an East-meets-West restaurant, and simple, light and healthy fare at Cuisine Légère.

Ideal for: Couples, singles and fitness addicts.

What to pack: Fitness gear and casually elegant clothes for evening (no jeans, shorts or T-shirts are allowed in the dining room).

Elysée Spa at La Samanna

★★★

Address: PO Box 4077, 97064 St Martin Cedex,
French West Indies
Telephone: (+590) 590 876 400
Booking details: reservations@lasamanna.com
Website: www.lasamanna.orient-express.com

La Samanna is cloaked in verdant foliage and colourful flowers, and overlooks 22 hectares (55 acres) of spectacular beachfront that's recognized as one of the finest and most secluded in the world. The hotel is built in a whitewashed Mediterranean style with the accent on space and natural light. There are about eight rooms and suites on the property; although a little 'busy' decor-wise, they are very comfortable and have private terraces or balconies opening onto the beach.

St Martin's vibrant cocktail of Caribbean paradise and French sophistication is reflected in the mini spa, which is run hand-in-hand with the French beauty company Phytomer. There are three soothing massage rooms, two hydrotherapy rooms and a separate bright, sunny salon for the nitty-gritty work – manicures, pedicures, waxing, and so on. As you would expect from the glamorous French, there is a treatment for every beauty whim. If you revel in people telling you how well you look when you get back from a holiday, this is the place to come. When you're not busy hopping on and off the beauty beds in the spa, you can hop on a boat with a picnic and lunch alfresco on another island.

The ambience: Relaxed and low-key, in an unspoilt natural setting.

Regular guests: Publicity-shy celebrities, Italian fashion designers Dolce & Gabanna, and everyday Americans.

Treatment menu: Phytomer laboratories have developed a range of treatments for legs, body contouring, dry and dehydrated skin and general relaxation. Some are hands-on and others use newfangled machines, but all pamper and improve. Choose from massages, body scrubs and peels that reveal the younger-looking body lurking beneath all of us (whatever our age). Effective facials include Sun Burn Rescue Aloe Treatment for those who have had too much sun. Slimming body wraps will help your confidence on that first day on the beach.

House speciality: The Phytomer Seaweed Wrap, containing a nourishing combination of marine ingredients, seaweed, healing gels or oils, relaxes, detoxifies and slims the body. It is performed either with a heated blanket or in a new Thalatherm machine (like a horizontal steam cabinet), which enhances the treatment effects.

Cuisine: A combination of French and Caribbean specialities are complemented by an extensive wine cellar. In addition to an abundance of healthy salads, snacks, grilled fish and virgin-cocktails to keep you happy and healthy, there are also low-fat dining options available in the spa.

Ideal for: Bonding, whether matrimonial, family or corporate.

What to pack: Your own snorkel. The waters are so clear here that you'll want to fish-watch at least once a day.

Shambhala Spa at Parrot Cay

✳ ✳ ✳

Address: PO Box 164, Providenciales,
Turks & Caicos Island, British West Indies
Telephone: (+1) 649 946 7788
Booking details: parrot@tciway.tc
Website: www.parrot-cay.com
www.shambhalaretreat.com

Parrot Cay is situated on an otherwise uninhabited, unspoilt tropical island and, with its palm-fringed coastline, powder-fine white sand and turquoise, turquoise sea, it is the ultimate Caribbean fantasy. Designed with the landscape at heart, the 60 rooms and villas all have ocean or garden views and a dozen or so larger villas have their own private swimming or plunge pool. With whitewashed walls, crisp white bedlinen, four-poster beds swathed in white muslin, and a spa with mind-body treatments to die for, you can see why it attracts Hollywood's tired and harassed. Be warned: Parrot Cay is shockingly expensive, but absolutely heavenly.

Shambhala is definitely more of a 'spaaah' than a spa. A weathered wooden lodge, set amid abundant vegetation and overlooking the ocean, creates a sanctuary where mind, body and spirit get a holistic holiday. Three massage rooms, a Vichy hydrotherapy room, saunas, steams, an infinity-edged swimming pool and a lofty yoga pavilion and movement studio, allowing peaceful meditation with inspirational views of the seas, will aid you on your way to a deep state of relaxation and calm. For guests who want total privacy, the separate Shambhala Cottage is the ultimate treatment room, with a private whirlpool, treatment tub and meditation pavilion.

Dedicated to mental and physical wellbeing, the Shambhala Retreat is host to week-long 'guided healing' therapies, featuring world-renowned yoga teachers and alternative health specialists.

The ambience: Upmarket but natural and spiritual. Although the resort is exclusive and attracts the elite, people are generally here just to *be* rather than to be seen.

Regular guests: The rich and famous; the beautiful and stylish. It's fashion's darling Donna Karan's favourite retreat, and actors Sylvester Stallone, Julia Roberts, Robert De Niro and supermodel Naomi Campbell visit, too. Bruce Willis is even building his own airstrip on the island.

Treatment menu: Choose from a healing and 'quietly' indulgent list of Asian-style treatments, fused with natural therapies from the sea and earth. The therapies take the form of facials, sensuous body massages, scrubs, soaks in open-air teak tubs overlooking the lagoon, healing therapies and traditional beauty treatments. All sessions are polished off with a complimentary cup of Shambhala's home-brewed ginger tea and the expert therapists have all been hand-picked from Bali.

House speciality: The Caribbean Delight begins with your fatigued body being scrubbed all over with lime, bay or clove while you lie under a shower of rainwater. You are then indulged in an hour-long massage to ease tension and revitalize your entire being.

Cuisine: A healthy and exotic blend of Asian and Mediterranean flavours are prepared daily alongside a tasty but elegantly prepared spa menu that offers bikini-friendly dishes, such as udon noodles with a lime-soy vinaigrette. During the special Shambhala Retreat weeks, the chef from top-notch Japanese restaurant Nobu is flown in to create über-healthy, calorie-conscious diets, including wheat-free, sugar-free and dairy-free dishes.

Ideal for: A lottery-win spa holiday where money is no object.

What to pack: A millionaire.

Ikal del Mar

**

Address: Playa Xcalacoco, Riviera Maya,
Quintana Roo 77710 Mexico
Telephone: (+52) 984 877 3000
Booking details: info@ikaldelmar.com
Website: www.ikaldelmar.com

Ikal del Mar is a secluded seaside luxury hotel and spa located in the Caribbean along 11.5 km (7 miles) of beach. Just north of the Mayan Riviera resort of Playa del Carmen, Mexico, it has 29 private *cabanas,* built from wood and stone indigenous to the region – all more spacious than most five-star hotel rooms and each with its own plunge pool, outdoor shower and terrace, complete with hand-crocheted hammock.

The full-service spa at Ikal del Mar offers a holistic experience, rather than a programme dedicated to reducing the size of your thighs. With its steam room, Jacuzzi, Swiss shower jets with adjustable water pressure, individual treatment areas and beachside Temazcal bath (see House speciality, below), the spa has all the amenities you need to enjoy the massages, facials, therapies and beauty treatments available. You can also explore other activities: tai chi, yoga, horse-riding, fishing, boating, snorkelling, parasailing, diving, golf, tennis and bird-watching, and there are nature walks and jungle tours, too.

The ambience: A secluded, intimate hideaway in rustic luxury.

Regular guests: Flush new-age travellers who want to mix nature with modern conveniences.

Treatment menu: The traditional therapies on offer incorporate local herb and plant extracts. The Sea and Land Body Treatment uses tepezcohuite, which comes from the bark of the mimosa tree and was used by the Mayans for its healing properties. Bentonita, a mineral-rich mud, is slathered over your body during the Ikal del Mar Massage, and it leaves skin feeling as soft as the day you were born.

House speciality: The Temazcal Bath is a sweat-inducing, deep-cleansing sauna, scented with herbs and flowers, and with accompanying background music. The soak itself is followed by a soothing massage, performed in a *temazcal* (meaning 'bath home'), a small stone igloo right next to the sea.

Cuisine: There are two restaurants. Unique dishes at Azul draw on Mediterranean, Asian and Mexican influences, while, for steadfast dieters, there is a 'lite' menu available at The Grill.

Ideal for: Anyone wanting somewhere with soul, right away from the beaten track.

What to pack: A torch (flashlight). City-dwellers might find nights a bit spooky with no artificial lighting, even with star-filled skies.

Las Ventanas al Paraiso

✳ ✳ ✳

Address: KM 19.5 Carretera Transpeninsular,
San Jose del Cabo, Baja California Sur 23400 Mexico
Telephone: (+52) 624 144 0300
Booking details: reservations@lasventanas.com.mx
Website: www.lasventanas.com

The magical Las Ventanas al Paraiso resides at the southern tip of Mexico's beautiful Baja Peninsula, where the Pacific Ocean joins the Sea of Cortez. A thrilling combination of sea, mountains and desert surround the resort, providing the most wonderful, natural setting for nurturing the mind, body and soul. All 60 or so of the exclusive suites combine simplicity with state-of-the-art sophistication in the hand-carved cedar doors, marble showers, wood-burning fires and a personal telescope for gazing up at the heavens' shimmering stars or out to the ocean for a spot of whale watching. Personal splash-pools, swimming pools, Jacuzzis and private terraces feature in the more luxurious suites.

The spectacular spa is located in a secluded flower-filled garden and has indoor treatment rooms. An outdoor, specially woven, pavilion on the sand, at the edge of the water, enables you to see out, but won't let others see in. At night, massages are performed

here by the light of burning torches. Attention to detail is excellent. Each room has a set of headphones connected to a stereo system so you can tune in and zone out during your treatment. This place is paradise through and through.

The ambience: This resort is what dreams are made of: it's utterly luxurious, unbelievably glamorous and wonderfully serene.

Regular guests: The beautiful people – such as Brad Pitt, Gwyneth Paltrow and Cindy Crawford – spa junkies and affluent jet-setters, who want to slow down their minds as well as their bodies.

Treatment menu: An enticing and extensive list of time-honoured treatments, therapies and rituals from around the world is available. Most use indigenous natural ingredients such as aloe vera, mud and desert clay. Indulge in facials, wraps, body scrubs, massages, Ayurvedic treatments and Balinese rituals, or experiment with the more fascinating array of spiritual-based treatments that, in essence, give your emotions a mental massage.

House speciality: The Holistic Crystal Healing Massage employs energy-filled crystals and Shamanistic techniques. The aim of this holistic and spiritual treatment is to put you into a state of relaxation and inner healing, melting away any doubt, anger and fear to leave your mind and spirit balanced and in harmony. As for your outer ego, the Tepezcohuite Healing Wrap will restore sunburnt skin and frazzled minds, thanks to the soothing and cellular-regenerating properties found in extracts of tepezcohuite (an indigenous tree).

Cuisine: The main restaurant serves Baja-Mediterranean cuisine inspired by the region's abundant natural resources. The Sea Grill at the water's edge features modern renditions of Mexican classics – grilled fish, shellfish and meats. Beach barbecues serve meat and seafood grilled over local-style barbecue pits in the sand and are so good they should be compulsory. Spa-reprobates will find their way to the Tequila & Ceviche Bar, which boasts 100 of Mexico's most exclusive, aged tequilas. You can even give tequila lessons, the distinctly Mexican version of wine tasting, a 'shot'.

Ideal for: Those who want to be spoilt rotten and pampered silly in the sun (the region gets 350 days of sunshine a year).

What to pack: The one you love.

Arizona Biltmore Resort & Spa

***

Address: 2400 East Missouri, Phoenix,
Arizona 85016 USA
Telephone: (+1) 602 955 6600
Booking details: (+1) 800 950 0086
Website: www.arizonabiltmore.com

Set in the foothills of Squaw Peak, the 15.8-hectare (39-acre) resort, designed in the 1930s in a geometric pattern inspired by the trunk of a tree, is an architectural landmark. Deservedly crowned the 'Jewel of the Desert,' the grounds feature magnificent flowering plants, palms and cacti.

There are around 750 guest rooms, each one tastefully decorated in the desert-friendly colours of beige, sand and ivory, and with a distinctive Southwestern flair. Most are available with a balcony or patio and overlook Squaw Peak Mountain, the Paradise Pool or any one of the magnificent lawns, fountains and flower gardens. If you have come here to do nothing, there are plenty of ways to do it in the spa. Otherwise, you can take advantage of the eight swimming pools, daily fitness classes, hiking trails, special winding jogging track, or horse-riding, to name just a few of the activities on offer.

The ambience: Professional, non-fussy pampering in first-class desert surroundings.

Regular guests: Celebrities, heads of state, captains of industry and business tycoons.

Treatment menu: The symbol of the spa, as seen on the letterhead and at the entrance to the spa, is the Water Goddess, who represents the balance of mind and body. Inspired by Native American tribes, the spa's holistic approach to wellbeing can be seen in treatments entitled Raindrop Therapy, Cactus Flower Wrap and Dreamcatcher Therapy. There is also a wide variety of other better-known beauty treatments, plus basic grooming necessities such as waxing and nail services.

House speciality: The Water Goddess Mud Purification treatment is a unique detoxifying Native American healing therapy that begins with a dry-brush massage. Mineral-rich Sedona mud is then applied to the entire body, and as the mud soothes muscles and nourishes the skin, it also draws out impurities and toxins from the body's systems. The mud is showered off and then a nourishing lavender-sage aromablend oil is gently massaged into the skin.

Cuisine: The resort specializes in 'New American' cuisine, which is a creation of the executive chef and a fusion of Asian, French and Southwestern flavours, blended with richly flavoured oils and herbal infusions. Classic American cuisine, grills and snacks are also served here.

Ideal for: Corporate men and their uncorporate wives.

What to pack: Swimwear, and golf and running shoes.

Camelback Inn Resort, Golf Club & Spa

✳✳

Address: 5402 East Lincoln Drive
Scottsdale, Arizona 85253 USA
Telephone: (+1) 480 948 1700
Booking details: mpps@camelbackinn.com
Website: www.camelbackinn.com or
www.marriotthotels.com

Although Camelback first opened in 1936, it has moved elegantly
with the times. Well over 400 pueblo-style *casitas*, suites and villas
are situated on 53 hectares (129 acres) of unique Sonoran Desert
landscape. The fitness centre runs a number of excellent wellness
programmes designed by Dr Kenneth Cooper, the founder and
president of the Institute for Aerobic Research in Dallas, Texas,
so they really do work. A computerized system analyses your
body composition, and you are given nutritional counselling,
stress management and personal training designed to improve
your health and wellbeing.

The spectrum of daily classes has something to appeal to everyone's exercise personality, from power-walking, Latin groove and step classes to meditation, yoga and tai chi. If, after all that physical exertion, the steam rooms, Finnish saunas, heated lap pool, Jacuzzi, hot tubs and icy-cold plunge pools don't rejuvenate you, nothing will.

The ambience: Buzzy with activity but relaxed and informal.

Regular guests: Hotel guests on business and pleasure, and families and locals taking time out. Throughout its long-running history, the resort has been host to stars of the silver screen (Clark Gable, Jimmy Stewart, Bette Davis), US presidents and, more recently, Oprah Winfrey and model Cindy Crawford.

Treatment menu: The 16 massage rooms offer traditional spa treats such as aromatherapy, massage, herbal body wraps, detoxifying mud masks and exfoliating body scrubs. In addition, there are more unusual and up-to-date offerings, including the Adobe Clay Purification, which is an exfoliating, nourishing and detoxifying treatment for the body, and the Deluxe Bindi Herbal Face and Body Treatment, which uses blended oils and heated herbal sheets to reduce tension and stress.

House speciality: The Camelback Signature Body Treatment is not just for the body. It is a head-to-toe, vitamin C preparation that treats skin everywhere. Your entire body is polished and hydrated with a silkening scrub containing vitamin C, sugar, silica beads, jojoba oil and essential oils of grapefruit, orange, lemon and jasmine. An aromatic citrus oil hair and scalp massage follows, and then a facial cleanse and exfoliation with gentle papaya enzymes. A layer of rich, firming serum, a plumping and firming lip treatment and a face-saving sunscreen complete the package.

Cuisine: The seven restaurants offer everything from Arizona-inspired cuisine to rotisserie-cooked chicken and juicy burgers. Waist-watchers can save a few calories in the day at the excellent, healthy Sprouts restaurant at the spa, which offers heart-friendly menu selections of fresh salads and innovative sandwiches.

Ideal for: Dieters and fitness fans, couples and families. The activity-filled Hopalong programme will keep children amused.

What to pack: A little willpower if you intend to shift a few pounds.

Canyon Ranch

★★★

Address: 8600 East Rockcliff Road,
Tucson, Arizona 85750 USA
Telephone: (+1) 520 749 9655
Booking details: 520 749 9000
Website: www.canyonranch.com

Located in the foothills of Tucson's Santa Catalina Mountains, Canyon Ranch is a year-round luxury destination dedicated to healthy living. Treatments are endless, and qualified specialists offer workshops on topics that include medical issues, nutrition, stress management, smoking, ageing, plus alternative healing disciplines such as acupuncture. The spa complex includes six gyms, a spinning room, strength training and cardio-fitness equipment, a yoga and meditation dome, squash and basketball courts, and locker rooms, as well as steam, sauna, plunge pool, sunbathing decks and whirlpools.

The ambience: An adult's adventure playground, with restaurants, a spa and a wellbeing centre instead of swings.

Regular guests: Top businessmen taking care of themselves and middle-aged couples taking time out.

Treatment menu: A full range of treatments, including massages, bodywork, hydrotherapy, facials, mud masks, Ayurvedic and seaweed therapies, as well as grooming services.

House speciality: Euphoria, a body treatment lasting 110 minutes, comprises a head-to-toe massage, body mask and sauna in a tub doused with grapefruit oil.

Cuisine: Canyon Ranch prides itself on its nutritious gourmet cuisine, which includes regional specialities, fish and vegetarian fare. You can even take a cookery course and continue your new food plan at home.

Ideal for: Those wanting to turn over a new leaf without living off lettuce leaves.

What to pack: The active and casual lifestyle means you only need comfortable, casual clothing – no dressy rhinestone dinner outfits.

Four Seasons Resort Scottsdale

＊＊

Address: 10600 East Crescent Moon Drive,
Scottsdale, Arizona 85255 USA
Telephone: (+1) 480 515 5700
Booking details: scottsdale.reservations@fourseasons.com
Website: www.fourseasons.com/scottsdale/index.html

The secluded location of this Four Seasons, among a rugged, sun-drenched nature reserve, high up in the Sonoran Desert, offers a rough-but-very-ready outdoor experience. Large boulders and jaggy saguaro cacti pepper the landscape and Mexican 'frontier'-style *casitas* nestle into the hillside. When you've finished recharging your batteries in the spa, get your heart racing and skin glowing with outdoor activities, such as hot-air ballooning, horse-riding, mountain biking, hiking, fishing and hunting, and rock climbing.

The ambience: Very tranquil and earthy, the resort makes you feel as though you're in the middle of nowhere.

Regular guests: Corporate retreaters, golfers and families.

Treatment menu: The extensive range has a special focus on Native American rituals. Massages can be performed in the privacy of your *casita* terrace or balcony and are available until 10 pm.

House speciality: In the Native American-inspired Willow Herbal Wrap, linens are soaked in a willow-herbal infusion, then wrapped around the body to create a cocoon of comfort that relieves tension.

Cuisine: Regional and Italian cuisine, plus steaks and seafood, are available at the elegant Acacia or the hacienda-style Javelina. Sipping cocktails in the Lobby Lounge is a must for the view of Pinnacle Peak.

Ideal for: Golf fanatics. The resort is home to the Troon North course, described as the 'best desert course ever built'.

What to pack: The kids. The resort's Kids For All Seasons caters brilliantly for children between 5 and 12.

Golden Door Spa at the Boulders

✷✷✷

Address: 34631 North Tom Darlington Drive,
Carefree, Arizona 85377 USA
Telephone: (+1) 480 488 9009
Booking details: gdres@adnc.com
Website: www.wyndham.com/luxury

Nestled among 12 million-year-old rock formations in the scenic desert foothills near Scottsdale, Arizona, the Boulders is one of the country's most prestigious resort destinations, and has armfuls of awards and distinctions to prove it. Nature plays a huge role in the experience here. The terrain and plant life have been left virtually untouched and even the building's interior reflects the outdoors – the doors are crafted with rubbed woods, ceilings are wood-beamed, restaurants have cascading waterfalls and most of the *casitas* and Pueblo villas (available as one, two or three bedrooms) have open, wood-burning fires.

The Golden Doors Spa, inspired by the ancient Honjin inns of Japan, where innkeepers called upon the arts of massage, therapeutic baths and refreshing food to rejuvenate weary travellers, is split into two wings. The action-based west wing has a state-of-the-art fitness centre, mind/body movement studios and a Spa Café; the tranquil east wing concentrates on meditation, self-awareness/acceptance and relaxation. Wrapped around the boulders that give the resort its name, the spa blends the Zen-like ambience of the original Golden Door in Escondido, California, with its unique settings.

There are 24 treatment spaces, a hydrotherapy tub, Japanese bath, shiatsu room, and outdoor pool with Jacuzzi, cascading waterfall and lap lane. The yoga studio is equipped with special lighting that replicates sunrise and sunset, and a ceiling painted with a mural of the sky. The Ultimate Spa Suite has private access to its own steam showers, outdoor shower, Jacuzzi, patio and outdoor massage tables. With its incredible attention to mental and physical comfort, its positive, relaxing atmosphere and its vast selection of indoor, outdoor and spa facilities, this place has absolutely everything going for it.

The ambience: This is a desert hideaway inspired by nature's finest raw materials. The atmosphere is almost mystical; the mood is positive, optimistic and relaxing.

Regular guests: Peace- and pleasure-seekers, golfers and those with a sense of worldly adventure.

Treatment menu: In addition to the usual spa treatments, there are more unusual Eastern therapies, such as a two-therapist massage, Shirodhara and other holistic face and body treats. A handful of Native American-inspired treatments include Raindrop Therapy, which involves essential oils drizzled along the spine, the Adobe Clay Wrap, which aims to purge the body of impurities (even those of the mind, albeit temporarily) and the Native Grain Exfoliation, which leaves the skin soft and smooth.

House speciality: Based on the Native American belief that turquoise is a protective colour, the Turquoise Wrap treatment involves all things turquoise – a bath, massage and wrap, involving essential oils, aimed at purifying the spirit and shifting negative energy. It concludes with a honey mask and warm rosehip lotion, which instils a sense of peace and wellbeing.

Cuisine: The sights, tastes and smells of the Southwest permeate most of the five restaurants at the Boulders. All of them use only the freshest local ingredients sourced from local farmers and ranchers. Delicious healthy spa cuisine, created in conjunction with the resort's chefs and spa professionals, is also on offer.

Ideal for: Flagging spirits, weary bodies and sapped souls.

What to pack: Rock-climbing equipment for scaling the heights of crystalline granite and metamorphic rock.

Mii amo Spa

★★★

Address: 525 Boyton Canyon Road,
Sedona, Arizona 86336 USA
Telephone: (+1) 928 282 2900
Booking details: info@miiamo.com
Website: www.miiamo.com

Mii amo means 'journey' or 'passage' in the Yuman dialect, and it couldn't be a better name for this special spa, nestled in the slope of a canyon wall. Surrounded by national forest and wilderness, Mii amo has borrowed the wisdom and traditions of Native Americans to create modern-day treatments that nurture body and soul, and help put you on the right path to better health, emotional wellbeing and spiritual renewal. A land bridge connects Mii amo to the Enchantment Resort, but you can book into one of the 16 *casitas* adjacent to the spa. Built in harmony with the red rock terrain, these cosy hideaways feature fireplaces and a courtyard or balcony. Mii amo consists of four main areas: the treatment centre, activities, and pool and food areas.

The ambience: Incredibly spiritual without being too wacky.

Regular guests: Modern-day hippies, new-age travellers and serious spiritual seekers.

Treatment menu: Most of the sensual treatments contain a spiritual element, such as Reiki Energy Healing. Ceremonies in the Crystal Grotto involve drumming, chanting, meditation and crystal therapy.

House speciality: The Mii amo falls under the 'connect with spirit' category and begins with sage-burning to help release negativity. The therapist then brushes your skin with sweet grass, massages you lightly with oils, and places crystals on your chakras.

Cuisine: The Mii amo Café combines Oriental and Southwest flavours with classic Provençal, and utilizes organic and macrobiotic produce.

Ideal for: Weary urbanites in need of nature and spirituality.

What to pack: Any issues you have with your life, your heart or your soul. This is the place to look them in the eye and send them packing.

Miraval Life in Balance Resort

✳ ✳ ✳

Address: 5000 East Via Estancia Miraval,
Catalina, Arizona 85739 USA
Telephone: (+1) 520 825 4000
Booking details: reservations@miravallifeinbalance.com
Website: www.miravalresort.com

Guests at this first-class destination spa don't come all the way here to be told what to do and when to do it. Here, there are no mandatory lengths of stay, no required classes and no rules against drinking alcohol. Miraval helps you achieve your personal goals, whether they are to improve your fitness, diet or relaxation. With the choice of pursuits, activities experts and treatments on hand, your days can be as high-energy or relaxed as you like. You can learn trust through grooming horses, reduce stress via meditation or cookery, or embrace the present with stargazing.

The ambience: Miraval is like a luxury hotel, but instead of guests overindulging in the bad stuff, they overindulge in the good.

Regular guests: Health and beauty tourists who have bought a first-class ticket to wellbeing.

Treatment menu: A comprehensive A-Z of treatments, from Ayurvedic to Zero Balancing, with lots in between, is on offer. Even the most seasoned spa aficionado will discover something new.

House speciality: Hot Stones massage using heated basalt stones.

Cuisine: Two full-service restaurants and two snack bars serve healthy, nutritious, satisfying, vibrant and plentiful food.

Ideal for: Those wanting to go on holiday and come back with less baggage, mentally and physically, and those craving a healthy-eating, get-in-shape break from the all-work-and-no-play mode.

What to pack: A metaphoric toolbox to carry home newly found 'life tools' that will help you with any wellbeing-orientated do-it-yourself.

Bacara Resort & Spa

★★★

Address: 8301 Hollister Avenue,
Santa Barbara, California 93117 USA
Telephone: (+1) 805 968 0100
Booking details: (+1) 877 422 4245 or
reservations@bacararesort.com
Website: www.bacararesort.com

Nestling between the Pacific Ocean and the Santa Ynez mountains, Bacara is like a mini Mediterranean village. All the intimate and relaxed facilities are luxurious but understated. The 311 elegant rooms, 49 suites and one-, three- and four-storey villas, made up of clusters of rooms, are scattered among lush gardens. Each one has breathtaking views of the ocean, garden or mountain and a private patio or balcony; many have a wood-burning or gas fire.

Just soaking up the atmosphere of this beautiful spa will make you feel totally pampered, and the impressive range of treatments and holistic pursuits will have you spoilt for choice. Personal training from one of the fitness professionals is available at the state-of-the-art gym, and other activities include beachside yoga, outdoor tai chi, Pilates, horse-riding, golfing and mountain biking. The numerous hikes and walks that wind through sunlit trails and avocado trees will have the colour back in your cheeks in no time.

The ambience: This luxury retreat exudes old-fashioned Hollywood glamour – from the poolside palm trees to the poolside divas in white towelling robes and Manolo Blahniks. Even their ever-so-stylish brochure is full of images of the young and beautiful, and their sleek black-and-white website could be mistaken for a trailer for the latest romantic blockbuster.

Regular guests: A playground for Hollywood's elite, Bacara attracts its fair share of superstars (too many to mention), plus those who simply want to feel like they are.

Treatment menu: The full-service spa and salon is nearly 4,000 square metres (42,000 square feet) dedicated to gorgeousness. The 36 individual rooms and four private suites offer every conceivable treatment to get you smoothed, buffed, polished, tightened, toned, relaxed and renewed. There are body scrubs, masks, massages and facials, as well as more alternative delights such as Shirodhara, reiki and Earth Crystal Therapy.

House speciality: To leave your skin super-soft and your mood similarly eased, try the Oatmeal Sage Body Polish. A scrub is used to exfoliate your skin before you are wrapped, loofahed, showered and finally massaged with essential oils.

Cuisine: All three restaurants serve organic produce grown in a kitchen garden on Bacara's 405-hectare (1,000-acre) avocado and lemon farm. Miro serves inspired California-French cuisine, along with the world's finest wines. The Bistro has a more casual, though richly flavoured, Mediterranean menu. Meals that are low in fat but high in nutrition are served in the 'casually elegant' Spa Café. Organic wines are available, as are low-fat and soya milk desserts, including soya ice cream and sugarless chocolate soufflé.

Ideal for: Modern-day Liz Taylors and Marilyn Monroes who want pampering and beautification during the day and glamour, champagne and delicious food in the evening.

What to pack: The largest pair of black Chanel sunglasses you can find, and an empty hold-all for all your feel-good beauty purchases.

Cal-a-Vie Spa

★ ★ ★

Address: 29402 Spa Havens Way, Vista,
California 92804 USA
Telephone: (+1) 760 945 2055
Reservations: info@cal-a-vie.com
Website: www.cal-a-vie.com

Cal-a-Vie is a private hideaway nestled in a secluded valley 66 km (40 miles) north of San Diego, where the climate is considered to be the best in the country. Each of the 24 guest cottages has been decorated to recall the understated elegance of a European country villa, with windowboxes brimming with flowers and breathtaking views of the rolling hills. Natural beauty enhances the experience of vigorous workouts and rejuvenating treatments. The seven-day programme integrates American-style fitness with European-style pampering and includes plenty of inspirational activities.

The ambience: Secluded, intimate, down to earth and friendly.

Regular guests: A-list celebrities, including Julia Roberts, Michelle Pfeiffer, Sharon Stone, Russell Crowe and Robin Williams, have been known to visit; otherwise 'normal' people wanting to shape up.

Treatment menu: Along with massages and facials, there are lots of mind- and body-boosting sessions ending in 'therapy' (thalassotherapy, hydrotherapy and aromatherapy).

House speciality: The Body Glo is a facial for the body. Using Indian herbs and clays, a full-body slough cleanses and detoxifies the skin and is followed by toxin-eliminating thalassotherapy.

Cuisine: Once you have decided whether you want to lose, gain or maintain weight, Cal-a-Vie takes care of the rest and manages to make nutritious food interesting; in fact, so much so that the guests have demanded a cookbook. No alcohol is served on the property.

Ideal for: Those who need other people's willpower, not just their own, to get them in shape and looking and feeling great.

What to pack: An emergency bottle of wine.

Givenchy Spa at the Merv Griffin Resort Hotel

✶✶

Address: 4200 East Palm Canyon Drive,
Palm Springs, California 92264 USA
Telephone: (+1) 760 770 5000
Booking details: www.palmspringsusa.com
Website: www.merv.com

Palm Springs and the surrounding area has an interesting history. The Agua Caliente Indians settled in the region and the fabulous year-round climate and spectacular scenery attract many visitors from Hollywood and beyond. The resort is geared up for fitness-and-health tourists and spa visitors.

The ambience: Overlooking a rose garden, it is Versailles meets the White House – America's take on ostentatious European style.

Regular guests: Warren Beatty and Annette Bening, older Californians, and young spa fans seeking old-time elegance.

Treatment menu: The spa is decadent and appealing, with many traditional treatments on offer. A facial to tone, cleanse and moisturize is a good way to start your stay, or choose the more daring all-over clay pack for drawing out impurities. Reflexology, shiatsu, Swedish massage and wraps using French seaweed are also available, or for a special treat, try the 120-minute body scrub.

House speciality: The Sacred Stone Therapy is a detoxifying pressure-point massage using warm stones and oil to stimulate the lymphatic system and re-energize and soothe your body and soul.

Cuisine: The Spa Café serves low-calorie, low-salt and low-fat options all day by the pool, while GiGi's, famed for its Franco-Californian dishes and elegant atmosphere, serves the high calories.

Ideal for: An anniversary treat for the young at heart.

What to pack: A California road map. Although you can fly to Palm Springs, you may want to take a trip to Las Vegas or Death Valley.

Ojai Valley Inn & Spa

✳✳

Address: Country Club Road, Ojai,
California 93023 USA
Telephone: (+1) 805 646 5511
Booking details: (+1) 800 422 6524
Website: www.ojairesort.com

Ojai Valley is nicknamed 'the Nest' and its first inhabitants, the Chumash Indians, revered it as a place of healing. Today more contemporary spiritual-seekers come to soak up the valley's mystical powers, and it has become a haven for artists, writers and movie stars looking for inspiration and serenity. Located on the California Gold Coast near Santa Barbara, Ojai Valley Inn & Spa is surrounded by the commanding Topa Topa Mountains; it has panoramic views of the valley that was portrayed as the mythical paradise of Shangri-La in Frank Capra's classic movie, *Lost Horizon*. With 100 or so rooms (some with their own open fires), the Inn has a Spanish colonial design and sits on 81 tree-shaded hectares (200 acres) that include expansive gardens.

In keeping with the Andalusian architecture of the inn, the health-orientated, holistic spa is a self-contained Mediterranean-style spa village. It has a staggering 28 treatment rooms, many with their own rustic fireplaces. Serious privacy searchers (that are also seriously rich) can hire the huge top-floor penthouse, only accessible by private elevator, which has four private guest rooms, two living areas, a treatment room, sauna, sunrise and sunset terraces with

whirlpools, and a meditation loft. Daily pursuits at Ojai Valley include tai chi, yoga, qi gong, meditation, spinning and water aerobics, and some more unusual offerings, such as tribal and salsa dancing. Those who would rather exercise their creativity than their body can try pastels, oil painting or watercolours in the art studio. The outstanding golf course, ranch and stables are also available to guests.

The ambience: Mystical, enchanting and incredibly relaxed, the resort combines the feel of an exclusive, sophisticated sanctuary with that of a Spanish country estate.

Regular guests: A-list celebrities, wound-up city slickers who need a hand unwinding, and families who want to share some unforgettable time together (Camp Ojai takes care of the children).

Treatment menu: The 'community' of wellness experts here offers a host of top-to-toe favourites, all of which have been given the nurturing Ojai twist. More unusual treatments and therapies are inspired by nature or ancient healing traditions. Medical assessments and customized healthcare strategies are also available.

House speciality: Kuyam (pronounced 'koo-yham') is a 50-minute purifying session, which means 'a place to rest together' in the Native American Chumash dialect. Taken from traditional healing methods, this communal (up to eight people) takes place in a warm, cocooned room and commences with a self-application of cleansing Moor mud, followed by guided meditation. Herb-infused steam softens the mud before you walk through a Swiss shower to rinse. You then slather yourself in moisturizing lotion before being wrapped in warm linen and sent off to relax in the outdoor loggia.

Cuisine: The two main restaurants are the fine-dining Maravilla and the alfresco Oak Café. The Franco-Californian cuisine, light snacks, fabulous wines and spa food with a distinct Mediterranean flair all use locally grown ingredients.

Ideal for: Those who want to be pampered in rustic luxury and breathe in the great outdoors.

What to pack: A camera to capture forever Ojai's legendary 'pink moment'. It's a magical time of the day when the sunset burns the sky, turning it into a marvellous fuchsia ceiling.

Post Ranch Inn

★ ★ ★

Address: Highway 1, PO Box 219, Big Sur,
California 93920 USA
Telephone: (+1) 831 667 2200
Booking details: (+1) 800 527 2200
res@postranchinn.com
Website: www.postranchinn.com

Situated on the clifftops of the rolling Ventana Mountains at Big Sur, on the coast between San Luis Obispo and Monterey, the Post Ranch Inn is a real getaway experience for spa travellers who want to be beautified in a natural setting. This stunning part of the world has long been known for its dramatic coastline and rugged beauty, and has historically drawn people searching for new experiences and a spiritual communion with nature.

The residential buildings have been designed to work in harmony with their specific locations by the architect Mickey Muenning, a proponent of eco-friendly, organic principles and the work of Bruce Goff and Frank Lloyd Wright. You can choose from the six-room Butterfly House, two-person treehouses, circular mountain and coast houses, an ocean house with a curved roof carpeted with grass and wildflowers, a south coast house with floor-to-ceiling windows overlooking the Pacific, or the Post House. Each of the 30 unique rooms has a king-size bed, fireplace, pull-out massage table and indoor spa tub.

Here, time isn't spent, it's invested in. Early morning yoga classes with a private instructor take place in a *yurt* – a Mongolian circular tent – beneath the mountains. You can relax in the outdoor basking pool that's kept at a constant 37ºC (99ºF), picnic in sun-drenched meadows or be massaged on your private deck in your room, alone or with your partner. A number of activities, from nature walks and mountain biking to astronomy and meditation, can be enjoyed. There are no TVs to disturb the serenity of the resort, but it's so romantic and cosseting here, and you'll look so gorgeous after all those his'n'hers facials and body wraps, that watching TV is the last thing you'll want to do together.

The ambience: Inextricably romantic, secluded and unaffected.

Regular guests: Adventurous spa-goers, who want an earthy back-to-mother-nature experience without any pomp and ceremony.

Treatment menu: A great range of massages, facials and more spiritually aware mind-and-body specialities, such as reiki, reflexology and craniosacral therapy.

House speciality: The Post Ranch Massage integrates Swedish massage, pressure point therapy and energy-balancing techniques to release stored-up stress and tension. It is performed in your room in front of a crackling open fire.

Cuisine: Wonderful organic Californian food is available from the Sierra Mar restaurant. Breakfast buffets are laden with fresh fruit and home-baked breads and pastries, and evening dinner plates offer dishes such as house-cured salmon Napoleon with crispy potato cakes, or curried pumpkin and mussel soup.

Ideal for: A very private romantic escape for couples, where spa treats are a prerequisite.

What to pack: Your soul mate or your best mate (ideal if they are one and the same), and cosy cardigans for the early mornings and evenings, which can be chilly.

Tea Garden Springs

✴✴

Address: 38 Miller Avenue, Mill Valley,
California 94941 USA
Telephone: (+1) 415 389 7123
Booking details: (+1) 415 389 7123
Website: www.teagardensprings.com

Here, you will embrace the wisdom of wellness from within. Feng shui-inspired design, treatment rooms with lighting tailored to individual therapies (from warm sunshine to serene moonlight), surround-sound stereo systems that emit ambient sounds, and fragrant gardens create a relaxing, caring environment – and that's before you've even had a massage. Guests travelling from afar tend to stay at the nearby Mill Valley Inn (www.millvalleyinn.com).

The ambience: Tranquil, peaceful and Zen-like.

Regular guests: Local professionals, plus an eclectic mix of visiting writers, artists and actors dropping in for treatments and half-day retreats between screenings at the Mill Valley Film Festival.

Treatment menu: Tea Garden Springs believes that true beauty and wellbeing can only be found through holistic healthcare. Their practitioners work with new-generation therapies that focus on treating the body from the inside out.

House speciality: The six-hour Tea Garden Getaway consists of aromatherapy bathing, a 3D Slimming or Ocean Thermo treatment, massage, a light lunch, reflexology and a deep pore-cleansing facial.

Cuisine: Nutritional light meals based on the Chinese holistic view of moderation and balance. Abstinence or overindulgence in any food group is not the Tea Garden Springs way to a healthy life.

Ideal for: A holistic journey for the mind, body and soul. If you want to take the weight of the world off your shoulders and lose a few pounds, this is a great place to start.

What to pack: Loose, flowing clothes for the spa and 'street' clothes for transit to and from the inn if you're making a week of it.

Two Bunch Palms

✳✳

Address: 67-425 Two Bunch Palms Trail,
Desert Hot Springs, California 92240 USA
Telephone: (+1) 760 329 8791
Booking details: (+1) 800 472 4334
Website: www.twobunchpalms.com

This desert oasis in the Coachella Valley is a hideaway for the Hollywood elite, with privacy and peace and quiet the priorities. Two Bunch Palms is a dedicated destination spa without a trace of conventional hotel mentality. Their speciality is the natural hot springs, enriched with minerals, and the curative water is cooled in tanks before free-falling into a rock-rimmed grotto. Here, Hollywood hotshots peruse scripts as they relax and rehydrate, and soaking under the stars is a popular evening pastime.

The ambience: Relaxed, unpretentious and very, very quiet. The only sounds you'll tend to hear during the day are the palm and tamarisk trees rustling in the breeze and bubbling water from the springs.

Regular guests: Hollywood stars have been flocking here since the early 1930s. It also attracts a high percentage of male guests because it feels more like a rich uncle's cattle ranch than a prissy beauty farm.

Treatment menu: Whether you want to wallow in mud baths, dip into Aqua Soma therapy or liquefy tension with shiatsu, you can do it here. The more offbeat options, like reiki, colour therapy, aqua-reflexology, and polarity-relaxing sessions, are well worth trying.

House speciality: Watsu is a sort of underwater shiatsu-stretching treatment in which you are cradled in the supporting arms of a therapist. Get over the initial embarrassment and leave feeling taller.

Cuisine: The Casino Dining Room serves fine Californian cuisine with fine wines. While not calorie-controlled, mostly low-fat, low-sodium ingredients are used and, where possible, non-fat dairy products.

Ideal for: People wanting to chill out rather than work out.

What to pack: A waterproof pen and autograph book.

Golden Door Spa at Wyndham Peaks Resort

★★★

Address: 136 Country Club Drive, PO Box 2702,
Telluride Mountain Village, Colorado 81435 USA
Telephone: (+1) 970 728 6800
Booking details: (+1) 800 789 2220
Website: www.thepeaksresort.com

Located 4,270 metres (14,000 feet) up the San Juan Mountains, Wyndham Peaks overlooks Telluride, the local mining town that was the target of Butch Cassidy's first bank robbery in 1888. If only the resort was built back then, Cassidy would have had a real choice of what to spend his stolen dollars on. Here, you will find outdoor activities, like golfing, mountain biking, horse-riding, hiking and fly-fishing in the summer, or skiing, ice-skating, dog-sledding and snowshoeing in the winter, as well as indoor activities, such as a fitness centre with pool, weight room and studios, as well as the spa. The resort has luxurious, modern facilities and friendly, hospitable staff. The well-designed accommodation includes rooms, penthouse suites and the See Forever cabins, which are authentically rustic but first class. There is even a ballroom.

The Golden Door Spa is inspired by ancient Japanese *hoijin* inns, where weary travellers would come to seek sanctuary, and this is reflected in the treatments. The bodywork programme represents a cross-section of Eastern techniques, including shiatsu, acupuncture, reflexology and reiki. The impressive treatments are complemented by the alpine air that is so clean it's actually got a natural taste.

The ambience: The ancient East meets the Wild West.

Regular guests: Wealthy winter skiers and healthy summer hikers. Tom Cruise is building a house nearby.

Treatment menu: The sheer size of the facilities and range of therapies available is as breathtaking as the view from the spa. The 44 treatment rooms cater for every whim, from reiki to reflexology, massage to manicure, and facials to fitness. The maternity massage and couples massage reveal an attention

to detail, while their oils, scrubs, body wraps and skincare products all incorporate local mountain-forest ingredients, which add to the bracing effect of fresh air at high altitude.

House speciality: The Deep Forest Exfoliation starts with a skin exfoliation using pine, Colorado clay, organic corn and oats. A massage using botanical oil to rehydrate and nourish the skin follows. Finally, you are wrapped in a warm herbal sheet, letting the nourishing oil soothe your skin. Another recommended treatment is the High Altitude Aromatherapy Facial. Soothing, cleansing and hydrating, you'll experience deep relaxation and rebalancing. It uses marma-point massage and essential oils to help you acclimatize to the Telluride atmosphere.

Cuisine: The spa has a low-fat menu, which makes the most of using no oil, cream or butter. The hotel offers two dining facilities: Legends is a daytime poolside restaurant with freshly grilled entrées and excellent cocktails; and Appaloosa is a slightly more formal evening dining room serving local game, lamb and seafood – but beware the huge portions.

Ideal for: Outdoor types who also enjoy being pampered indoors.

What to pack: The spa provides shorts, T-shirts, robes and slippers, so all you need to bring with you is proper footwear – for working out, chilling out and dining out.

Agua Spa at the Delano Hotel

***

Address: 1685 Collins Avenue, South Beach,
Miami, Florida 33139 USA
Telephone: (+1) 305 672 2000
Booking details: (+1) 800 695 8284
Website: www.ian.schragerhotels.com

Pushing open the white wooden gate that sits inconspicuously in the middle of the perfectly pruned, green garden hedge concealing the entrance of the Delano is almost certainly the nearest you'll ever get to feeling like Alice in Wonderland. Once through, you are met with a 15-story, five-star, luxurious, Art Deco, Ian Schrager hotel, with unusual touches like oversized lampshades, gigantic rooms, wacky furniture and knick-knacks.

The tiny penthouse Agua Spa is a bit like a rabbit's warren and, although in need of a little bit of beautifying itself, has wonderful, but expensive treatments. Treatment areas are separated by white curtains and voices carry, so you never quite get the feeling of

switching off and logging out. As an alternative, you can have a massage in the gardens, the private tents surrounding the swimming pool or on the fabulous penthouse sundeck.

The outdoor pool – for all hotel guests, not just spa-goers – has underwater music, and a spacious, well-equipped gym with first-rate personal fitness trainers is located in the basement. The big advantage of this city spa is the rooftop sundeck with 360-degree views of the Atlantic Ocean. It is painted bright blue and has comfortable, double sun-loungers. But the shy and retiring beware: if you nod off while wearing your bikini, you may wake up surrounded by porn-star lookalikes sunbathing nude – which is totally acceptable as Agua has sex-designated opening times and you are in Miami.

The ambience: Mega-stylish, mega-cool and mega-pricey.

Regular guests: Miami-loving celebrities, such as Madonna and Jennifer Lopez.

Treatment menu: Advanced, rejuvenating treatments from around the world include upmarket favourites such as Eve Lom facials, plus massage, meditation, aromatherapy and reflexology.

House speciality: Milk and Honey is an Ayurvedic-based body treatment involving a gentle 60-minute massage with a specialized blend of warm honey, organic sesame oil and milk.

Cuisine: A handful of restaurants and bars offers Delano-devotees a wide array of dining choices. Blue Door serves 'French cuisine with a tropical twist' and, diet or no diet, is too good to miss. The Blue Sea bar has an extensive selection of sushi and seafood, as well as more traditional fare, and is one of the hotel's most popular and healthier dining spots.

Ideal for: Located in the heart of the trendy Art Deco district, the Delano is just a short walk away from restaurants, bars and the infamous South Beach nightlife. It's the perfect deluxe base for a Miami break combining spa-ing, art galleries, museums and shopping with a bit of sunbathing on the penthouse sundeck and on the beach, located at the foot of the Delano's back garden.

What to pack: Hot beachwear, cool spa-wear and funky nightwear.

Spa at the Mandarin Oriental

* * *

Address: 500 Brickell Key Drive, Miami, Florida 33131 USA
Telephone: (+1) 305 913 8332
Booking details: momiaspa@mohg.com
Website: www.mandarinoriental.com

The only downtown thing about the spa at the Mandarin Oriental is its location in trendy Brickell Key, Miami's prestigious commercial and residential district. This deluxe three-level spa has a spectacular waterfront position, 17 stylish treatment rooms and six private suites located on the top floor. As you would expect in the land of the body beautiful, there is a state-of-the-art gym, an outdoor infinity-edge pool, male and female sauna and steam rooms, Jacuzzi and a hydrotherapy bath with colour therapy lighting.

The ambience: Luxurious, sensual and tranquil.

Regular guests: Hotel guests and minted Miamians.

Treatment menu: The top-notch, innovative and restorative treatments are inspired by Chinese, Indian, European, Balinese and Thai traditions and incorporate E'Spa aromatherapy products.

House speciality: Time Rituals are individually tailored to your physical and emotional needs. Simply reserve an amount of time (a minimum of two hours) and, on arrival, a therapist will assess what treatment you will benefit from most.

Cuisine: No healthy restaurants as such, but anything calorific that passes your lips in Azul, the hotel's signature restaurant, will be well worth the calories. Café Sambal serves light, tasty snacks all day, including special wok creations. M-Bar offers the largest selection of martinis in South Florida (over 250).

Ideal for: A day and night of pampering for you and your partner.

What to pack: Comfortable clothes for mooching around the spa and a sexy number for smooching in the bar.

Spa Palazzo at the Boca Raton Resort & Club

***

Address: 501 East Camino Real,
Boca Raton, Florida 33432 USA
Telephone: (+1) 561 447 3000
Booking details: resinfo@bocaresort.com
Website: www.bocaresort.com

The Boca Raton Resort & Club, located on Florida's fabled Gold Coast, is a private estate thriving with exotic birds, tropical flora and historic architecture. In true Florida style of bigger and better, it boasts two 18-hole golf courses, 30 tennis courts, several pools, three fitness centres and a private beach offering watersports. Spa Palazzo, designed after Spain's Alhambra Palace, backs onto a courtyard and gardens, and has a waterfall, whirlpools, a pool with underwater music, two terraces for sunning your newly buffed body, and the elegant Great Room, which is ideal for reading.

The ambience: Very everything: very elegant surroundings, very laid-back guests and very attentive staff.

Regular guests: Big families with big wallets and Premier Club members making use of the facilities.

Treatment menu: The eclectic mix of treatments combine modern techniques with Native American healing rituals and European spa therapies, and use local ingredients (seaweed, sea salts and citrus).

House speciality: The detoxifying Mineral Trilogy, using medicinal mud, healing waters and massage, takes an unhurried 80 minutes.

Cuisine: The numerous restaurants serve practically every dish under the sun, from 'new world' to Tuscan and buffets to burgers. The spa's juice bar offers juices, hot drinks and a heart-healthy menu.

Ideal for: Families – there's more than enough to keep parents happy, and child and teen activities will keep everyone smiling.

What to pack: Empty stomachs and full wallets.

Grand Wailea Resort

✱✱✱

Address: 3850 Wailea Alanui Drive,
Wailea, Maui, Hawaii 96753 USA
Telephone: (+1) 808 875 1234
Booking details: (+1) 800 888 6100 or spa@grandwailea.com
Website: www.grandwailea.com

The Grand Wailea is a vast resort with incredibly high standards and an impressive attention to detail. Despite the 780 rooms, 14 tennis courts and three golf courses, the resort is immaculate. The Spa Grande also places its emphasis on grooming: for a price you can even have your toe hair removed. Children will love the kids club, which includes a flowing canyon river, with rope swings, pools, white rapids, caves and the world's only water elevator.

The ambience: Just this side of ostentatious, the resort is perfectly maintained and very friendly.

Regular guests: American holiday-makers and lucky executives.

Treatment menu: Spa Grande has 42 rooms offering 13 types of massage, as well as facials, tropical scrubs and Ayurvedic treatments. There are some Hawaiian treatments of note, including lomi lomi Wela Pohaku, a massage using a bag full of heated lava pebbles.

House speciality: The Terme Wailea Hydrotherapy circuit begins with a brief shower, a soak in a Roman tub, then a sauna and steam, before jumping (or rather tiptoeing) into a cold plunge pool. A loofah scrub, waterfall shower, mud bath and a Swiss jet shower follow.

Cuisine: The unpronounceable 'Humuhumunukunukuapua'a' restaurant, a cluster of 'floating' Polynesian huts, serves local favourites, or choose more formal food at Japanese Kincha or Grand Dining Room Maui. Calorie-counters will prefer Bistro Molokini and Café Kula.

Ideal for: Families looking for a one-stop summer destination with guaranteed good weather and palm trees.

What to pack: A compass so you can find your way around.

Canyon Ranch Spa Club

*

Address: The Venetian Resort-Hotel-Casino,
3355 Las Vegas Boulevard South, Suite 1159,
Las Vegas, Nevada 89109 USA
Telephone: (+1) 702 414 3600
Booking details: (+1) 877 283 6423
Website: www.canyonranch.com

Canyon Ranch is situated in the centre of a Venetian-style garden atop a 2-hectare (5-acre) pool deck. The high-tech facility comprises treatment rooms; gyms and weight rooms; a spinning gym; studios; and a 12-metre (40-foot) rock-climbing wall. In addition, a first-class wellness centre employs fully qualified experts that will help you achieve optimal health through nutritional consultations, physical therapy, assessments and exercise programmes.

The ambience: Opulent, luxurious and fun, it's literally Las Vegas meets Venice.

Regular guests: Convention delegates and holiday-makers who want to push the boat out (and I'm not talking about the imported gondolas floating in the re-created canal).

Treatment menu: What's your pleasure? Swedish, exotic Thai or a Canyon Stone massage? How about a mud, clay or seaweed body cocoon? There are 120 services here so you won't be disappointed.

House speciality: The Royal King's Bath begins with a dry body-brush, followed by a relaxing soak in a bronze bath filled with essential oils and flower petals, and finished with a sensual massage.

Cuisine: A host of restaurants pepper the Venetian, offering cuisine from all four corners of the globe. The Canyon Ranch Café has an additive-, preservative-free menu, full of flavour rather than calories.

Ideal for: Beauty-gambling junkies and those needing to take a breather from the slot machines.

What to pack: Everything here is big, glitzy and spread out, so pack comfortable evening shoes (your stilettos will soon start to hurt).

Elemis Spa at the Aladdin Hotel Casino

**

Address: 3667 Las Vegas Boulevard South
Las Vegas, Nevada 89109 USA
Telephone: (+1) 702 785 5555
Booking details: reservations@aladdincasino.com
Website: www.aladdincasino.com

The Aladdin, as with all big Las Vegas resorts, aims to cater for every whim, so you won't even need to leave the complex; there's a shopping arcade, a performing arts theatre, a gym and a Morocco-themed casino. This is the city of dreams, gambling and excess, and fortunately the hotel's spa provides a sanctuary where you can lose the shirt off your back in the positive sense, rather than at the gaming tables.

The Elemis Spa opened in December 2001 and in true Las Vegas style, no expense was spared. The attention to detail, from the decor to the personal care that the therapists provide, is excellent, and with its vast range of therapies and 30 treatment rooms, appointments are not difficult to book.

The ambience: Mystical Morocco, rich in earthy textures and exotic furnishings. A true escape from the hectic Las Vegas strip.

Regular guests: Families, couples of all ages, high-powered Vegas workers needing a rest, and gamblers needing a break.

Treatment menu: Sole-to-soul therapies focused on simplicity and sensuality – rare commodities in Las Vegas. World renowned Elemis aromatherapy and wellbeing experts offer a range of modern treatments that take inspiration from the past, such as ayurveda, shiatsu and craniosacral massage. Skincare includes Algae-Detox, marine wraps, bath floats and oxygen facials. Salon services are abundant – you name it, they do it.

House speciality: Jasmine Lulur Ritual is a 150-minute skin therapy traditionally practised by Javanese royal princesses before their weddings. The skin is prepared with a body polish containing turmeric, red rice, ylang ylang and jasmine, then a wellbeing massage and soothing yogurt cleanse is followed by a jasmine flower bath and an anointment with jasmine body oil.

Cuisine: The spa only serves fruit, juices and light snacks, but some of the hotel's 20 other restaurants have healthy options and will serve guests in the spa on special request. The Towering Palms is the hotel's poolside grill, Zanzibar is a 24-hour café and the elegant St James is a multinational gourmet restaurant.

Ideal for: Gluttons for reward, as opposed to punishment.

What to pack: A flexible credit facility.

Ten Thousand Waves

*

Address: 3451 Hyde Park Road,
Santa Fe, New Mexico 87501 USA
Telephone: (+1) 505 992 5025
Booking details: (+1) 505 982 9304
Website: www.tenthousandwaves.com

Ten Thousand Waves is primarily a day spa, and it's not the kind of place where you rock up and stay for a week, although there are eight fully feng-shui'd Zen-like rooms for the odd overnight stay. You can choose from minimalist Japanese cabins to a lavish Emperor's Court suite with all the trimmings. Families may bring their pets for a small day supplement charge, but if you do, the pets need to be accompanied at all times.

Santa Fe has one of the largest concentrations of massage therapists and alternative healers in the world, due to the many schools in the area for acupuncture, Ayurveda, reflexology and a variety of bodywork techniques. If, however, you prefer hands-off to hands-on treatments, chilling out in a forest hot tub while looking up at the clear night sky is hard to beat.

The ambience: A weird and wonderful culture clash where Zen philosophy, paper lanterns and kimonos meet the turbulence of New Mexico's border history.

Regular guests: Skiers from the local Sangre de Cristo mountain range, New Mexicans and spa tourists, who flock to Santa Fe for its many natural hot springs.

Treatment menu: As a dedicated day spa, Ten Thousand Waves has a well-constructed menu. Most people hire the private spa pools, bath houses or outdoor hot tubs, but committed spa-goers can experiment with Japanese cleansing rituals, hot oil, and herbal and mineral body wraps. Massage is varied; choose from Swedish (undressed), Thai (clothed), Watsu (underwater), LaStone (hot stones) and Four Hands One Heart (double therapist massage). Massage can take place in treetop group rooms (where massage tables are separated by screens), private rooms, double rooms or in stand-alone pagodas for master-class treatments.

House speciality: Used for centuries by geishas in Japan, the Japanese Nightingale Facial uses processed nightingale droppings, which have been dried, pulverized and sanitized with ultraviolet light, before being blended with essential oils formulated to your skin type and then packed onto your face. A unique experience.

Cuisine: Light-snacks, baked goods, fresh fruit, bottled water and soft drinks are available for purchase in the lobby. Food is not the point of the spa, though, and if you hanker after some Southwest fare, Sante Fe's many restaurants provide a good nearby choice, or you can book a self-catering lodge at the spa.

Ideal for: A family or friends on a weekend or a day visit to break up a longer trip.

What to pack: Your own swimwear. Although nudity is common, the not-so-tantalizing alternative is to hire one.

The Away Spa & Gym

* *

Address: The W Hotel, 541 Lexington Avenue,
4th Floor, New York, New York 10022 USA
Telephone: (+1) 212 407 2970
Booking details: (+1) 212 407 2970
Website: www.theawayspa.com

Deemed the best day spa in Manhattan by *New York Magazine*, The Away Spa is tucked away in the super-chic W hotel. It is a full-service spa featuring a variety of body and skincare therapies that treat the inside as well as the out. Like the hotel, the decor is modern, stylish, minimal and immediately calming. The majority of Away's guests are regulars so you may feel a little out of place but you can rest assured that they're all regulars for a good reason.

The ambience: A city hotspot teeming with body beautifuls. It's been described as a 'stylish sanctuary' by regulars.

Regular guests: Members, hotel guests and day-trippers.

Treatment menu: The menu includes facials, massages, wraps and more alternative healing treatments. It features Javanese Lular, a beautifying wedding-day ritual, and Star of India, an Ayurvedic face and body treat, plus pranic healing (energy rebalancing) and reiki.

House speciality: The 90-minute Urban Renewal Antioxidant Body Mask is designed to combat the harsh effects of city life. Potent antioxidants found in green tea and tea tree are used in the clay-and-herbal-extract mask. An exfoliation is followed by the body mask, a scalp treatment, and a massage using pine or geranium oils.

Cuisine: Only an antioxidant tea bar is available in the spa, but there are two hotel eateries that have healthy-ish options – Heartbeat, serving organic food, and the Cool Juice Bar.

Ideal for: Locals and tourists who want workouts and pampering.

What to pack: Non-members need only their cross-trainers (sneakers), as the spa provides T-shirts, shorts and socks. Potential regulars need their chicest, most flattering gym kit for showing off.

Helena Rubinstein Beauty Gallery

✲✲

Address: 135 Spring Street,
New York, New York 10022 USA
Telephone: (+1) 212 343 9963
Booking details: (+1) 212 343 9963
Website: www.helenarubinstein.com

The Helena Rubinstein Beauty Gallery, a small, calming oasis slap-bang in the middle of the bustling Big Apple, is a retail store/spa that combines spa treatments with hands-on playtime with products. Although primarily for hectic women, relaxation is key here, and the treatments are about looking good first, feeling good second. Apart from the La Spa Center, there is a make-up bar, vitamin C skincare bar, consultations with dermatologists, high-tech diagnostic equipment and lots more to play with in the quest for looking good. Here, you'll feel like a little girl in a candy store.

The ambience: Elegant and calm.

Regular guests: Professional women needing grooming for their next meeting or to be spruced-up for a weekend in the Hamptons.

Treatment menu: The menu is small but offers body treatments, facials, manicures and pedicures dedicated to those with more time or no time. All use products from the Helena Rubinstein range.

House speciality: The 60-minute Plumper is a decadent but effective facial combined with a paraffin-wax hand treatment.

Cuisine: There is not a café as such, but there is a help-yourself tray stacked with 'snackettes' and refreshments.

Ideal for: Locals and tourists needing a pit-stop while shopping, or those who travel to NY regularly for business (or for the business of shopping), who need an oasis of calm for a couple of hours.

What to pack: Just yourself, everything else is on hand, even make-up for you to use afterwards.

Mezzanine Spa at Soho Integrative Health

✳✳

Address: 62 Crosby Street, New York, New York 10012 USA
Telephone: (+1) 212 431 1600
Booking details: (+1) 212 431 1600
Website: www.sohoderm.com

Soho Integrative Health is basically a one-stop beauty shop where all your needs are catered for under one roof, whether they are medical, aesthetic or alternative. This newly renovated loft is split into separate areas dealing with anything from plastic surgery to skin peels, reflexology to dermatology, fake tans to luxurious body wraps. The Mezzanine Spa is where you head for relaxation.

The ambience: A hub of inactivity – as far as the client is concerned. With only eight treatment rooms, it is calm, quiet and intimate.

Regular guests: Trendy downtowners feeling downtrodden, mothers-to-be feeling weary and resident New Yorkers feeling ugly.

Treatment menu: Unique and advanced. Eastern specialities, like the Wu facial and Shirodhara, are alongside Western treatments, such as microdermabrasion and Epilight hair removal. East–West combinations like reiki will help you cope with any type of surgery.

House speciality: The Tan Lepa – Ayurvedic Wrap aims to restore vital energy flow through your chakras. Herbal oils are dripped, mineral scrubs are rubbed and herbs suited to your Ayurvedic constitution are blended with milk, cream or flower waters and smoothed all over your body. You are then wrapped in nutrient-rich banana leaves before being rinsed with a hand or monsoon shower.

Cuisine: Herbal teas are available in the meditation/relaxation area.

Ideal for: Absolutely anyone, any sex, any age. Pre- and post-surgical care, stress control through yoga, mothers-to-be treatments and menopausal facials cover every life stage and mind set.

What to pack: A Polaroid camera to capture the befores and afters.

Grove Park Inn

✶✶

Address: 290 Macon Avenue, Asheville,
North Carolina 28804 USA
Telephone: (+1) 828 252 2711
Booking details: (+1) 800 438 5800 or
info@groveparkinn.com
Website: www.groveparkinn.com

Designed at the turn of the twentieth century, Grove Park Inn has recently been renovated and expanded, and has over 500 rooms, meeting spaces, ballrooms, 40 conference rooms, plus golf, tennis, two pools, a sports complex and a fitness centre, not to mention the spa, set into a hillside just below the main inn. In keeping with the mountainous architectural feel of the resort, the spa has been decorated like a grotto with granite boulders arching over pools and sunlight streaming in through skylights. The aim was to bring the Blue Ridge Mountains indoors and they've certainly succeeded.

The ambience: Steeped in history, it is quite rustic and grand.

Regular guests: Presidents of countries and presidents of companies mixing business with pleasure, and couples and families just mixing.

Treatment menu: The full selection includes European facials, aromatherapy, stone to shiatsu massage, specialized balneotherapy, and exfoliating, detoxifying and hydrating body treats.

House speciality: The 80-minute Fire, Rock, Water and Light provides a taster of treatments: a buttermilk and honey whirlpool bath; scalp massage; full-body exfoliation; body wrap; facial massage with cool stones; and a waterfall massage.

Cuisine: Most of the food puts taste in front of waist, but the spa serves tasty low-calorie cuisine, such as vegetarian dishes, garden vegetables and salads, lean meats and smoothies and juices.

Ideal for: Couples where relaxation means golf and a massage for him, and exercise and lots of pampering treatments for her.

What to pack: A torch (flashlight). It gets very dark at night.

Green Valley Spa

✷✷

Address: 1871 West Canyon View Drive,
St George, Utah 84770 USA
Telephone: (+1) 435 628 8060
Booking details: (+1) 800 237 1068 or request@infowest.com
Website: www.greenvalleyspa.com

Set in the middle of red rock canyons in Utah, it's no wonder that many of the spa treatments and fitness programmes have been inspired by the landscape, from the full-body Canyon Mud Pack to a host of guided hiking trips over the rugged terrains and rolling desert. The accommodation at Green Valley is in the form of cosy Southwestern-style suites that feel like a home away from home (only nicer), which have arched entries, tiled roofs and outdoor relaxation areas surrounded by brightly coloured flowers.

Not just a place for the body beautiful, Green Valley has a fully equipped medical wellness programme under the direction of Dr A Gordon Reynolds, which aims to help you live a healthier, fitter, not to mention longer, life. You can be tested for potential diseases, including the latest markers for cardiovascular problems and screened for conditions such as diabetes and anaemia.

The site of the resort is on an ancient salty lake, famous for its rich minerals, clays, sands and the abundant vegetation that grows there – all elements which are made into the spa's therapy products at the on-site lab. The list of treatments is virtually endless, and you can choose the setting for that, too – your suite, the garden treatment area or the spa itself. There are lots of exercise activities, from Pilates, cardio-boxing, aquacise, power cycling, yoga and tai chi to aerobics, as well as golf, tennis (at an impressive camp), and guided hikes into the Snow Canyon and Zion National Park through air smelling of sage-brush. There's masses to do, but you needn't do any of it; you can just lounge by the pool with a cold drink, pampering yourself occasionally or changing your whole perspective on health and wellbeing.

The ambience: Low-key and easy-going.

Regular guests: Health-seekers, hikers and the harassed.

Treatment menu: There is everything on offer, from sports massage and Hawaiian lomi lomi to herbal wraps and facials. There is an emphasis on water therapies and also new-age treatments for the mind and soul, which are classed as 'energy medicine'. The Gem Therapy, an energy-balancing, herbal wrap and stone therapy treatment is recommended, as is the Vision Journey, delicate, repetitive native drumming, which takes self-awareness deep into your 'inner heart' – a meditative experience.

House speciality: With the Painted Desert Clay treatment, you are smoothed with wet mineral- and salt-rich clay. When it has dried, it is brushed away, taking with it excess water weight and leaving behind firmer, softer skin.

Cuisine: The one dining room serves delicious, low-fat gourmet food based on the 'heart-healthy' guidelines of the American Heart Association. Spices are used to enhance flavour, so there is no need for added sugars, salts or fats. You can lose inches and pounds without even getting hungry.

Ideal for: Those wanting to give themselves a body overhaul and indulge in some out-and-out pampering.

What to pack: Comfortable but robust shoes and lots of layers for hiking, so you can adapt to the day's weather.

Red Mountain Adventure Spa

✷✷

Address: 1275 East Red Mountain Circle, Ivins,
Utah 84738 USA
Telephone: (+1) 435 673 4905
Booking details: (+1) 800 407 3002 or
reservations.worldres.com
Website: www.redmountainspa.com

A long horse ride or a short road trip from the Grand Canyon, Red Mountain's facilities include some exciting outdoor activities. Cycling or walking across the red desert trails is a must, while the more athletic can take kayaking or rock-climbing trips in the canyons. For those who want less adventurous activity, there are over 65 lively gym classes and a large pool. Remember, when you book, that the changing seasonal temperatures and weather conditions may affect the activities available. Finding space on organized trips is not a problem, however, as the resort has a maximum capacity of just over 200 guests. To complement the beneficial effects of the fresh mountain air on your sense of wellbeing, the spa itself focuses mainly on rejuvenating body treatments and skin-boosting facials.

The ambience: Modern, robust but intimate; set in red mountain formations – home of cartoon stars Roadrunner and Wily Coyote.

Regular guests: Billed as an 'adventure spa', sporty executives of LA and Las Vegas venture here, sometimes with their lively parents.

Treatment menu: Catering for those who want spa treats to be a part of, rather than their entire holiday, the options are broad and basic. Basic hair and beauty treatments are available, as well as aromatherapy, reflexology and sports massage; there are body wraps, too, which come with mud, aloe vera or fruit options.

House speciality: Red Mountain Four Elements leaves your aching body and stressed mind eased, soothed and relaxed. Your skin is buffed with grains, covered in purifying, mineral-rich clay, and then you are cleansed, massaged and rehydrated with juniper oil.

Cuisine: The food policy here is 'good produce in good measures'. The Canyon Café serves organic snacks and healthy takeaway lunches for the days you decide to head out on a day trip. The Canyon Breeze restaurant uses nutritious ingredients to create corn waffles with syrup, herb-crusted fish and cheesecake that wont leave you feeling guilty.

Ideal for: Couples and small groups who want a massage and Martini by the pool, but who enjoy the rugged sense of outdoor adventure. A great place to lose weight without losing out.

What to pack: Strong walking shoes and a camera with a panoramic viewfinder, as the vibrant colours are quite remarkable.

The Greenbrier

***

Address: 300 West Main Street, White Sulphur Springs,
West Virginia 24986 USA
Telephone: (+1) 304 536 1110
Booking details: (+1) 800 624 6070
Website: www.greenbrier.com

Set in 2,600 hectares (6,500 acres) of lush West Virginian valley
in the Allegheny Mountains, the Georgian-style Greenbrier looks
like a grand version of the White House. With 739 rooms, ranging
from individual guest rooms to luxury suites, roomy guesthouses
and elegant estate houses, it isn't short on space or facilities.

The recently refurbished and expanded Greenbrier Spa looks after
your fitness, nutrition, stress levels, and overall mind and body.
It works with old- and new-age cures, from the natural mineral
spring water that flows into the spa's hydrotherapy baths to the
latest technology at the Greenbrier Clinic, which offers diagnostic
sessions to assist you with everything from nutritional counselling
to cardiovascular scans and preventative medical care. Healthy
Living programmes can be geared towards exercise, health or

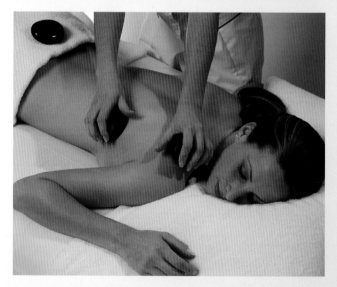

pampering, or a combination of all three. Classes, including yoga, aqua-aerobics, high-low aerobics, kickboxing, body sculpting and spinning, will help you burn off last night's dinner.

For the easily distracted, there are over 50 recreational activities, including indoor and outdoor tennis, horse-riding, fishing, biking trails, bowling, swimming and even Land Rover driving. There are three golf courses as well as a practice range, putting green and golf academy. And on the subject of the easily distracted, the Brier Bunch is a programme of supervised activities for youngsters from three- to five-years-old; the Tweeners programme is for children aged 6 to 9, and the Clubbers programme takes care of the 10- to 12-year-olds. The teenagers get sports schools to help them learn or improve their golf and tennis skills, plus there are a wide variety of lawn games available for the little people, and even kiddie cooking classes for budding chefs.

The ambience: Grand, impressive and runs like clockwork.

Regular guests: Politicians to actresses (from George W Bush Junior to Cameron Diaz), golfers and spa-goers.

Treatment menu: The menu ranges from the sublime to the ridiculous. An example of sublime is Neptune's Gift, a soak in minerals from Canadian glacier lakes in the Zephyr hydrotherapy tub, followed by a Swedish massage. The circulation-boosting Swedish shower, which involves being hosed down with freezing jets of water, might well be considered ridiculous.

House speciality: The Greenbrier starts with a soak in the sulphur waters of White Sulphur Springs, for which Greenbrier is famous, followed by a steam or sauna, a Swiss shower and a Scotch spray (an icy mist of water) to refresh and invigorate. A massage follows, which makes all the detoxifying hosing-down worthwhile.

Cuisine: The Rhododendron Spa Café is open daily and serves low-calorie, low-salt and low-sugar snacks and drinks. Otherwise you can choose from fine-dining at the Main Dining Room, the Tavern Room and Tavern Wine Cellar or Sam Snead's at the Golf Club.

Ideal for: Families – there's lots of space and lots to do.

What to pack: A desire for an action-packed experience.

AUSTRALASIA
THE PACIFIC

	PAGE	TYPE	PRICE	LUXURY	HEALTHY FOOD	GYM	POOL	OUTDOOR SPORTS	ALTERNATIVE TREATMENTS
Aman Spa at the Amandari Hotel, Indonesia	206	Hotel/Resort	✱✱	✓			✓	✓	✓
Aman Spa at the Amanpuri Hotel, Thailand	228	Hotel/Resort	✱✱✱	✓			✓	✓	✓
Angsana Resort & Spa, Australia	195	Hotel/Resort	✱✱	✓			✓	✓	✓
Angsana Resort & Spa, Indonesia	214	Hotel/Resort	✱	✓			✓	✓	✓
Aurora Spa Retreat, Australia	196	Hotel/Resort/Day	✱	✓				✓	✓
Banyan Tree Bintan, Indonesia	215	Hotel/Resort	✱✱✱	✓	✓		✓	✓	✓
Banyan Tree Bangkok, Thailand	230	Hotel/Resort	✱✱✱	✓	✓	✓	✓	✓	✓
Banyan Tree Phuket, Thailand	232	Hotel/Resort	✱✱✱	✓	✓	✓	✓	✓	✓
Begawan Giri Estate & Source Spa, Indonesia	208	Destination/Mineral Springs	✱✱✱	✓	✓	✓	✓	✓	✓
Chiva-Som International Health Resort, Thailand	234	Destination	✱✱✱	✓	✓	✓	✓	✓	✓
Club Jin Mao at the Grand Hyatt Shanghai, China	204	Hotel/Resort	✱✱✱	✓		✓	✓	✓	✓

	PAGE	TYPE	PRICE	LUXURY	HEALTHY FOOD	GYM	POOL	OUTDOOR SPORTS	ALTERNATIVE TREATMENTS
Day Spa at the Observatory Hotel, Australia	197	Hotel/Resort/Day	✶✶	✓		✓	✓	✓	✓
Eagle's Nest, New Zealand	224	Destination	✶✶	✓	✓		✓		
Four Seasons Hotel, Singapore	225	Hotel/Resort	✶✶✶	✓	✓	✓	✓	✓	✓
Four Seasons Resort, Indonesia	210	Hotel/Resort	✶✶✶	✓	✓	✓	✓	✓	
Fullerton Singapore Hotel & Asian Spa, Singapore	226	Hotel/Resort	✶✶	✓	✓	✓	✓		
Golden Door Resort Spa at Cypress Lakes, Australia	198	Destination/Resort/Day	✶✶	✓	✓	✓	✓	✓	✓
Inn Seiryuso, Japan	217	Destination/Resort/Day /Mineral springs	✶✶✶	✓		✓	✓		✓
Jamu Nature Spa at the Andaman, Malaysia	218	Hotel/Resort	✶✶✶	✓	✓	✓	✓	✓	
Mandara Spa at the Datai, Malaysia	220	Hotel/Resort	✶✶✶			✓	✓	✓	
Mandara Spa at the Hotel Padma Bali, Indonesia	211	Hotel/Resort	✶✶			✓	✓	✓	
Nusa Dua Beach Hotel & Spa, Indonesia	212	Hotel/Resort/Day	✶✶			✓	✓	✓	

	PAGE	TYPE	PRICE	LUXURY	HEALTHY FOOD	GYM	POOL	OUTDOOR SPORTS	ALTERNATIVE TREATMENTS
The Oberoi, Indonesia	216	Hotel/Resort	★★★	✓		✓	✓		✓
Oriental Spa, Thailand	236	Hotel/Resort	★★★	✓	✓	✓	✓		✓
Peninsula Hotel & Spa, China	205	Hotel/Resort/Day	★★★	✓	✓	✓	✓		
Pimalai Resort & Spa, Thailand	237	Hotel/Resort	★★	✓	✓	✓	✓	✓	
Regent Chiang Mai Resort & Lanna Spa, Thailand	238	Hotel/Resort	★★★	✓	✓	✓	✓		✓
Retreat on Spring, Australia	200	Day	★	✓	✓	✓	✓		✓
St Gregory Javana Spa, Singapore	227	Hotel/Resort/Day	★★	✓	✓	✓	✓		✓
Spa Chakra, Australia	201	Day	★★★	✓	✓	✓	✓		✓
Spa Village at the Pangkor Laut Resort, Malaysia	222	Hotel/Resort	★★	✓		✓	✓	✓	✓
Sun Spa at the Hyatt Regency Coolum, Australia	202	Hotel/Resort/Day	★★	✓	✓	✓	✓		✓
WakaGanga Resort, Indonesia	213	Hotel/Resort/Day	★★	✓		✓	✓	✓	✓

Angsana Resort & Spa

✴✴

Address: 1 Veivers Road, Palm Cove, Great Barrier Reef,
Cairns QLD 4879, Australia
Telephone: (+617) 4055 3000
Booking details: (+617) 4055 3000
(cairns@angsana.com)
Website: www.angsana.com

Nestled snugly in the beautiful village of Palm Cove just a short drive from Cairns, the Angsana is a gateway to the longest coral reef and oldest rainforest on earth. It has the best beach in the region, which looks directly onto the awe-inspiring Great Barrier Reef. Treatments can be carried out on your balcony overlooking the beach with the sound of *real* waves crashing on the shore (as opposed to mood music). All the 67 luxurious suites have a balcony, verandah or private tropical garden and fully equipped kitchenette.

The ambience: Tranquil, laid-back and very friendly.

Regular guests: Targeted at Australian holiday-makers.

Treatment menu: Includes three facials, eight types of massage and detoxifying and invigorating body wraps and scrubs using über-natural ingredients (you can be wrapped in tomato or orange pulp and buffed with sea salt, honey and sesame oil).

House speciality: Creamy banana wrap – a super-cleansing and moisturizing tropical body wrap.

Cuisine: Far Horizons restaurant and bar offers imaginative cuisine with an Asian touch. The resort doesn't have a dieters' menu as such, but an abundance of healthy, fresh local produce, fish, rice dishes and salads galore means that those wanting to lose a few pounds can do so without missing out.

Ideal for: Anyone who wants to take advantage of some of the world's best diving during the day and exotic cocktails by night.

What to pack: Sunscreen and a good book to read while lazing in a hammock under a palm tree.

Aurora Spa Retreat

*

Address: The Prince Hotel, 2 Acland Street,
St Kilda VIC 3182, Australia
Telephone: (+613) 9536 1130
Booking details: info@aurorasparetreat.com
Website: www.aurorasparetreat.com

The Aurora Spa Retreat is a big, uptown beauty salon in an adjoining building to the Prince Hotel. Like its neighbour, the spa has a sharp style and funky vibe. Although broad and exciting, the treatment menu doesn't venture too far beyond the superficial and is more given over to pampering than spiritual rejuvenation.

The ambience: A hip boutique hotel and ultra-modern spa, cool enough for *Vogue* to do a fashion shoot in the corridors.

Regular guests: Melbournites, touring rock stars and young, funky visitors with money and style.

Treatment menu: Unique treatments include a staggered three-month bride-to-be programme and cell-regenerating stretchmark and bust-firming courses. In addition, the Mayi Mapi body wrap calms nervous tension, the Miriki facial releases toxins and the Kitya Karnu water therapy, a steam room with attitude, leaves you radiant.

House speciality: Essential Calm is a six-hour journey to deep relaxation. After a geisha tub soak, you are massaged from top-to-toe, given a Mirri facial and a hair mask. A detoxifying body wrap and Polama hand treatment complete the package.

Cuisine: Circa is a stylish and theatrical fine-dining experience at the adjoining Prince Hotel. The food is modern and varied with a subtle urban edge, though not without a calorie or three. Opposite the hotel, Il Fornaio, an old 'workshop' bakery and café, serves traditional French-style pastries and exceptional bread.

Ideal for: A group of girlfriends preparing for a night out on the town.

What to pack: Your sassiest party dress and a desire to chill out, scrub up, then get on down.

Day Spa at the Observatory Hotel

**

Address: 89-113 Kent Street, Sydney NSW 2000, Australia
Telephone: (+612) 9256 2222
Booking details: email@observatoryhotel.com.au
Website: www.orient-express.com

Superbly located under Sydney Harbour Bridge with views of the Opera House, the Observatory is the prime base from which to explore Sydney. The modern spa has a state-of-the-art gym and a 20-metre (66-foot) heated pool, mirrored by a ceiling of fibreoptic lights designed to re-create the constellations of the southern hemisphere. Tennis can be played at the court across the road.

The ambience: The hotel is fairly traditional, whereas the spa has a generally more modern look and feel.

Regular guests: Business executives wanting to fit in a massage and a meeting, and holiday-makers.

Treatment menu: Holistic and beautifying treatments include facials, body wraps, mud masks, massage and flotation. There is something for everyone, from Ancient Massage therapies for the hippies at heart and Time for Men and Beautiful Mother packages.

House speciality: Tibetan Bell Therapy is a sacred treatment incorporating massage, which resonates harmonic tones to switch off the mind, open the heart, enhance clarity and restore balance.

Cuisine: The Galileo, specializing in delicious modern Australian cuisine with an Italian influence, is Sydney's leading five-star hotel restaurant. Calorie-counters and detoxers beware: Galileo is consistently recognized for its fine food and excellent wines.

Ideal for: Those wanting to sample Sydney's famous relaxed lifestyle from a luxurious vantage point.

What to pack: A guidebook to the Rocks, Sydney's uniquely historical Australian quarter where the Observatory is located.

Golden Door Resort Spa at Cypress Lakes

✷ ✷

Address: Corner of McDonalds and Thompsons Roads,
Polkolbin, Hunter Valley NSW 2320, Australia
Telephone: (+612) 4993 1555
Booking details: reservations@cypressresort.com.au
Website: www.cypresslakes.com.au

A 90-minute drive north of Sydney, the Golden Door Resort Spa is light and breezy, taking advantage of its surrounding greenery with big windows and wide verandahs. Although permanently busy, the spa has an air of natural calm. The many diverse treatments on offer make the spa a 'jack of all trades' and, unusually, a master of them all. The use of native Australian wild flower essences, Ayurvedic techniques and soulful energy balancing, along with yoga and tai chi classes, perfectly complements the less spiritual joys of manicure, pedicure, hairdressing and leg waxing.

Australians traditionally love the outdoor life, and Cypress Lakes' scenic golf course, organized bike rides and fitness walks confirm this. Dietary advice and women's lifestyle programmes may make the resort sound like a cross between a boot camp and beauty farm, but everything is geared towards relaxing, and smiling, as you spoil yourself. The Hunter Valley boasts some of Australia's premier vineyards, so it would be a missed opportunity if you didn't take time to sample the local wines.

The ambience: A spacious, friendly, country club environment that offers a touch more spirituality than you might expect.

Regular guests: Melbournites and Sydneysiders looking for a short, indulgent break from their hectic lifestyles, as well as anyone who enjoys golf, spirituality and relaxation in the great outdoors.

Treatment menu: The treatments are remarkably spiritual, considering the athletic feel of the resort. Schooled in the popular ancient Indian techniques of Ayurvedic and Samvahan massage (vibration therapy, which harmonizes the body), practitioners work to restore energy, relieve stress and balance chakras (energy meridians) in the body. Reiki, the hands-on art of healing, is also practised, which, with the more traditional facials, mud packs, reflexology and merely skin-deep pamperings, make the treatment possibilities at Golden Door endless.

House speciality: In recruiting expert male and female therapists from many disciplines, the spa delivers exceptional quality across the wide range of treatments. Choosing one speciality is therefore nearly impossible. Recommended, though, is the Golfer's Special, a combined crystal-healing foot soak, revitalizing Vichy shower and tension-relieving massage that is perfect before a round of 18 holes.

Cuisine: Pipette, a relaxed yet elegant restaurant with an outdoor terrace and valley views, has a seasonal, modern Australian menu. Mulligans, a more informal dining experience, looks onto the golf course and swimming pool, and serves a selection of classic brasserie food. Icons Bar is the place for hanging out at night, while Lagoons Bar is for chilling during the day.

Ideal for: Anyone holidaying in Australia who wants to fit in a hard-earned spa reward; management training groups for lucky executives; and couples or honeymooners who want an adventurous and pampering getaway.

What to pack: Sunscreen, your golf clubs and a good pair of walking shoes for enjoying the nature trails.

Retreat on Spring

*

Address: 49 Spring Street, Melbourne VIC 3001, Australia
Telephone: (+613) 9654 0909
Booking details: info@retreatspas.com.au
Website: www.retreatspas.com.au

Retreat on Spring, an Aveda Concept Salon, is a three-level holistic urban oasis – a one-stop spa for wellbeing for the body and soul. Here, traditional towelling robes have been swapped for Japanese kimonos and minimal Zen-like rooms offer mollycoddling treatments. Beautiful relaxation areas and an open-air deck make the spa the perfect spot to revive and rejuvenate. The mezzanine-level Revamp Nail Spa offers spur-of-the-moment manicures and pedicures. If you need some space, this is the place to come.

The ambience: Calming and quiet, it will still even the most chaotic mind. The spacious open-plan layout is flooded with natural light and the colour palette of whites, yellows and golds is soothing.

Regular guests: Burnt-out executives, urbanites looking for an escape and groups of girlfriends.

Treatment menu: The full range of Aveda signature treatments is on offer, plus an extensive list of therapies, from aromacocoons (a relaxing body wrap) to multijet Vichy showers.

House speciality: Himalayan Rejuvenation is an exclusive two-hour-long Aveda treatment focusing on the mind and body. An invigorating dry exfoliation is followed by a warming friction massage and then a 'pure-fume' steam. Finally, a plant-based concentrate is directed in a steady stream onto the forehead.

Cuisine: Juicettaria, the juice and brunch bar, serves healthy fast food six days a week, as well as natural boosters like echinacea, spirulina, brewer's yeast, guarana and wheatgrass.

Ideal for: Regular pit stops or the occasional full service.

What to pack: Your credit card. The endless treatment list is tempting and you're sure to find something you need in the shop.

Spa Chakra

***

Address: The Wharf, 6 Cowper Wharf Road, Woolloomooloo,
Sydney NSW 2011, Australia
Telephone: (+612) 9368 0888
Booking details: spachakra@chakra.net
Website: www.chakra.net

Located in the chic W Hotel in the recently redeveloped Finger
Wharf, Spa Chakra is a favourite with Sydney's trendy set.
Dedicated to the busy urbanite who likes to work and play hard,
Spa Chakra is the Rolls Royce of spas. While your beauty therapist
cares for your body, the special Chakra Concierge will take care of
your life, organizing anything you need to accomplish during your
visit, from washing your car, buying gifts, sending flowers, ironing
clothes or booking dinner.

The ambience: Calming but buzzy at the same time. The decor
is sleek and minimal.

Regular guests: Sydney's cash-rich/time-poor individuals.

Treatment menu: Treatments range from traditional grooming
services like manicures, pedicures and waxing to more advanced
aesthetic treatments, including a rejuvenating programme for sun-
damaged skin. Skincare technicians, massage therapists and holistic
healthcare professionals use a combination of ancient therapies
and cutting-edge technologies to focus on the body's energy
centres – the chakras – and to maximize your natural beauty.

House speciality: The Spa Facial is a 90-minute relaxing facial to
cleanse, exfoliate, massage and de-puff the complexion. And here, a
facial means an eyelash tint, eyebrow shape and hand massage, too.

Cuisine: The organic juice bar serves healthy snacks, or you can
get 'spa chakra' meals in the many restaurants located in the hotel.

Ideal for: Moneyed individuals who need to buy relaxation and
time, and are prepared to pay big bucks to get it.

What to pack: A 'to do' list for the concierge.

Sun Spa at the Hyatt Regency Coolum

✳✳

Address: Warran Road, Coolum Beach QLD 4573, Australia
Telephone: (+617) 5449 3456
Booking details: resorthostcoolum@hyatt.com.au
Website: www.coolum.hyatt.com

The Hyatt Regency Coolum is set in a rainforest in the lee of Mount Coolum, fronting the Pacific Ocean beach on Queensland's Sunshine Coast. Hailed as Australia's most outstanding international spa and golf resort, it sprawls over 150 landscaped hectares (370 acres) of picturesque countryside with private beachfront access. It's particularly famous for its 18-hole PGA championship golf course set among natural bushland. In addition, there are nine swimming pools, seven tennis courts and superb spa rooms. Accommodation consists of luxury suites, villas and residences arranged in discreet clusters around the resort.

White walls, sunshine filtering through skylights in the showers, wooden-slatted massage beds, chocolate-brown towels and divine treatments provide a haven for all the senses. The private therapy rooms have their own courtyards, complete with sunken spa baths inspired by Japanese plunge pools.

The ambience: East-meets-West, minimalist, Zen-like surroundings create a tranquil, calming atmosphere, which is further enhanced by the black stone courtyards, water and pebble features, and natural vegetation.

Regular guests: Corporate big cheeses and working parents needing rejuvenation (a kids' club keeps little ones safe and happy while frazzled mothers and fathers are looked after in the spa).

Treatment menu: With around 140 pampering health and beauty treatments to choose from, you can probably book in for almost any treatment under the sun (from traditional to unique). The spa draws on Mother Nature, using local land and sea ingredients, and the cycle of the sun: Sun Rise (invigorating), Sun Day (for reflection) and Sun Set (relaxation).

House speciality: The Body Zone treatment, which takes place in an open suite with a private garden and geisha-style bathtub. The treatment incorporates a full-body exfoliation, a face and body massage using fresh fruits, and a head massage.

Cuisine: A wide choice of restaurants and bars is on offer: a light snack takeaway, T'Go; a pizzeria; a more health-conscious grill; a superb seafood restaurant; Italian and Asian Noodle cafés. Most food outlets and shops are in the Village Square, an Italian-style piazza that is set slap-bang in the middle of the resort. In addition, room service operates from 6.30 am to midnight, and breakfast can be served in garden rooms set in each accommodation cluster. Those who prefer to venture further afield in search of nourishment can head for the chic town of Noosa, which is only a 15-minute drive away.

Ideal for: Golf and sports enthusiasts, conference delegates and the health-conscious who want a break with health, fitness and beauty facilities, without compromising on good food and wine.

What to pack: Hiking shoes so you can join the guided walk to the top of Mount Coolum and take in the spectacular views.

Club Jin Mao at the Grand Hyatt Shanghai

★★★

Address: Jin Mao Tower, 88 Century Boulevard, Pudong,
Shanghai 200121, People's Republic of China
Telephone: (+86) 21 5049 1234
Booking details: info@hyattshanghai.com
Website: www.shanghai.hyatt.com

Located in Shanghai, China's largest city, this hotel and spa fuses ancient and modern, Asian and Western, cultural and commercial. Truly dedicated to high-flyers, it is situated in the Jin Mao Tower, the third tallest building in the world, making the hotel, located on floors 53 to 87, the highest in the world. Every one of the 555 guest rooms has spectacular views of the Bund, Huang Pu River or the city. The spa is at the very top of the tower in a pagoda-shaped structure and consists of a warren of little rooms with no-nonsense decor. Not dedicated to one-to-one pampering, the rooms have treatment tables next to each other, so don't expect to be alone.

The ambience: This contemporary hotel offers guests a heady experience, with breathtaking cityscape and panoramic views.

Regular guests: Business clientele from around the world, including some of the world's leading tycoons and entrepreneurs.

Treatment menu: All of the usual spa treatments, plus a cross-section of Chinese therapies. The renowned Dr Guo practises a Chinese version of osteopathy, but seeing him is almost impossible – he's often whisked away to treat under-the-weather VIPs.

House speciality: Any of Dr Guo's treatments.

Cuisine: With a choice of 13 restaurants, from open-show kitchens to an Italian trattoria, the hotel caters for all palates.

Ideal for: Business travellers, heads of state and VIPs seeking traditional Chinese treatments.

What to pack: Your head for heights and a guidebook.

Peninsula Hotel & Spa

***

Address: Salisbury Road, Kowloon, Hong Kong SAR
People's Republic of China
Telephone: (+852) 2920 2888
Booking details: pen@peninsular.com
Website: fasttrack.hongkong.peninsula.com

Consistently ranked as one of the world's top hotels, the Peninsula is set in the middle of Kowloon's business and entertainment district. Huge rooms with the latest high-tech facilities and a lobby that is reputedly the most elegant rendezvous in Hong Kong attract guests with limited time, but not money.

The ambience: A modern twist on classic Roman; arches and pillars appear throughout, from the pool to the eighth-floor garden terrace.

Regular guests: Stressed Hong Kong executives, Oriental lunching ladies and transient business guests needing a spa fix.

Treatment menu: Any beautifying treatment is welcome after battling with Hong Kong's noise, pollution and grime. The gentle facials, Clarins lymphatic massages, reflexology and many grooming treatments are enough to warrant a visit.

House speciality: The two-person Pen-Ultimate Experience includes one night in a suite, a chauffeured Rolls Royce, dinner, a helicopter tour, a private tai chi class, and a massage and facial.

Cuisine: Spa dining is limited to hotel guests only and includes low-fat, low-sodium breakfasts, light lunches, snacks and health drinks. At the hotel, Felix is a 28th-floor restaurant with views over Victoria Harbour and the city skyline, Gaddi's is for social gourmet lunches, Spring Moon is an Art-Deco Chinese, Imasa is contemporary Japanese, Chesa is a Swiss fondue joint and the Verandah is a sea-facing Mediterranean buffet.

Ideal for: A weekend hideaway for two lovers.

What to pack: Restaurant attire and swimwear – the hotel shops are pricey if you forget.

Aman Spa at the Amandari Hotel

* * *

Address: Kedewatan, Ubud, Bali, Indonesia
Telephone: (+62) 361 97 5333
Booking details: reservations@amanresorts.com
Website: www.amanresorts.com

This is the ideal destination for those who hanker after a beautiful natural setting, exceptional service and the exclusive intimacy ensured by the small number of rooms. Located only a few minutes from the art community of Ubud in central Bali, the Amandari Hotel consists of 30 traditional thatched-roof suites with Balinese-style stone-fronted gateways. If you want to go up in the world, book a two-storeys-high duplex suite; the second floor is entirely dedicated to a bedroom with a queen-size bed. Some suites have their own private swimming pool, but all have an outdoor sunken marble bath surrounded by ferns and bamboo.

The mini spa looks like a traditional thatched Balinese house floating in the middle of a tranquil lake. Treatment bungalows (*burras*) are open-air, so you can enjoy a massage while listening to the gurgling sounds of the river flowing past. The more adventurous can go white-water rafting down the Ayung River and mountain biking or elephant-riding in the surrounding mountains and valleys.

The ambience: Amandari means 'peaceful spirit', and the name certainly reflects the mood. Said to be the most authentic Balinese hotel on the island, it resembles a Balinese village and sits at the edge of the Ayung River.

Regular guests: Fans of the Aman group of small luxurious resorts, as well as spa veterans who prefer a discreet sanctuary off the beaten track.

Treatment menu: The Aman Spa makes wonderful use of natural resources, and although the menu is small, the treatments are perfectly formed. There are lots of massage and body treatments in addition to traditional Javanese therapies.

House speciality: Mandi Lulur, a traditional Javanese body mask originally used to give brides ultra-soft skin for their wedding day.

Cuisine: The open-air restaurant is crafted largely out of teak and overlooks Amandari's swimming pool and the Ayung River gorge. It serves Western and Indonesian dishes morning, noon and night, but for a slightly less formal and more romantic dining experience, meals can be served in an open-air gazebo next to the restaurant.

Ideal for: Honeymooners and lovers who want utmost privacy, and budding novelists in need of quiet and some time to muse.

What to pack: A pen and journal for recording your innermost thoughts or sketching the exotic surroundings.

Begawan Giri Estate & Source Spa

***

Address: Desa Melinggih Kelod,
Banjar Begawan, Payangan, Ubud, Bali 80571, Indonesia
Telephone: (+62) 361 97 8888
Booking details: reservations@begawan.com
Website: www.begawan.com

The Begawan Giri Estate, meaning 'old man of the mountain', is an exceptional place. Tucked away amid sprawling, dense tropical gardens in Bali's serene rural heartland, it has been built over nine years to ensure the natural beauty of the area remained intact and undisturbed. It comprises five residences named after the natural elements of fire, wind, water, forest and earth, which have their own butler and private pool and between them house 22 suites. You can rent a suite to hide out in with your loved one or book the entire complex for an entourage.

The beautiful Source Spa has treatments to die for and an exotic location. Muslin-draped pavilions on raised platforms are set in the jungle amid spectacular waterfalls and overlooking the Ayung River. And as if all this wasn't enough, there is even a natural spring with a stream that winds its way through the estate. The locals believe it to be holy water, and judging by the rest of the place, it probably is ...

The ambience: Like no hotel you've ever been to – this is more of a hotel retreat. It's amazingly tranquil yet buzzing with jungle activity.

Regular guests: Funky 30- and 40-somethings who want luxury without the commercial trimmings. Actors and actresses who just want to be themselves are also known to visit – Susan Sarandon, Tim Robbins and Richard Curtis, to name a few.

Treatment menu: Exotic body treatments incorporate nature's best offerings, such as volcanic clay, sea salt, flowers and local plants and herbs, and the Balinese massage uses aromatic oils direct from the island itself. The Begawan Giri Estate also has a handful of visiting masters who aim to help you 'connect with your body' through gentle treatments, such as Balinese herbal remedies, meditation or massage. Those who would rather work on a deeper level than just their muscle tension can try the 'guidelight trance journey' session, a combination of yoga, meditation, emotional release and clearing.

House speciality: For a start, the spa comes to you. You can be treated in the comfort of your own suite, by a waterfall, alongside the pool or in the jungle. Treatment-wise, the Bali Boreh Spice ritual is a must. After a massage, you are covered with an invigorating paste made from ginger, clove and nutmeg. While it is drying, you enjoy a reflexology treatment to boost wellbeing. You are then rinsed down and led to an outdoor bath, scattered with rose petals. After the alfresco soak, you are smoothed down with an aromatic body lotion. What more could you ask for?

Cuisine: Eating here mirrors the same principal as the massage routine: you can eat anytime (round the clock) and anywhere in the resort (even deep in the jungle if you desire). The chef at the contemporary Biji restaurant and bar prepares Aussie-Asian/New World cuisine, whereas the Kudus House restaurant rustles up more authentic Indonesian food. For that straight-off-the-tree freshness, the estate grows its own fruit and vegetables, and tends its own fish and seafood farms.

Ideal for: Hiding away with your lover, whatever the scenario – the proposal, honeymoon, anniversary ...

What to pack: Jet-lag remedies if you're coming from the West; you don't want to miss a day in this one-in-a-million retreat.

Four Seasons Resort

✳ ✳ ✳

Address: Sayan, Ubud, Gianyar, Bali 80571, Indonesia
Telephone: (+62) 361 977577
Booking details: as above
Website: www.fourseasons.com

This low-rise luxury resort sits snugly in the lush central highlands of Bali, with stunning views over rice terraces, rainforest and the Ayung River far, far below. Stylish villas and suites are scattered down the hillside, blending unobtrusively with their natural, unspoilt surroundings. Every villa has its own private plunge pool, gardens and outdoor shower; the free-for-all 33-metre (112-foot) swimming pool with natural cascading waterfall will make working off lunch to make room for dinner a pleasure rather than a chore.

The ambience: Discreet, quietly stylish and very, very languid.

Regular guests: Wealthy Europeans and Australians, couples and families with more grown-up children. Celebrities are rumoured to choose it for its privacy and integrity.

Treatment menu: The treatments focus on Balinese and Ayurvedic therapies, using clay, spices, herbs and flowers from the region.

House speciality: Suci Dhara translates as 'awakening and balancing of the body, heart and soul' and begins with a scalp massage, followed by warm herbal oils dripped onto the forehead, a massage and finally a soothing yet energizing steam bath. Or try the Coconilla, a body scrub using freshly grated coconut, coconut milk and vanilla beans to leave skin super-moisturized and glowing.

Cuisine: A handful of restaurants offer everything from noodle dishes and Indonesian-inspired specialities to wood-burning oven pizzas, pasta and health-conscious spa cuisine.

Ideal for: Getting married, or those wanting a luxurious holiday.

What to pack: An autograph book. You never know who you might be sitting next to at dinner, but be subtle as the staff are quite rightly protective of their guests' privacy.

Mandara Spa at the Hotel Padma Bali

**

Address: Jalan Padma No 1, Legian, Bali, Indonesia
Telephone: (+62) 361 75 2111
Booking details: reservation@hotelpadma.com
Website: www.mandaraspa-asia.com

Set on Legian Beach just outside Kuta, the Hotel Padma Bali exudes hospitality. All the rooms have private balconies overlooking serene courtyards. The swimming pool sprawls over approximately 1,000 square metres (17,000 square feet), and has a children's pool next to it. Other facilities include two floodlit tennis courts, two squash courts and a gym with instructors on hand. The spa adds an extra touch of paradise for those seeking to restore and rejuvenate. Take your treatment in any one of the five indoor rooms or indulge away from other guests in one of the three Deluxe Spa Villas with daybed, ensuite bathroom, outdoor tub, private garden and fountain.

The ambience: A village-style hideaway, this resort is set among spacious landscaped gardens and offers a sense of privacy.

Regular guests: Couples wanting to spend quality time with each other, and families – the resort has a kids' club.

Treatment menu: The choice is not extensive, but there are plenty of well-balanced packages for the whole body, including Balinese massage, Mandara massage with two therapists, and Ayurvedic treatments, including Shirodhara – a hands-on Asian facial.

House speciality: Padma Tranquillity is a Balinese massage combined with a choice of manicure or pedicure.

Cuisine: Dine among the lotus ponds at the Taman Ayun Coffee House or take the alfresco option by the sea at the pizzeria. There is also a fine-dining Japanese-style restaurant within the gardens.

Ideal for: Families and couples.

What to pack: The kids – this is a child-friendly resort.

Nusa Dua Beach Hotel & Spa

✳ ✳

Address: Kawasan Pariwisata Nusa Dua, Lot North 4,
Nusa Dua, PO Box 1028, Denpasar, Bali, Indonesia
Telephone: (+62) 361 771210
Booking details: sales@nusaduahotel
Website: www.nusaduahotel.com

The Nusa Dua is situated on a private stretch of golden beach on Bali's southern shores. A monster of a hotel (it has nearly 400 rooms and suites), this is not a get-away-from-it-all kind of resort, although there are acres of peaceful gardens. Treatments are carried out in the main spa villa and in garden pavilions. A workout in the gym, followed by an aerobics class and a few laps in the pool is as energetic as it gets; otherwise, engage in mountain-biking, wall-climbing, beach volleyball or Balinese dance classes.

The ambience: Traditional Balinese hospitality and decor is combined with familiar touches from around the world.

Regular guests: International travellers, families and couples wanting to be at the hub of Bali.

Treatment menu: The spa offers three traditional body rituals – Coconut Scrub, Javanese Lulur and Balinese Boreh – plus massages. A blend of native herbs, flowers and spices are applied with hands-on techniques to soothe the mind and smooth the body.

House speciality: The Balinese Boreh is a spicy hand-crushed paste applied to the body to warm the muscles, stimulate blood circulation and rejuvenate even the most sluggish systems.

Cuisine: The resort has five restaurants, three bars, regular buffets, and beach, pool and 24-hour room services, offering a selection of international, Asian-Pacific and healthy dishes.

Ideal for: Couples and families wanting peace, but some of the action.

What to pack: Plenty of beach gear and casual eveningwear.

WakaGangga Resort

✳✳

Address: Tabanan, Bali, Indonesia
Telephone: (+62) 361 416256
Booking details: sales@wakaexperience.com
Website: www.wakaexperience.com

WakaGangga Resort is located in Banjar Yeh Gangga, approximately 22 km (13 miles) from Ngurah Rai International Airport and 8 km (5 miles) from Tanah Lot Temple, one of Bali's most sacred places. There are 12 bungalows – called *burras* – with thatched roofs, and two villas perching on gently sloping rice terraces, overlooking a black sand beach. Each comfy bungalow (ideal for two) is furnished in the unique Waka style: textures and colours of nature, slate tiles, smooth unpainted wood and lots of natural bamboo. Some have air-conditioning, and all have king-size beds, an outdoor enclosed bathroom with sunken tub, garden shower and an outside sundeck. Pricey local stables provide horses for riding on the beach.

The ambience: The Waka philosophy is based on a deep and enduring love for the natural environment of Bali and Indonesia. Here is a place that is restful, quiet and oozing with tradition.

Regular guests: Intrepid travellers who want to experience the beauty of rural Bali.

Treatment menu: The menu centres around traditional Balinese massage. The massage profession is well-respected in Bali and a wealth of skilled therapists are available. Waka's top-quality, Balinese-speaking therapists perform first-class treatments at a very reasonable price, so you can enjoy several treatments a day.

House speciality: Balinese massage. A deep, effective treatment that uses a variety of different strokes.

Cuisine: There is only one restaurant and one type of cuisine – local dishes created from local ingredients.

Ideal for: Those wanting to get away from it all and rough it in style.

What to pack: All your worries. This is the place to leave them.

Angsana Resort & Spa

✶

Address: Site A4 Lagoi, Bintan Island, Indonesia
Telephone: (+62) 770 693 111
Booking details: (+62) 770 693 111 (bintan@angsana.com)
Website: www.angsana.com

Angsana takes its name from the exotic Angsana tree – a tall, tropical rainforest tree noted for its crown of fragrant, golden flowers, which burst into bloom for a day, close and then bloom again unexpectedly. The resort is set in picturesque Tanjung Said Bay, overlooking the breathtaking South China Sea. Unpretentious hospitality meets low-key, comfortable accommodation. Of the 135 traditional Balinese-style rooms, the suites are ideal for families and groups as they offer spacious dining and living areas, a sundeck, outdoor shower and spa bath, and a private landscaped garden. At the Angsana, you can be as active – with fabulous watersports and an 18-hole golf course – or as inactive as you wish.

The ambience: Stylish but cosy, you can dress up or down and you'll fit in either way.

Regular guests: Business travellers needing conference rooms and a chance to unwind after hours, and families.

Treatment menu: The spa offers invigorating massages using aromatic oils such as rosemary, lavender, jasmine and frangipani. Other treatments include the Creamy Banana Wrap, Purifying Potato Mask and a Sunburn Soother.

House speciality: The 90-minute Angsana massage uses euphoria oil (extracts of ylang ylang and sweet basil) and combines slow palm strokes with thumb pressure to relieve tension and aid circulation.

Cuisine: The Lotus Café, overlooking tropical gardens and the sea, offers flavours from the East and West.

Ideal for: A family holiday, a break away with friends or corporate groups wanting to build sandcastles as well as team spirit.

What to pack: Flip charts and flip-flops.

Banyan Tree Bintan

* * *

Address: Site A4, Lagoi, Bintan Island, Indonesia
Telephone: (+62) 770 693 100
Booking details: (+62) 770 693 100
(bintan@banyantree.com)
Website: www.banyantree.com

This Banyan Tree resort is located on the spectacular beach of Tanjong on the island of Bintan in the Riau archipelago. Prepare to be mesmerized by the tropical forest, hillside terrain and secluded golden beach. Each villa is built on stilts, and if you really want to splash out, choose one with its own private open-air Jacuzzi and swimming pool. The spa is an absolute sanctuary, but to top it all, they have created a package that combines the facilities of an exclusive Pool Villa with a hedonistic spa treatment. One bedroom is designed as an exquisite pavilion with relaxing music, flowers, oils, incense and candles. What with the private pool and open-air Jacuzzi just outside the door, you will be pampered like royalty.

The ambience: Very relaxed and calm, with understated luxury and lots of privacy.

Regular guests: Couples and small groups of close friends.

Treatment menu: The list of Asian healing and relaxation techniques and European rejuvenation therapies is extensive. They are also happy to put together your own tailored package.

House speciality: Perfect for couples, the Javanese Lulur pampers from head to foot with an Indonesian massage, an exfoliating body scrub using yellow-coloured spices and herbs, and a yogurt rubdown.

Cuisine: Saffron, the fine-dining restaurant, creates wonderful Thai and Southeast Asian food. The other two restaurants offer brasserie-style seafood specialities and Mediterranean cuisine.

Ideal for: People wanting to tie the knot on the beach or have their knots untied in the spa.

What to pack: Golf clubs for the nearby 18-hole course and a sarong.

The Oberoi

★ ★ ★

Address: Medana Beach, Tanjung, Metaram 83001,
West Lombok NTB, Indonesia
Telephone: (+62) 370 638 444
Booking details: reservations@theoberoi-lombok.com
Website: www.oberoihotels.com

The Oberoi in Lombok is a secluded cluster of around 50 single-storey, thatched-roof villas and terrace pavilions set in acres of tropical gardens along the golden sands of Medena beach. While these incredibly private 'cottages' look rustic from the outside, don't be fooled. Inside, they're decked out with traditionally styled furniture, comfy beds, marble bathrooms and sunken baths, not to mention the modern conveniences of air-conditioning, satellite TV, video and sound systems, mini-bar and hairdryer. Most also have their own swimming pool. Here is the place to kick back in style and indulge in a few beauty treatments for the body and soul.

The ambience: Relaxing and, due to everything being so well spaced out, very peaceful; lavish without being pretentious.

Regular guests: Couples who want time by themselves, together.

Treatment menu: Though not a huge selection on offer, there's a great choice of massages, from Balinese and Ayurvedic to shiatsu, as well as facials, reflexology and basic grooming treatments.

House speciality: Mandi Lulur is a traditional pre-wedding ritual for Javanese brides. It commences with an hour-long massage, followed by a specially blended herbal scrub, then a refreshing yogurt rubdown and finally a floral body lotion.

Cuisine: The resort offers Asian and international fine-dining, and more relaxed alfresco buffet dinners and a cosy cocktail bar.

Ideal for: Those craving a bit of solitude but not wanting to forsake their comforts or feel cut-off.

What to pack: Your favourite DVDs and CDs to play on the in-room equipment, and bath oil.

Inn Seiryuso

✴✴✴

Address: 2-2 Kochi, Shimoda-shi,
Shizuoka-ken 415-0011, Japan
Telephone: (+81) 558 22 1361
Booking details: info@seiryuso.co.jp
Website: www.seiryuso.co.jp

There are 30 traditional rooms, each with their own bathroom
with cedar tub, situated in beautiful gardens near Naoshima village.
If you want to work out, swim lengths in a manmade pool and get
dressed up for dinner, don't come here. Inn Seiryuso is more like
a bathing paradise, where a maid leads you to the tranquil gardens
for hot soaking, meditating and cleansing of the spirit. The idea
is to bring space, time and self into harmony, so be prepared to
embrace a very different style of relaxing.

The ambience: Silent. Steeped in Japanese traditions and style.
Stone paths lead into Zen gardens and hot springs located in
isolated forests turn bathing into an art form.

Regular guests: US presidents and Japanese aristos.

Treatment menu: Although shiatsu, massage and reflexology are
all available in your room, Seiryuso is a *ryokan*, or bath house, and
so prides itself on its hot springs set in gardens of rustic purity.

House speciality: Hot spring baths. The bathing ritual is as soul-
soothing as the actual sensation. After washing from a pail, you
slip into the thermal springs, which naturally moisturize the skin.

Cuisine: There is no dining room, so meals are served in your
room in keeping with traditional *ryokan* culture. The two-hour
ceremonial dinner is worth the journey; each of the ten courses
is served like a miniature artwork featuring vegetables, seafood
and fruit, carved and delicately flavoured to perfection.

Ideal for: Those wishing to go on the 'missing' list for a few days.

What to pack: Credit cards, a camera and best-selling book
Memoirs of a Geisha by Arthur Golden.

Jamu Nature Spa at the Andaman

* * *

Address: The Andaman Datai Bay, PO Box 94, Jalan Tuluk
Datai 07000 Langkawi, Kedah Darul Aman, Malaysia
Telephone: (+60) 4 959 1088
Booking details: reservation@theandaman.com
Website: www.theandaman.com

Translucent, pristine waters that gently wash onto the white sandy
beach of Datai Bay form a sort of blue, watery, front garden to this
virgin-rainforest resort. The grand ballroom, six meeting rooms, an
enormous lagoon-style swimming pool and an 18-hole golf course
will give you an indication of its size. Even so, the Andaman is
truly a pocket of peace and tranquillity, famed for its protective
obligation to surrounding natural flora and wildlife.

The Jamu Nature Spa is a white duplex-style pavilion that cuddles
up to the hills, giving bountiful views of the Andaman Sea. Each

treatment room has two massage beds, a large bathtub, a garden shower and a relaxation terrace. Real treat-seekers can hire out the fabulous Sari Villa, a lavish private villa within the nature spa, complete with Jacuzzi and terrace. The curative combination of rejuvenating influences from the sea, the healing life-force that seems to seep out of the rainforest and the divine, drawn-out treatments by the skilled therapists can only leave you feeling younger, taller, more glowing on the outside and more peaceful within.

The ambience: The grand but not gaudy five-star Andaman hotel has been designed in traditional Malaysian style, which fuses with a good deal of Western finery.

Regular guests: Honeymooners, families and couples, plus prominent people including South African President Nelson Mandela, French President Jacques Chirac and Formula One racing driver Michael Schumacher.

Treatment menu: The spa boasts a modest selection of indulgent treatments, such as exotic body scrubs, warm fragrant baths and traditional and aromatherapy massages.

House speciality: Despite its name, there is no need to get up early for the Andaman Sunrise package, though you may want to go to bed early as it will zonk you out. The four-hour treatment involves aromatherapy or traditional massage, a body scrub and a soak in a healing sea-salt bath, followed by a facial and head massage while gazing out at the Andaman Sea (if you can still keep your eyes open by that stage).

Cuisine: Authentic Mediterranean, Japanese à la carte, teppanyaki, Malaysian curries, Indian tandooris, wood-fired pizzas, light snacks and sandwiches should give you a taste of the diverse choice on offer at the eight restaurants.

Ideal for: People who like nature to be close at hand, or want to explore until they drop and then be massaged back into action. Or for those who, like Mr Schumacher, just need to slow down.

What to pack: Walking shoes and a video camera to capture images of the chattering leaf monkeys, giant red flying squirrels, tree snakes and the varied birdlife that live here.

Mandara Spa at the Datai

∗∗∗

Address: Jalan Teluk Datai, 07000 Pulau Langkawi,
Kedah Darul, Aman, Malaysia
Telephone: (+60) 4 959 2500
Booking details: datai@ghmhotels.com
Website: www.ghmhotels.com

The five-star Datai hotel is situated on the northwestern tip of the Malaysian island of Langkawi and provides an idyllic natural retreat within the depths of a centuries-old virgin rainforest. Sitting atop a secluded cove, it has its own white sand beach, where you can dip your toes into the blissfully warm waters of the Andaman Sea. Freestanding villas, all with spectacular views of the natural landscape from their verandahs, have been crafted from local materials. They are scattered throughout the forest, connected to the resort's central areas only by a series of pathways. Two-thirds of the island is covered by hills and natural vegetation, making it the perfect landscape for jungle trekking and cool forest walks. Sports enthusiasts can enjoy mountain biking, golf, tennis and watersports.

The walk along meandering jungle paths and across a mountain stream to get from the hotel to the spa starts your mental and physical journey of relaxation, and you'll notice how the stress starts to ebb away at every step. The Mandara Spa consists of four open-air pavilions, each with a spacious double treatment room, oversized terrazzo bathtub facing onto a wall of jungle green, and a timber deck over the stream. Twittering birds, rippling water and jungle music of the natural variety fills the air. Here is where the world stops.

The ambience: Langkawi is a mystical island which blends wild, scenic beauty and aquamarine seas with a past that's steeped in mysterious legends full of romance. The Datai has harnessed this magical mood.

Regular guests: Hip, 'in the know' travellers from Malaysia and all four corners of the world.

Treatment menu: A host of modern, exotic spa treatments combine the spirit and traditions of Bali with the mysticism of Langkawi's ancient rainforests. Indulge in herbal scrubs made from coconuts, coffee and local herbs, or massage treatments for couples as well as individuals. The treatment names themselves are otherworldy. Datai Dreams is 80 minutes of salt exfoliation and massage, the Rainforest Harmony is similar but with reflexology to boot, and the Langkawi Luxury is almost two hours of exfoliation using gentle, natural ingredients, steam infusion, a warm floral bath and Balinese massage.

House speciality: The Mandara massage is an unforgettable experience. Two spa therapists work on one person in synchronized harmony and employ five different types of massage: Japanese shiatsu, Thai, Hawaiian lomi lomi, Swedish and Balinese.

Cuisine: Traditional Thai food is served amid the treetops in the open-air Pavilion restaurant. Partake of Malaysian and Western cuisine in the Dining Room or try the lighter snacks and salads that are available from the Beach Club and Lobby Lounge.

Ideal for: Those looking for a quiet, peaceful beach holiday and completely natural spa experience.

What to pack: The appropriate gear for golfing, tennis, jungle trekking and deep-sea fishing.

Spa Village at the Pangkor Laut Resort

✳ ✳

Address: Pangkor Laut Island, 32200 Lumut,
Perak, Malaysia
Telephone: (+60) 5 699 1100
Booking details: travelcentre@ytlhotels.com.my
Website: www.pangkorlautresort.com

Pangkor Laut is a privately owned island located 5 km (3 miles) off the West Coast of Malaysia in the Straits of Malacca. The island boasts 125 hectares (300 acres) of land, most of which runs wild with lush, unspoilt, 2-million-year-old rainforest. The island is only accessible to resort guests, which is ideal if you don't want people to find you.

There are just under 150 Malaysian-style luxury accommodations in various locations, including the hill villas, garden villas, sea villas, beach villas and spa villas. These form the main part of the resort with eight magnificent estates in a nearby secluded cove. Every villa, suite and estate is spacious and has a private balcony, ensuite bathrooms and, depending on the type of residence, a separate shower and oversized tub in a private outdoor courtyard or by huge windows that open out onto the tropical gardens or sea.

The spa complex comprises eight healing huts, a restaurant and spa boutique. Inspired by Eastern philosophy, the condition of your mind, spirit and soul, and how you feel on the inside takes priority over how you look on the outside (although they do a wonderful job of that, too, with manicures, pedicures, and so on). So, if it's nurturing you want as well as immaculate pink toenails, this is the place to come.

The ambience: Private, remote and unhurried. Even though you are just off the coast of Malaysia, you feel a million miles away from anywhere.

Regular guests: Couples, groups of friends and families. The resort has a good babysitting service.

Pangkor Laut Island, Malaysia

Treatment menu: An eclectic mix of healing practices from around Asia. Categories of treatments are Rejuvenation and Longevity, Beauty and Slimming, and Relaxation and Stress Reduction. Try the Chinese 'foot pounding', a Malay 'circulating' bath, Japanese-style cleansing treatment or an exfoliating Shanghai Scrub. In the Wrap House, the menu changes daily, alternating between Ayurvedic, Herbal, Seaweed and Chinese Herbal wraps.

House speciality: The traditional two-hour Malay treatment includes a flowered footbath, a Chinese foot massage and a Malay bath and body scrub, followed by a top-to-toe massage.

Cuisine: The nine restaurants (including a teak boat anchored in a quiet cove) serve Malaysian, Chinese and international favourites.

Ideal for: The run-down and stressed-out, particularly those with young children who want to run around and let off some steam.

What to pack: Insect-repellent for exploring the protected rainforest.

Eagle's Nest

✱✱

Address: 60 Tapeka Road, Russell,
Bay of Islands, New Zealand
Telephone: (+64) 9 403 8333
Booking details: eagle@eaglesnest.co.nz
Website: www.eaglesnest.co.nz

Aimed at an upmarket clientele, the natural environment of Eagle's Nest makes it a unique destination. Designed by biodynamic architect, Reinhard Kanuka-Fuchs, the wood, glass and steel structure sits comfortably on the gentle slopes, and no chemicals were used in the construction. Even the interior designers have considered ecological and human energy, using bed mattresses without springs to reduce magnetic fields, low-energy refrigerators and barbecues rather than microwaves. This secluded paradise is more a wellbeing destination than a white-robe hotel. The benefits of fresh air, healthy food and breathtaking views rarely combine to such effect, and you can't help but leave with a clearer mind, a cleaner body and a more nourished soul.

The ambience: Uncluttered Japanese simplicity marries with raw, tropical, New Zealand energy, with a stunning horizon at every turn.

Regular guests: Yoga-loving celebrities and people looking for a prolonged break from the rigours of modern life.

Treatment menu: A wide variety of different massages.

House speciality: Massages in the comfort of your own villa.

Cuisine: There is an excellent range of fresh seafood, New Zealand lamb and locally grown vegetables and fruit. All food can be prepared by the resort chef at your villa, and recipes can be adjusted to accommodate individual dietary needs.

Ideal for: Well-off families wanting a holiday surrounded by nature, and environmentally appreciative friends, aged 35-plus, looking for a chance to hang out in natural luxury and drink good wine.

What to pack: Walking shoes, binoculars, books and board games.

Four Seasons Hotel

★ ★ ★

Address: 190 Orchard Boulevard,
Singapore City, 248646, Singapore
Telephone: (+65) 734 1110
Booking details: (+65) 734 1110
Website: www.fourseasons.com

Many touches make the Singapore Four Seasons special, including the 20th-floor Cabana swimming pool and terrace (phew, the view!) and four tennis courts – two indoor air-conditioned ones and two outdoor, which are floodlit. The internationally influenced spa treatments include Swedish, Indonesian and shiatsu techniques, and there is also aromatherapy, sports and foot reflex massage.

The ambience: A discreet blend of old-school Asian business charm and young, successful Singaporian luxury.

Regular guests: Singapore's rich and beautiful, high-powered men with highly powdered women, and Westerners seeking solace from the city. Popular with travel writers, which is a valid endorsement.

Treatment menu: A comprehensive head-to-toe menu features extensive body and facial treatments, massages and manicures, pedicures and waxing. All massages are available in-room. The Hormo Mask, Vitamin C Facial or Collagen Mask are a must.

House speciality: Home to the only floatation tank, to date, in Singapore. You are suspended free from the forces of gravity in a solution of Epsom salt heated to skin temperature. With ear plugs in and lights off, you can drift off into a state of deep relaxation.

Cuisine: One-Ninety is vibrant and casual, with seafood a speciality and the occasional live jazz. Jiang-Nan Chun, the Cantonese restaurant, offers lunchtime dim sum or an à la carte evening choice of more traditional Chinese plates.

Ideal for: Couples or two girlfriends wanting a slice of glamour, luxury and self-indulgence, and an escape from city stress.

What to pack: A tennis racket and your most stylish swimwear.

Fullerton Singapore Hotel & Asian Spa

✶✶

Address: Fullerton Square, Singapore 049178
Telephone: (+65) 6 733 8388
Booking details: info@fullertonhotel.com
Website: www.fullertonhotel.com

You can't fail to be impressed with the surroundings of this former post office building. The neo-classical colonial architecture, complete with Doric columns and arches, gives the Fullerton a grandeur that is only matched in Singapore by City Hall and the Supreme Court. The infinity pool, designed to look as though the water drips over the edges, has amazing views across the river, and provides business leaders with a chance to recharge before negotiating their next deal. Just across the river, within a minute's walk from the Fullerton, is Merlion Park, showcasing the legendary half-lion, half-fish sculpture.

The ambience: A neo-classical hotel that is stylishly chic.

Regular guests: Olivia Newton-John, Singapore's Prime Minister Goh Chok Tong and the occasional colonial military type.

Treatment menu: The exotic-sounding, slightly chi-chi treatments are ideal for ladies who lunch (or ones who want to look like they do).

House speciality: The spa is big on treatments for couples, with names like Sweetheart's Delight and Just U and I. Their use of oceanic mud packs, minty massages, juniper berry foot rubs and petal baths is certain to help you relax alone, together.

Cuisine: The Town restaurant offers riverside dining with Western and Asian favourites, as well as a bar with snacks. Jade is a more refined affair, serving modern gourmet Chinese. And the Lighthouse, ahhh, the Lighthouse – set 37 metres (120 feet) up with views across Marina Bay, you will definitely feel the majesty of this classic building.

Ideal for: Romantic older couples or for a wedding anniversary treat.

What to pack: A partner and an appetite – the food is delicious.

St Gregory Javana Spa

✳✳

Address: Plaza Club Fitness & Spa, Plaza Hotel, Beach Road,
Singapore City, Singapore 119591
Telephone: (+65) 6 290 8028
Booking details: plazafitness@pacific.net.sg
Website: www.stgregoryspa.com

St Gregory's Spa technically consists of three separate spas, the Javana, Marine and Therapeutic, with Javana being the largest and most evolved. Although adjoining the busy Plaza hotel, the grounds are sufficiently calming to offer a temporary escape. Make sure you book treatments in advance as demand is high.

The ambience: A calming sanctuary in a heaving city. This opulent complex brings together business, pleasure, tourism and leisure.

Regular guests: Affluent locals who fancy a treat or tourists seeking a recharge before venturing beyond Singapore.

Treatment menu: The treatments are not considered very 'cosmetic', but the reward is a series of innovative skincare, bathing, detoxifying and soothing therapies, which will leave you feeling like a million dollars. Make the most of the four varieties of skin buffing: Boreh for aching muscles, Lulur for enhancing skin lustre, Tropical Mint for cooling and purifying, and Orange and Honey for nourishing.

House speciality: The tropical Javanese massage is a heavenly combination of a honey-and-yogurt rubdown with the revitalizing strokes of a body massage to ease tension, invigorate and moisturize.

Cuisine: The hotel has a well-regarded Chinese restaurant for evening dining and a buffet at the Café Plaza for daytime eating. Healthy food is available in the Club lounge.

Ideal for: A three-day stopover between taking on the cities of Hong Kong, Bangkok or Shanghai and the jungles of Southeast Asia.

What to pack: The *A-Z of Singapore City* and a CD Walkman, in case the pool gets a little too noisy.

Aman Spa at the Amanpuri Hotel

***

Address: Pansea Beach, Phuket Island, Thailand
Telephone: (+66) 76 324 333
Booking details: reservations@amanresorts.com
Website: www.amanresorts.com

The Amanpuri, meaning 'place of peace', is built on a coastal hillside on Phuket, only a 20-minutes drive from Phuket Island but far enough away from the throng. The island is connected to Thailand's Phang-Nga province by bridge and is surrounded by the Andaman Sea, which joins the Indian Ocean to the south. On Phuket's west coast is Pansea Beach, where a discreet stairway leads up to the resort's main pool and facilities. There are plenty of fascinating places to visit locally. Government House, built a century ago, was used as a location in the movie, *The Killing Fields*; the central market bustles from early morning to noon; and if you want to justify that massage, climb the hill that gives the island its name (*bukit* is the Malay word for 'hill'). Butterfly Gardens, a National Park and about 30 Buddhist temples on the island are other attractions that may tempt you.

The hotel accommodation is made up of about 40 pavilions and 30 Thai-style villa homes, connected by elevated walkways with colonnades and interspersed throughout a coconut plantation. The pavilions are nice and roomy with private outdoor terraces. Rates are determined according to the view and location; some have better views of the Andaman Sea than others. While exploring the resort, you may stumble across a cluster of privately owned Amanpuri villas hidden away among the coconut palms and most with oceanfront settings. These are available to rent and are inclusive of a live-in maid and a cook who prepares delicious Thai food in your own kitchen.

The charming Aman Spa opened in December 2001 and is made up of three double rooms for couples plus three smaller single rooms. Each room has its own private changing area, steam shower, treatment area and an outdoor *sala* (terrace) for lounging. Rest assured, after the treatments here, you'll want to lounge.

The ambience: Gentle Thai hospitality is combined with a warm, friendly and very, very welcoming atmosphere.

Regular guests: Thai holiday-makers and foreign travellers wanting a taste of authentic Thailand.

Treatment menu: A range of massage therapies, facials, scrubs, body wraps, baths and beauty treatments, as well as meditation and yoga sessions on the *salas*.

House speciality: Thai massage, where you lie fully clothed on a bed or the floor and the therapist stretches and exercises your body.

Cuisine: The Terrace restaurant offers casual, all-day, alfresco dining and features many Thai and European specialities. The Restaurant serves Italian cuisine. At last light, half a dozen tables and chairs are set out along the terrace between the pool and the steps leading to the beach so you can watch the sun set on the Andaman Sea.

Ideal for: Those who want to absorb local culture as well as essential oils.

What to pack: Your deck shoes. Amanpuri boasts the largest, most comprehensive hotel charter fleet of professionally crewed vessels in Thailand with boats ranging from 6-28 metres (20-90 feet). Don't bother taking a book, as the sun-lit library keeps over 1,000, ranging from novels to travel guides and coffee-table books about Southeast Asia.

Banyan Tree Bangkok

★★★

Address: 21/100 South Sathon Road,
Bangkok 10120, Thailand
Telephone: (+66) 26 791 200
Booking details: bangkok@banyantree.com
Website: www.banyantree.com

The Banyan Tree is 63 floors up in one of Bangkok's tallest buildings and offers an exquisite and unique city spa experience; if you want your head to be in the clouds, this is the place to come. On the top floors of this partly shared building (although you wouldn't know it), you'll find the executive suites and spa, both of which have incredible panoramic views of the city. Here, you can have a massage in a room with floor-to-ceiling glass windows, overlooking spectacular skyscrapers and a frantic city, where you can see others, but they can't see you.

Like all Banyan Tree resorts, this one takes a holistic approach to physical and spiritual wellbeing and provides a sanctuary for the senses. Using Asian traditions that date back centuries, this away-from-it-all retreat blends romance and serenity with exotic sensuality. The decor is modern and minimal, but the dark wood, exotic flowers and unflustered atmosphere shouts, or rather whispers, Thailand. Want more privacy? Book a treatment suite that comes complete with its own steam or sauna room and relaxation area. The spa may be in the middle of a bustling city, but you'll feel like you're miles away from everything.

The ambience: Slap-bang in the middle of one of the most in-your-face, 24-hour, traffic-jammed, polluted cities in the

world may not seem the ideal location for a spa, but this a Banyan Tree resort, so it has ended up being a sanctuary in the middle of mayhem. But the stunning panoramic views, outdoor showers and swimming pool on a decked rooftop garden may disorientate you a little, making you forget that you're in the middle of a concrete jungle.

Regular guests: Business executives, tourists stopping off on the way to Thailand's fabulous beaches, and holiday-makers breaking up a long journey elsewhere.

Treatment menu: The 23 stunning treatment rooms offer a blend of some of the best therapies in the world, using aromatic oils, herbs and spices combined with ancient healing remedies. An amazing fusion of East-meets-West means you're spoilt for choice, with face and body treatments including massages, facials, body scrubs and deep-cleansing masks. All of the treatments aim to promote inner calm as well as outer beauty.

House speciality: The Royal Banyan is a three-hour hedonistic treatment drawing on the centuries-old massage traditions used in the Royal Thai Palaces. An oil-free, Thai acupressure massage is performed to improve blood circulation and alleviate muscle tension. Banyan Herbal Pouches, filled with lemongrass, cloves and coriander (cilantro), are then used to apply warm sesame oil onto the body, and the Banyan Massage that follows helps restore balance to your mind, body and soul.

Cuisine: There are nine different restaurants in the hotel, offering Thai specialities and Chinese and international dishes with that five-star touch. Each one offers healthy options if you need help resisting the tendency to overindulge. The stylish, open-air rooftop grill, located on the 61st floor and aptly named Vertigo, is a must for barbecued steaks, seafood and a generally uplifting vibe.

Ideal for: Lone business travellers, especially female high-flyers, who need pampering between business meetings. The spa is a great place for an overnight stay to break up a long journey – the only problem is that you might not want to go onto the next leg. So many treatments, so little time ...

What to pack: Bundles of cash for a spree on 'nearly' designer items in Bangkok's famous Patpong market.

Banyan Tree Phuket

✱ ✱ ✱

Address: 33 Moo 4 Srisoonthorn Road, Cherngtalay,
Amphur Talang, Phuket 83110, Thailand
Telephone: (+66) 76 324 374
Booking details: phuket@banyantree.com
Website: www.banyantree.com

Surrounded by the golden sands and gentle waves of the
Andaman Sea, the Banyan Tree in Phuket is an oasis of peace
and tranquillity, and a treat for all the senses. This exotic paradise
couldn't be further away from a weight-watchers exercise farm;
it's more of a haven for luxurious pampering with its Spa Pool
villas situated in tropical gardens. For the ultimate in privacy
and relaxation, you can book a massage in your villa.

While you can choose to eat healthily, take some long-overdue
exercise, lose a few pounds and indulge in some serious de-stressing,
you can also enjoy the local food, top up your tan on the secluded
beach and pamper yourself silly with the long list of incredible
spa treatments. You can also take advantage of the many sports
facilities on offer, including an 18-hole golf course, tennis and
squash courts, and watersports.

The ambience: Light, airy and incredibly relaxed. The open-air
design in both the spa areas and the hotel give this boutique
resort an incredible sense of space and brightness. The exotic
location and understated luxury make it one of the most romantic
resorts in the world.

Regular guests: Golfers, honeymooners, love-struck couples and
high-flyers that need to come down to earth.

Treatment menu: Choose from the Thai Honey Facial that's
perfect for moisturizing sun-kissed complexions, the skin-softening
Herbal Enricher body wrap or the Romance Salt Scrub.

House speciality: The Banyan Massage is, according to those who
have experienced it, 'the best massage in the world'. Rhythmic
strokes and intricate massage movements help melt away long-
held stress and tension. But be warned: don't book anything to do

afterwards, as the treatment may leave you feeling slightly floppy. For the ultimate in romance, book the Intimate Moment ritual. On returning to your room at night, you will find it magically transformed with lit candles, burning incense, cotton sheets swapped for fresh silk ones, a bath doused with essential oils and a bottle of champagne on ice. The rest is left up to you ...

Cuisine: The food on offer at the nine restaurants ranges from delicious and surprisingly low-fat traditional Thai and Japanese to Western-style dishes. The Tamarind Spa restaurant specializes in healthy light dishes, which are just as tasty as more calorific dishes. Dining in a longboat floating on the lagoon is not to be missed.

Ideal for: A romantic and luxurious holiday with your partner. The resort also boasts an award-winning golf course and excellent watersports, should you get bored of being pampered.

What to pack: A partner to share the experience, and simple clothes for the evening and swimwear for the day. You are presented with your own matching kimono and slippers, which make you look, not to mention feel, at home here.

Chiva-Som International Health Resort

✳ ✳ ✳

Address: 734 Petchkasem Road, Hua Hin, 77110, Thailand
Telephone: (+66) 32 536 536
Booking details: reservation@chivasom.com
Website: www.chivasom.net

Chiva-Som, meaning 'haven of life', gives the impression of being paradise on earth, with its palm-tree-lined beachfront position and honour of Asian traditions. But the resort hasn't lost its roots as a traditional health farm; here, you get appointments with doctors and nurses, time allocated to exercise bikes and monitored food portions. If it's pigging out on Pad Thai and wallowing in petal-strewn baths you're after, you'll be disappointed; however, this exclusive retreat is perfect for getting your mind and body back on track.

The à la carte spa menu offers treatments from all corners of the globe, from a Thai Body Glow to a traditional Sisley facial, and you are given an empty timetable to fill in with personally tailored therapies. As for exercise and activities, Chiva-Som has practically everything under the sun, including cooking classes and arts-and-crafts workshops for the less sporty.

The ambience: Situated on what feels like a deserted white sand beach, Chiva-Som is built like a traditional Thai-style village with well-spaced pavilions with pointed roofs and intricate, ornate interiors. Once inside the gates, you'll find walled gardens full of lush greenery and beautiful flowers, Buddha statues and relaxing fountains. Not a hippie hangout, Chiva-Som is very sophisticated and designed for health, wellbeing, relaxation and total pampering.

Regular guests: Thai royalty, stressed-out executives, British women who love spa-ing in the sun and celebrities that include Kate Moss, Kylie Minogue, Elizabeth Hurley, Naomi Campbell, Sadie Frost and Jude Law.

Treatment menu: Every kind of complementary therapy you can think of, and a lot more you can't, is available here. Acupuncture based on Chinese medicine is a popular choice and you will notice guests walking around with adhesive strips dotted all over their bodies; they've not been stung by something tropical, they've just had acupuncture.

House speciality: The Chiva-Som Experience is a two-hour-long, head-to-foot treatment. It begins with a luxurious herbal body rub, using sesame seeds, buckwheat kernel, fresh lemongrass and camomile flowers. This is followed by a spa bath with essential oils, a fresh papaya, pineapple and aloe vera body mask, and finished off with a mind-blowing scalp massage.

Cuisine: Don't expect traditional Thai cuisine at the resort, or you'll be disappointed. Instead, tightly calorie-controlled, low-salt, low-cholesterol, organic stir-fries, salads and soups are served. If you want to indulge in Thai cuisine without the calorie counting, you'll have to sneak out to the local town of Hua Hin – but keep it hush-hush as it's not encouraged.

Ideal for: A short detoxing, weight-loss break on your own, or with a girlfriend or your mother – especially good for before a wedding or after overindulging at Christmas. The Chiva-Som is *not* suitable for families with young children; under 16-year-olds are banned.

What to pack: Your bikini, sunscreen with a high SPF, yoga gear, and simple strappy dresses and flat sandals for the evening.

Oriental Spa

✲ ✲ ✲

Address: The Oriental Bangkok Hotel, 48 Oriental Avenue,
Bangkok 10500, Thailand
Telephone: (+66) 26 599 000
Booking details: reserve-orbkk@mohg.com
Website: www.mandarinoriental.com

The hotel is located on the banks of the Chao Phya River and the
spa itself is a short boat ride away on the opposite, quieter side.
Teak walls, a lily pond with koi carp, Chiang Mai antiques and a
meditation room that is home to a magnificent golden Buddha
create an opulent yet spiritual haven away from the bustling streets
of Bangkok. Privacy is paramount, and each treatment is conducted
in a luxurious suite, complete with its own changing area, shower
and raised platform with futon. A garland of fresh ginger is hung
outside your door to ensure you are not disturbed. It's not hard to
see why the spa has been nicknamed the 'temple of wellbeing'.

The ambience: Peaceful, calming and fragrant – the aroma from
the many lotus flowers, incense and exotic oils hangs in the air.

Regular guests: Business travellers, shopaholics and many famous
names, including Goldie Hawn and former US president George Bush.

Treatment menu: The extensive menu offers a wondrous blend of
ancient Thai herbal remedies and modern Western treatments.

House speciality: Thai massage – the lazy person's yoga – is the
perfect antidote to a long flight. The therapist works with you to
manoeuvre you into de-stressing body and mind stretches.

Cuisine: The hotel has eight restaurants and bars. Sala Rim Naam
offers healthy Thai cuisine, but the spa also has its own low-fat
menu with delicacies created by the hotel's cookery school.

Ideal for: Those who want to be pampered in between Thai cookery
lessons and boat cruises to the old capital and Summer Palace.

What to pack: A Bangkok guidebook. You can get to everything,
from temples to thronging markets, via the river.

Pimalai Resort & Spa

**

Address: 99 Moo 5, Ba Kan Tiang Beach, Lanta Yai Island,
Krabi 81150, Thailand
Telephone: (+66) 075 629 054
Booking details: reservation@pimalai.com
Website: www.pimalai.com

This boutique island resort is located in the heart of a rainforest
nestling in Ba Kan Tiang bay. There are roughly 75 rooms and
suites, some opening onto private sundecks and gardens planted
with ferns and tropical plants. Superior suites are set in 16 small
South-Thai-style houses, each containing four rooms decorated with
polished teak floors, rich fabric, bamboo curtains and beautiful
Siamese artefacts. The spa is located in a natural environment
away from the main resort. You won't get plinky-plonky relaxation
music playing in the background while having a massage here, not
when you've got the melodic sounds of a tropical rainforest.

The ambience: The beautiful beaches, stunning views over the bay
and green, mountainous backdrop create an intimate tropical haven.

Regular guests: Holiday-makers enjoying Thailand and spa-goers
who want to be pampered Thai-style.

Treatment menu: The spa offers herbal and natural products with
their Oriental-style treatments. Choose from Thai therapies to sports
massage, ideal after a day of scuba diving or mountain-trekking.

House speciality: The Royal Siam is a Thai massage that uses an
ancient method of aligning and balancing the energies of the body.

Cuisine: Dine overlooking the bay in the Baan Pimalai restaurant
and enjoy international and Thai cuisine, or take advantage of the
fresh seafood caught daily and grilled at the Rak Talay Beach & Bar.

Ideal for: Those wanting to get away from the hustle and bustle of
Bangkok or the larger Thai islands, and couples wanting a romantic
break with enough activities to keep them both happy.

What to pack: Your snorkel and a good pair of cycling shoes.

Regent Chiang Mai Resort & Lanna Spa

★★★

Address: Mae Rim-Samoeng Old Road, Mae Rim,
Chiang Mai 50180, Thailand
Telephone: (+66) 53 298 181
Booking details: rcm.reservations@fourseasons.com
Website: www.regenthotels.com

Lanna is Thai for 'the land of a million rice fields', and fittingly, the
Regent Chiang Mai Resort and Lanna Spa are set among rice fields,
complete with water buffalo. Just an hour's flight from Bangkok,
the resort is located in Thailand's 'rose of the north', Chiang Mai. It
has 79 suites – 64 Pavilion and 15 Residence – that harmonize with
their rural surroundings and come with one, two or three bedrooms
and a private plunge pool. Each suite is part of a two-storey building
and has its own lounge, oversized bathroom with glass-surrounded
sunken tub, which makes you feel like you're bathing outside, and
open-air terrace for eating alfresco. The decor, which follows the
principles of feng shui, is minimal, with white walls and stripped
wooden floors. In addition to the grass tennis courts and a health
club, the resort is also close to four world-class golf clubs and
orchid and butterfly farms. Adventure expeditions, such as
mountain-trekking and river-rafting, can be arranged.

As for the Lanna Spa, spas don't come better than this. A lavish
sanctuary, the seven spacious treatment suites offer total privacy.
Six of them have soaking tubs on semi-enclosed *salas*, or outdoor
terraces. Five of the suites have private herbal aromatherapy
steam rooms and two of them feature 'rain shower' massage
tables, where overhead jets gently caress your body with water.
The palatial Lann Chang penthouse suite has a stunning sunken
bathtub in a turret, with soul-stirring views of the resort and Doi
Suthep and Doi Pui mountain ranges.

The ambience: Absolutely magical. This place will balance your
spirit and put your life back into perspective.

Regular guests: Northern Thailand fanatics, honeymooners and
the Queen of Denmark.

Treatment menu: The spa offers a fabulous range of traditional Southeast Asian treatments using Thai herbs, aromatic oils, pastes, unguents and poultices. Many are geared towards couples.

House speciality: Toss a coin to choose between the Lanna Sampler and the Tropical Rain treatments. The first includes a Thai Herbal Steam, Traditional Thai Massage, Lanna Herbal Facial, Ginger and Honey Elixir, all in a mind-altering three hours. The second is a four-hour rhapsody that includes a Thai Herbal Steam, Sandalwood and Herbal Body Scrub, Tropical Rainshower, Aromatic Body Massage, Tropical Garden Bath and Tropical Hibiscus Elixir.

Cuisine: Choose from traditional, healthy and delicious Northern Thai, vegetarian and Western dishes in the Sala Mae Rim restaurant; or go to the Elephant Bar or Pool Terrace and Bar for leisurely lunches and informal alfresco dinners.

Ideal for: Couples, spa connoisseurs, VIPs and high-flyers in need of some serious grounding.

What to pack: Clothes and footwear for walking and exploring. The trekking and nearby attractions in this part of the world, including temples, elephant training camps and bazaars, are captivating, and the blend of Burmese, Laotian and Yunnan Chinese cultures just adds to the fascination.

MIDDLE EAST
AFRICA
ASIA

	PAGE	TYPE	PRICE	LUXURY	HEALTHY FOOD	GYM	POOL	OUTDOOR SPORTS	ALTERNATIVE TREATMENTS
Amanjena, Morocco	288	Hotel/Resort	✱✱✱	✓		✓	✓	✓	
Amarvilàs, India	252	Hotel/Resort	✱✱✱	✓		✓	✓	✓	✓
Angsana Oasis Spa & Resort, India	253	Hotel/Resort	✱	✓		✓	✓	✓	✓
Angsana Resort & Spa, Maldives	265	Hotel/Resort	✱✱	✓	✓	✓		✓	✓
Assawan Spa at Burj al Arab, Dubai	246	Hotel/Resort	✱✱✱	✓	✓	✓	✓	✓	✓
Banyan Tree Maldives, Maldives	266	Hotel/Resort	✱✱✱	✓	✓	✓	✓	✓	✓
Banyan Tree Seychelles, Seychelles	290	Hotel/Resort	✱✱✱	✓	✓	✓	✓	✓	✓
Caracalla Spa at Le Meridien Hotel, Dubai	248	Hotel/Resort	✱✱	✓		✓	✓	✓	
Carmel Forest Spa Resort, Israel	260	Destination/Day	✱✱		✓	✓		✓	✓

	PAGE	TYPE	PRICE	LUXURY	HEALTHY FOOD	GYM	POOL	OUTDOOR SPORTS	ALTERNATIVE TREATMENTS
The Cecil, India	254	Hotel/Resort	✱✱✱	✓		✓	✓	✓	✓
Dinarobin Hotel Golf & Spa, Mauritius	278	Hotel/Resort	✱✱✱	✓		✓	✓	✓	✓
Earth Nature Spa, South Africa	292	Hotel/Resort	✱✱✱	✓		✓	✓	✓	✓
Givenchy Spa at Le Saint Géran, Mauritius	280	Hotel/Resort	✱✱✱	✓	✓	✓	✓	✓	✓
Guerlain Imperial Beauty Centre, Mauritius	282	Hotel/Resort	✱✱✱	✓		✓	✓	✓	✓
High Rustenburg Health Hydro, South Africa	294	Hotel/Resort	✱		✓	✓	✓	✓	✓
Hilton Maldives Resort & Spa, Maldives	268	Hotel/Resort	✱✱✱	✓		✓	✓	✓	✓
Hilton Mauritius Resort & Spa, Mauritius	283	Hotel/Resort	✱✱✱	✓		✓	✓	✓	✓
The Island Spa, Maldives	272	Destination	✱✱	✓	✓	✓	✓	✓	✓

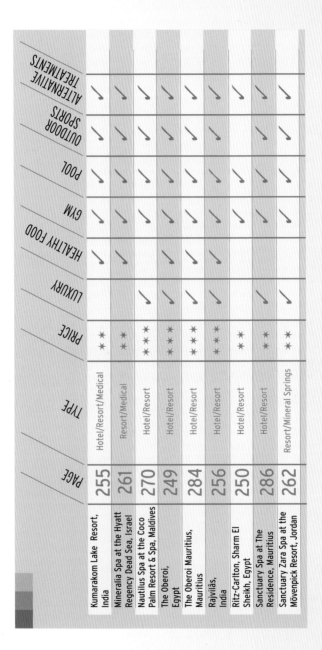

	PAGE	TYPE	PRICE	LUXURY	HEALTHY FOOD	GYM	POOL	OUTDOOR SPORTS	ALTERNATIVE TREATMENTS
Kumarakom Lake Resort, India	255	Hotel/Resort/Medical	✱✱		✓	✓	✓	✓	✓
Mineralia Spa at the Hyatt Regency Dead Sea, Israel	261	Resort/Medical	✱✱		✓	✓	✓	✓	✓
Nautilus Spa at the Coco Palm Resort & Spa, Maldives	270	Hotel/Resort	✱✱✱	✓		✓	✓	✓	✓
The Oberoi, Egypt	249	Hotel/Resort	✱✱✱	✓	✓		✓	✓	✓
The Oberoi Mauritius, Mauritius	284	Hotel/Resort	✱✱✱	✓	✓	✓	✓	✓	✓
Rajvilās, India	256	Hotel/Resort	✱✱✱	✓	✓	✓	✓	✓	✓
Ritz-Carlton, Sharm El Sheikh, Egypt	250	Hotel/Resort	✱✱			✓	✓	✓	✓
Sanctuary Spa at The Residence, Mauritius	286	Hotel/Resort	✱✱	✓		✓	✓	✓	✓
Sanctuary Zara Spa at the Mövenpick Resort, Jordan	262	Resort/Mineral Springs	✱✱	✓			✓	✓	✓

	PAGE	TYPE	PRICE	LUXURY	HEALTHY FOOD	GYM	POOL	OUTDOOR SPORTS	ALTERNATIVE TREATMENTS
Sérénité Wellness Centre, South Africa	295	Resort/Medical	*		✓	✓	✓	✓	✓
Soneva Fushi Resort & Spa, Maldives	274	Hotel/Resort	***	✓	✓	✓	✓	✓	✓
Taj Ayurvedic Centre, India	257	Destination/Medical	*		✓	✓	✓	✓	✓
Thermes Marins de Carthage at The Residence, Tunisia	298	Destination/Hotel/Resort	**	✓	✓	✓	✓	✓	✓
Ulpotha Sanctury, Sri Lanka	296	Destination	**					✓	✓
Veyoge Spa at the Kanuhura Resort, Maldives	276	Hotel/Resort	***	✓	✓	✓	✓	✓	✓
Wellness Centre at Ananda – in the Himalayas, India	258	Destination/Medical	***	✓	✓	✓	✓	✓	✓
Wild Fitness, Kenya	264	Hotel/Resort	**		✓	✓	✓	✓	✓

Assawan Spa at Burj al Arab

★ ★ ★

Address: PO Box 74147, Dubai, UAE
Telephone: (+97) 14 301 7777
Booking details: reservations@burj-al-arab.com
Website: www.jumeirahinternational.com

Soaring towards the sky like a giant sail, the Burj Al Arab dominates the Dubai skyline. Situated on its own exclusive manmade island in the Arabian gulf, next to Jumeirah Beach, it's linked to the 'real world' by only a causeway. Non-guests have to pay even to get onto the island. Once you've stepped out of one of the hotel's fleet of white Rolls Royces (or helicopter) into this all-suite hotel (there are no rooms here), you're hit with pure opulence and money, money, money. Not a dirham has been spared, not a corner cut. When you see gold, it's real. The duplex suites on two floors are larger than most people's homes and consist of rooms with panoramic views of the sea, stretching as far as the eye can see, a Hollywood-style sweeping staircase, an office and a 24-hour butler.

The spa occupies the entire eighteenth floor. Although slightly less elaborate than the rest of the hotel, it is decked out with marble and gold. The treatment rooms aren't as intimate as some other spas, but then again subtlety isn't the thing here. Males and females are segregated, but the culture and general ambience encourages a communal vibe, so the atmosphere is lively and fun, with lots of chatter. This is not the place to come if you want to detox – you're more likely to retox.

The ambience: Out-and-out decadent, unbelievably lavish and extraordinarily extravagant, this is the ultimate hotel-cum-theme park for grown-ups. Even Donatella Versace would feel under-dressed here.

Regular guests: Attracts the more flamboyant personality – the Versace customer rather than the pared-down Donna Karan devotee. Although, among the flashy there are also the more sophisticated; Nelson Mandela has also stayed here.

Treatment menu: Traditional Middle Eastern pleasures fuse with the best European-style treatments. The focus is on the aesthetic, with lots of facials, and slimming, firming and detoxifying wraps.

House speciality: La Prairie Caviar Body Treatment. This extravagant therapy has immediate – as well as long-term – firming effects and revitalizes even the dullest of skins.

Cuisine: Here, with six restaurants and bars to chose from, you can eat and drink to your heart's content, so you're not likely to lose any weight (unless you religiously stick to the calorie-controlled spa menu). The culinary highlight is the spectacular

Muntaha restaurant, situated on the top floor of the hotel, with striking views of Dubai – in those surroundings, who cares what the food is like (sophisticated Mediterranean, incidentally). Al Mahara, the award-winning seafood restaurant, is just as ground-breaking, literally. This undersea fantasy is reached by a three-minute simulated submarine journey and is centred around the biggest aquarium (real Arabian sea life) you've ever seen.

Ideal for: An extravagant hen night (bachelorette party) or girly weekend to remember. Having said that, the mirrored ceilings above the bed might encourage you to take a lover instead.

What to pack: A camera (your friends will think you're exaggerating about the place), your gold card and a sense of fun.

Caracalla Spa at Le Meridien Hotel

* * *

Address: Jumeirah Beach, Dubai, UAE
Telephone: (+97) 14 399 5555
Booking details: reservations@leroyalmeridien-dubai.com
Website: www.lemeridien-dubai.com

Le Meridien is one of those hotels that you could drop into any city in the world, leave it as is, and still please a lot of people. Inspired by cultures from all over the globe, its international-luxe vibe makes everyone feel at home – albeit a very royal version of home. Gold fixtures, elaborate ornaments, suites with their own Jacuzzis and a choice of 14 restaurants enable you to live like a king and, thanks to the three floors of hammam and massage rooms devoted to beauty (including Cleopatra-inspired milk baths), be pampered like a queen.

The ambience: Upmarket and classy – from the magnificent flower arrangements in the black-, white- and gold-tiled lobby through to the elegant and serene Roman-inspired spa in the royal tower.

Regular guests: Successful businessmen, affluent families and couples come here for business, pleasure, or both.

Treatment menu: Aimed at a more mature market, the treatments are designed for anti-ageing, firming, toning and energizing.

House speciality: Aromatherapy Top-To-Toe is a multisensory experience that uses Elemis products and incorporates a body massage, foot massage, facial, and scalp and hand massage.

Cuisine: In keeping with its cosmopolitan clientele, Le Meridien operates a staggering range of restaurants and bars, offering Thai, Chinese, French, Italian, Japanese and Spanish food, to name a few.

Ideal for: A business trip with some after-hours pampering, and couples for whom golfing (it has a PGA golf course) and shopping (it is situated by Dubai's infamous shopping district) are priorities.

What to pack: Tod's loafers so that you can shop till you drop.

The Oberoi

★★★

Address: Sahl Hasheesh, Hurghada, Red Sea, Egypt
Telephone: (+20) 65 440 777
Booking details: toshres@oberoi.com.eg
Website: www.oberoihotels.com

The Oberoi Sahl Hasheesh is the first all-suite luxury hotel on the Red Sea coast, and its combination of domes, arches and columns represents the traditional architecture of the region. The suites, a short walk from the beach, have their own living room, bedroom, marble bathroom with sunken bathtub and enclosed courtyard. The Grand and Royal suites have private swimming pools and butler service. The spa, found in the main building, is small, with three single treatment rooms and a twin massage room for couples. There is also a health club with a sauna, steam room and gym.

The ambience: Set on 20 hectares (48 acres), with a private beach and panoramic sea views, the Oberoi offers space and serenity.

Regular guests: A mix of people from all over the world; it has become one of the most popular tourist areas in Egypt.

Treatment menu: Pampering and soothing beauty treatments revolve around the traditional Egyptian philosophy of renewal and celebration of the body and soul. Prepare to be seduced and sedated with blended oils, herbs, spices and perfumes.

House speciality: The Red Sea Aromatic, their most popular spa package, includes a body polish with a blend of apricot kernels and exfoliating gel to cleanse and invigorate the skin, followed by a warm shower, aromatherapy massage and deep-cleansing facial.

Cuisine: You can choose from a fine-dining seafood restaurant, a more informal dining room serving Continental cuisine and a café offering light meals and snacks alfresco.

Ideal for: A spa/beach/snorkelling holiday. Hurghada's crystal-clear waters, reefs and shipwrecks offer escapism to another world.

What to pack: An underwater camera.

Ritz-Carlton, Sharm El Sheikh

**

Address: Om El Seed, PO Box 72, South Sinai, Egypt
Telephone: (+20) 69 661 919
Booking details: reservations.ritzcarlton.com
Website: www.ritzcarlton.com

The Sharm El Sheikh is the first dedicated spa in Egypt and is both luxurious and tranquil. Scuba diving is big business and the hotel overlooks the Amphora reef, a Mecca for divers. The hotel or a local school can arrange lessons, and the more experienced can take a short speedboat ride to a nearby twelfth-century shipwreck. Facilities also include a state-of-the-art gym with personal trainers, power-walking, aerobics, and stretching and toning classes. Children are well catered for, with many imaginative activities.

The spa menu takes great pride in – and is inspired by – ancient Egyptian practices. Traditional spices are used in treatments and include coffee, nutmeg, cardamon, cinnamon and tumeric, which give an authentic Middle Eastern flavour. Also cashing in on the Egyptian theme are a variety of treatments with tongue-in-cheek names such as Rameses Reign, Isis Bliss and Red Sea Ecstasy.

The ambience: It's a Ritz-Carlton, so there's no getting away from the fact that it's a corporate chain. However, the elegant Egyptian architecture and feeling of age-old decadence adds romance.

Regular guests: European families, American couples and divers.

Treatment menu: The spa has maintained the ancient tradition of skincare and rejuvenating bathing with a long list of treatments. A good range of body and scalp massages are also on offer and there's a focus on improving circulation and relieving stress. The Boreh Slush is typical of the treatment style, here – an original herbal blend of nutmeg, cloves and black pepper, is applied all over the body to ease muscle aches and improve circulation. The client is then wrapped in a thermal blanket to increase the effects before being unravelled and slathered in a skin-soothing yogurt and cucumber concoction.

House speciality: The three-hour Cleopatra's Indulgence includes a hand and foot scrub, aromatic oil mask, body glow and wrap, relaxing massage and Cleopatra Aromatic Milk Bath. Guests are also advised to enjoy a private massage at sunrise, which takes place in an Arabian cliff-top tent.

Cuisine: The Lebanese-influenced Fayrouz, complete with tableside belly dancers, serves touk kebabs, Sharma's couscous and other Middle Eastern plates, which, fortunately, are all fairly healthy. Those guests wishing to avoid rich food altogether may prefer the special spa menu that consists of low-calories meals, fresh juices and exotic fruits.

Ideal for: Couples, groups of friends and families who want to find a holiday where there's something to suit everyone. This is also the perfect place to learn how to dive.

What to pack: Scuba gear, the kids and an underwater camera.

Amarvilâs

★ ★ ★

Address: Taj East Gate Road, Taj Nagri Scheme,
Agra 282 001, Uttar Pradesh, India
Telephone: (+91) 562 23 1515
Booking details: reservations@amarvilas.com
Website: www.oberoihotels.com

Being situated no more than four minutes' walk from the Taj Mahal
(you can see it from every room) makes the Amarvilâs (an Oberoi
resort) a pretty special place. There are just over 100 rooms and
suites, most with private terraces, set in elaborate gardens decorated
with stunning fountains, pools, terraced lawns and discreet pavilions.
Like the hotel, the spa has an old-world charm with just enough
modern minimalism to stop it from being 'fusty'.

The ambience: Low-key, sensible, quiet and, being a short walk
from the greatest monument to love ever constructed, truly romantic.

Regular guests: Taj Mahal tourists and more spiritual spa-seekers.

Treatment menu: Aromaveda treatments, unique to Amarvilâs, are
an intoxicating combination of Ayurveda and aromatherapy. If one
doesn't get you into a heady state of relaxation, the other one will.

House speciality: The Rice Indulgence is an incredible treatment
that will leave skin soft and glowing. The skin is first exfoliated
with a blend of rice flour and buttermilk, and then the client is
cocooned in a honey body wrap that feels silky rather than sticky.
The final stage involves being slathered in aromatic body cream.

Cuisine: Continental and Asian dishes are on offer. If you want to
learn a thing or two about Indian cookery, book into the Esphahan,
where diners can watch how it's done in the display kitchen.

Ideal for: Foodies who want to have their excesses pummelled
away with massage rather than exercise.

What to pack: A notebook to write down Indian cookery tips and
a guidebook to explore the many architectural splendours of the
nearby sixteenth-century Agra city, Itmad-ud-Daulah.

Angsana Oasis Spa & Resort

*

Address: North West Country, Doddaballapur Main Road,
Rajankunte, Bangalore 560064, India
Telephone: (+91) 80 846 8893
Booking details: bangalore@angsana.com
Website: www.angsana.com

The Angsana is an oasis of calm in one of India's most enchanting regions, situated conveniently near Bangalore city. Luxurious air-conditioned rooms and suites are set amid tropical gardens and open onto spacious patios where you can bask in the sun. For the reflective, there's a well-stocked library and meditation and yoga room; the more active can make use of the pools, gym, aerobics centre, and squash and tennis courts. Sprawling landscaped gardens and magnificent pools add to the rustic charm of this serene sanctuary and encourage you to sit back and relax.

The ambience: A combination of guests stay here for pleasure and business, but either way, everyone is relaxed and smiling.

Regular guests: Business travellers chilling out before and after meetings, and couples and families wanting to holiday in India.

Treatment menu: The usual Angsana menu, which includes every sort of treatment, scrub and massage for the body and mind.

House speciality: Ayurveda massage – it would be rude not to take advantage of this ancient healing and nurturing wisdom.

Cuisine: A selection of 'low in fat, high in taste' cuisine, naturally healthy barbecues and Indian, Chinese and Continental dishes.

Ideal for: Those wanting to indulge in pampering and wellbeing, plus the chance to explore Bangalore, known as India's Silicon Valley and Garden City, and now one of the most attractive modern cities in India.

What to pack: A factual book on Bangalore for the days you want to get out and about, and a fictional one for the days when you don't.

The Cecil

***

Address: Chaura Maidan, Shimla 171 001, India
Telephone: (+91) 177 20 4848
Booking details: reservations@thececil.com
+800 1234 0101
Website: www.oberoihotels.com

Rising 2,200 metres (over 7,000 feet) above sea level in the foothills of the Himalayas, the Cecil (an Oberoi resort) was once the venue for glamorous balls and parties in the days when Shimla was the summer capital of the British Raj. Today the hotel has 71 rooms and eight suites, each one boasting a spectacular view over the Himalayan forests and hills. The spa is small and intimate, with two massage rooms, two therapy rooms, and individual sauna and steam baths. It's a tranquil haven, good for relieving tired legs that ache from too much trekking. An indoor stretch pool, whirlpool and fully equipped modern gym are also available.

The ambience: Here, you can feel the old-style colonial decadence and sophistication. The staff make you feel special and are attentive without being overintrusive.

Regular guests: Trekkers wanting luxury after a day out.

Treatment menu: The spa specializes in Ayurvedic and Western therapies, ranging from herbal body rubs to stress-relieving massage.

House speciality: The Oberoi Massage is a full-body massage that uses palms and fingertips to apply pressure in a series of flowing movements. It stimulates blood circulation and improves muscle tone.

Cuisine: The restaurant offers a selection of European, Indian, Continental and Thai gastronomy. You can get light snacks and drinks in the Atrium bar-lounge, which, like the restaurant, offers views of the picturesque Himalayas.

Ideal for: A base from which to discover the unique beauty of the Himalayan ranges, cedar forests and ancient monasteries.

What to pack: A book on the local history and walking shoes.

Kumarakom Lake Resort

**

Address: Kumarakom North PO, Pillichira, Kottayam 686 566, Kerala 686 566, India
Telephone: (+91) 481 524 900
Booking details: klresort@vnsl.com
Website: www.klresort.com

Located at the southernmost tip of India, Kerala has mountains on one side and blue sea on the other, along with silvery beaches, fertile plains and tropical forests. The surroundings are truly beautiful and peaceful, but it is the health-giving advantages of this resort that make it so attractive. At Ayurmana, the ayurveda centre, the emphasis is on holistic medicine, and treatments are structured to provide you with a nurtured soul – as well as a more svelte body. The resort offers yoga and meditation, in addition to health club facilities, to complement the treatments. Think seriously before coming here; although you will feel infinitely better after your stay, it will take a certain amount of commitment to benefit completely.

The ambience: A beautiful and poetic backwater paradise, bird sanctuary and holistic wellbeing haven.

Regular guests: Health-seekers and health-conscious tourists. Poets, writers, artists and creative and soulful travellers.

Treatment menu: An A-Z of Ayurvedic treatments. The medical aspects of Ayurveda are strongly adhered to and specialized treatments for skin, muscular and bone problems are available.

House speciality: The revolutionary weight-reduction programme blends yoga, diet, customized massages and herbal medicine.

Cuisine: The main restaurant, Ettukettu, focuses on local ethnic dishes, and vegetarians are also catered for. Although the food is extremely health-orientated, no-one will frown if you want a cold beer.

Ideal for: Hardcore wellbeing-seekers.

What to pack: Willpower and an objective – this is the place to jump-start a new purification and self-improvement lifestyle.

Rajvilâs

* * *

Address: Goner Road, Jaipur, Rajasthan 303 012, India
Telephone: (+91) 141 68 0101
Booking details: reservations@rajvilas.com
Website: www.oberoihotels.com

Rajvilâs is far removed from the India most people imagine. It's immaculate and calm; the only link you could make between Delhi and belly here would come in the form of a gently detoxifying Ayurvedic massage that included the stomach. The hotel itself is said to be the 'jewel in the crown' of the Oberoi resort group. Rich with Indian craftsmanship, it is lavish but tastefully elegant. In the bedrooms there are four-poster beds and sunken marble baths – which overlook private walled gardens – and saunas, plunge pools, and steam and treatment rooms in the two-wing spa complex. Even with all the material splendour, there is a very holistic feel. Early-morning yoga in a pavilion in the gardens is literally the most breathtaking way to start your day in this majestic place.

The ambience: So opulent, lavish, rich and luxurious that you feel like you're in a palace of a maharajah. And all this with intimacy, too.

Regular guests: The rich, the famous, and lottery winners ...

Treatment menu: The treatments have been designed to nourish more than just your skin. None are remotely clinical, as the emphasis is on pure pampering and relaxation.

House speciality: The 60-minute Ayurvedic Marma-Point Facial evolved from traditional Indian healing practices and aims to balance your karma as well as your complexion.

Cuisine: Real Indian food with an extra touch of class. A low-calorie menu is available for those who don't want to overindulge.

Ideal for: People who want no-holds-barred luxury, pampering and decadence, and who want to absorb some of the local culture.

What to pack: Chic comfy clothes for day and full-on glamour for night. You'll need a large suitcase for your purchases from the bazaar.

Taj Ayurvedic Centre

*

Address: Taj Residency Hotel, P.T. Usha Road,
Calicut 673 032, India
Telephone: (+91) 495 765 354
Booking details: residency.calicut@tajhotels.com
Website: www.tajhotels.com

Run by the renowned Arya Vaidya Pharmacy, a leading hospital in India, the Taj is a very focused Ayurvedic facility of the highest standards. Visiting this spa is not going to have any positive effect unless you are prepared to sacrifice some of your worst habits. There are also great products to take home with you and enough Ayurvedic teachings to last you for the rest of your recently extended life.

The ambience: A beautifully designed, holistic, medical centre that is serious about wellbeing.

Regular guests: The unwell, the earnest and those who are fully committed to health and self-improvement.

Treatment menu: Forget the manicure and makeover: this is a medical spa in the truest sense. The Ayurvedic techniques and treatments here are widely respected and are focused on your exact goals or ailments. Back pain, stress, obesity, insomnia, migraines, high blood pressure, diabetes and even paralysis are treated with comprehensive individual programmes that involve diet, yoga, meditation, massage and lifestyle assessment.

House speciality: Pizhichil helps to alleviate skeletal and muscular problems, including arthritis. Oil is poured in a continually flowing, single stream over the head and body by four therapists.

Cuisine: There is a restaurant, but don't expect a menu or wine. The chefs and doctors create every meal together, adhering to the recommendations and restrictions imposed by Ayurveda.

Ideal for: People recuperating from an operation or needing to take serious health measures to prevent illness, or worse.

What to pack: A personal keepsake, as you may feel a little homesick.

Wellness Centre at Ananda – in the Himalayas

* * *

Address: Ananda – in the Himalayas, The Palace Estate, Narendra Nagar, Tehri Garhwal, Uttar Pradesh 249175
The Himalayas, India
Telephone: (+91) 137 827 500
Booking details: reservations@anandaspa.com
Website: www.anandaspa.com

All those who have made the journey to Ananda in the Himalayas swear it's the most spiritual, calming, healing place they've ever visited. Maybe it's got something to do with the region being the birthplace of yoga and home of Ayurveda. Nestled in the foothills of the Himalayas, in the palace of the Maharajah of Tehri Garhwal in Uttar Pradesh, the hotel itself is beautiful without being overly lavish. The bedrooms and bathrooms are simple and tasteful, and if you go in winter, don't be surprised to find a hot-water bottle in your bed when you clamber in – they've thought of everything here. Yoga, meditation and breathing-technique classes, which take place in the palace's Music Pavilion in the gardens, are not just offered, they're positively encouraged. Make sure you catch an early morning class so that you can enjoy the sun rising over the valley.

The impressive Wellness Centre encompasses 13 treatment rooms, a relaxation area, cutting-edge gym and pebbled pools that massage your feet as you walk through them. Two doctors run the facility: one trained in orthodox medicine and one Ayurvedic physician. You can take full advantage of the Ayurvedic traditions to alleviate conditions such as recurring migraines, asthma, cystitis, arthritis, digestive problems – the list of ailments Ayurveda treats is endless. As for the holistic beauty therapists, they have a reputation for being some of the best in the world and perform the most beneficial treatments money can buy.

The ambience: Tranquil, healing and very, very spiritual.

Regular guests: Honeymooners and people wanting to escape. You're in the middle of nowhere, and you won't find a business conference full of working city-types here.

Treatment menu: It's endless. Pretty much all treatments on offer are based around the ancient Indian philosophy and science of Ayurveda – now the fastest growing complementary health system in the world, which attracts people from all walks of life. In addition, the facility offers aromatherapy, hydrotherapy, reflexology and other more familiar beauty treatments.

House speciality: Shirodhara is a treatment that induces an amazing sense of relaxation by pouring oil onto the 'third eye' (located somewhere on our foreheads, between the other two). It feels far better than it sounds and makes stress, headaches and insomnia a thing of the past.

Cuisine: The chef works strictly in accordance with common-sensical Ayurvedic principles, preparing fresh, delicious food suitable for each individual's *dosha* (your own holistic blueprint that needs to be kept in balance to prevent illness). Rest assured that you can have whatever you want, however you want it and whenever you want it (as long as it's right for your dosha, that is).

Ideal for: Anyone who's prepared to relax and take advantage of the amazing expertise that's on offer here. Particularly perfect for those wanting to embrace and take home a more balanced, fighting-fit Ayurvedic approach that will remain long after the memories of Ananda have started to fade.

What to pack: A good moisturizer, as the Himalayas are exceptionally dry, and a pair of lightweight walking shoes. The treks are breathtaking and will put a spring in your soul as well as your step.

Carmel Forest Spa Resort

✶ ✶

Address: Royal Garden Hotel, PO Box 9000,
Haifa 31900, Israel
Telephone: (+972) 4 830 7888
Booking details: carmelf@isrotel.co.il
Website: www.isrotel.co.uk

This spa, dedicated to relaxation and pampering, is Israel's largest and most luxurious. Enclosed by a nature reserve, it has a bubble-like atmosphere of total peace and quiet. The aim here is to recharge your batteries to help you cope with the pressures and pace of modern life on the 'outside'. There are dozens of health and beauty treatments, and a wide range of activities. Workshops, gourmet (kosher) cuisine and many pampering treats are all designed to renew body and soul in a truly life-enhancing experience.

The ambience: Nestled in a forest among high cliffs and natural flower groves, Carmel Forest nurtures the spirit as well as the body.

Regular guests: An eclectic mix of Tel Aviv's business executives reducing their stress and Jewish mothers reducing their bodies.

Treatment menu: The many treatments range from de-stressing massages, such as Ayurvedic, Swedish, Thai, lymphatic and reiki, to pampering mud wraps, facials and aromatherapy. Strict nutritional programmes and meditative therapy are also offered.

House speciality: The Butterfly Woodeep is a gentle seaweed peel, rich in vitamins and minerals, which leaves skin smooth and refreshed. It is followed by a relaxing massage using sesame oil.

Cuisine: All meals are included in the room rate, but don't expect flamboyant and wildly imaginative food. A meat menu is served at lunch and dinner, and low-calorie alternatives can be arranged.

Ideal for: A motivating start to a new health and fitness routine. Lounging around the pool drinking wine is frowned upon.

What to pack: Good footwear. Flip-flops for the spa and pool, trainers (sneakers) for the gym and comfortable outdoor shoes for exploring.

Mineralia Spa at the Hyatt Regency Dead Sea Resort

∗∗

Address: Hyatt Regency Dead Sea Resort, Ein Bokek,
Dead Sea 89 680, Israel
Telephone: (+972) 8 659 1234
Booking details: concierge@hyatt.com
Website: www.deadsea.hyatt.co.il

This resort is located on the western shore of the Dead Sea, framed
by the Judean Mountains. The deluxe rooms have balconies or
terraces facing the sea. There's a private beach a few minutes' walk
from the hotel, two large freshwater swimming pools, a children's
pool and spacious sundecks. The neo-classic Roman-style spa
is set among palm trees and thriving gardens, and has domed
ceilings and stone columns. There are around 23 treatment rooms,
saltwater and sulphur pools, a Jacuzzi, sauna and steam room. It
is deeply calming, yet the fresh air gives you a natural high.

The ambience: Peaceful. Although based in the Hyatt Regency
in bustling Ein Bokek, this spa sits away from it all on a hill.

Regular guests: People from all over the globe wanting to get
the health, beauty and wellbeing benefits from the Dead Sea.

Treatment menu: Highly trained specialists working with ancient
and scientific techniques offer health and beauty treatments. The
array of mud wraps not only pamper but alleviate complaints like
muscle pains and arthritis. The private medical clinic specializes
in post-surgery recovery and alternative medicine programmes.

House speciality: The Mineralia Natural-Mud Body treatment; you
are thoroughly exfoliated and then smothered in Dead Sea mud.

Cuisine: Five restaurants offer a wealth of international flavours.

Ideal for: Recuperating after an operation, and for those wanting
to try out the curative, beautifying benefits of the Dead Sea.

What to pack: A swimming hat to protect your hair.

Sanctuary Zara Spa at the Mövenpick Resort

✱✱

Address: Mövenpick Resort & Spa Dead Sea, Dead Sea Road, PO Box 815538, Sweimeh, Amman 11180, Jordan
Telephone: (+962) 5 356 1111
Booking details: (+962) 5 356 1110 or sanctuary-spa@zara.com.jo
Website: www.movenpick-deadsea.com

The five-star Mövenpick Resort and Sanctuary Zara Spa is located on the northeast shore of the historic Dead Sea. The hotel has been built like an old fortress in traditional Islamic style, with stone and plaster creating a close-to-nature 'village' feel. Even the guest rooms, equipped with modern luxuries, have traditional touches. The spa has been modelled on Castle Amra, a Jordan desert castle that was used as a getaway for the Ummayad kings in AD 700, the main purpose of which was to serve as a bathhouse and relaxation venue – in other words, a spa. Domed ceilings and mosaics, arabesque arches, luxurious surroundings and suites, not to mention the heavenly treatments, are fit for a modern-day king.

You needn't even set foot in the spa to receive the benefits from the Dead Sea salts and minerals. You can wallow in the large, outdoor hydropool and use the neck-massage jets, airseats, airbeds, whirlpools and geysers, or try the indoor flotation pool or whirlpool. Alternatively, you can splash around in the invigorating Kniepp foot-massage pool. All these water treatments have a Dead Sea salt concentration of between 3 and 23 per cent.

Separate male and female thermariums (Turkish hammams) offer hot dry rooms, warm steam rooms and refreshing tropical rain showers infused with mint. The Therapy Suite has around 16 rooms and four mud rooms, all geared up for around 70 treatments overall. Alternatively, the Royal Suite, a private wing of the spa, has four treatment rooms, two of which are designed for two people, and its own private reception area, showers and steam room.

The ambience: Incredibly relaxed and easy-going. You can lounge around in a robe or beachwear in the day, and then dress up for the fine-dining restaurant in the evening.

Regular guests: Spa-goers wanting to top up their tan as well as recharge their batteries.

Treatment menu: The number of health and beauty therapies on offer is huge. This is the largest luxury non-medical spa in Jordan and the myriad treatments on offer range from restorative Dead Sea-based body wraps and mud facials to high-tech, anti-ageing facials and Swedish massage.

House speciality: The resort has a superb range of one- to seven-day packages, but the real gems have to be their Dead Sea treatments, which use the mineral- and salt-rich mud that is famous for its therapeutic properties.

Cuisine: Five restaurants offer everything from fine-dining and Asian specialities to pizza, pasta and light snacks.

Ideal for: Particularly good for those who want to take advantage of the incredibly healing, soothing benefits of the Dead Sea.

What to pack: Beach gear and glamorous clothes for the evenings.

Wild Fitness

✦✦

Address: Baraka House, Watamu Beach, South East Kenya
Telephone: (+44) 207 368 1632
Booking details: info@wildfitness.com
Website: www.wildfitness.com

For anyone wanting to get fit and healthy, but as far away from a health club as possible, Wild Fitness is the perfect solution. Situated on long stretches of white sand beaches, this spa offers the ideal motivational and mental training ground for even the most inexperienced fitness hopeful. The accommodation is a grand house facing onto the Indian Ocean, which provides a sunny backdrop for early morning training sessions – it certainly beats watching MTV in the gym. If Wild Fitness's team of professionals can't get you in shape, nobody can. There are also activities such as canoeing, scuba diving, windsurfing and deep-sea fishing for when you need a rest.

The ambience: Homey and exclusive, catering for small groups who share the same private house. Not the archetypal beauty spa, this is a health and fitness retreat that buzzes with get-up-and-go.

Regular guests: Anyone wanting to get strong and healthy, from professional athletes to amateur fitness enthusiasts.

Treatment menu: Because fitness is the key here, the only 'beauty' treatments are in the form of massage, including sport, full-body, aromatherapy and cold stone. Don't expect any superficial half-hour jobs; your whole body gets the full works. Everything else is based around fitness assessments (postural, flexibility, endurance, etc.), sessions in the natural surroundings, nutritional advice and yoga.

House speciality: The Sports Massage, which is truly excellent.

Cuisine: Fresh, nutritious food sourced locally includes seafood, tropical fruit and vegetables.

Ideal for: Anyone wanting to get into peak shape or just get into shape. This is the place to lose weight and gain confidence.

What to pack: A good pair of cross-trainers (sneakers).

Angsana Resort & Spa

✴✴

Address: Ihuru, North Malé Atoll, Republic of Malidves
Telephone: (+960) 443 502
Booking details: maldives@angsana.com
Website: www.angsana.com

This Angsana resort is set on Ihura, an exclusive eco-island in the Maldives. Dazzling white sand and the bluest waters imaginable, teeming with astonishing corals and multicoloured fish, make this the perfect spa getaway. It's so small you can walk around the entire island in ten minutes. There are around 50 thatched beach-front villas, all with minimalist interiors painted in vivid lime-green, tangerine, burgundy and white. The Jacuzzi villas have waterfall-like, outdoor showers and open-air bathtubs sheltered with overhanging flowers. Every day petals are strewn and floating candles are lit in your villa. Most evenings involve eating and sipping cocktails in the bar before walking barefoot up the beach.

The ambience: Upmarket and hip with a young, funky vibe.

Regular guests: A young, stylish, multicultural crowd. Lots of couples, plus the odd fashion crew on a magazine shoot.

Treatment menu: The treatments range from soothing massages to beauty remedies and are dedicated to pampering. Emphasis is on aromatherapy combined with touch. Glow, Peace, Spirit and Bliss are some of the treatment names.

House speciality: The Natural Thai Herbal Wrap containing Thai white mud known as 'magic mud' cleanses and balances the skin.

Cuisine: The dishes are imaginative, fresh and healthy. Grilled fish, salads and tropical fruits are served daily, buffet-style. Romantic dining is their speciality; you choose the spot – your villa, a dune or a glass-bottom boat – and they do the rest.

Ideal for: Young honeymooners and groups of couples wanting to spend quality time with their loved ones and close friends.

What to pack: Slinky dresses and sandals for the evening.

Banyan Tree Maldives

✶✶✶

Address: Vabbinfaru Island, North Malé Atoll,
Republic of Maldives
Telephone: (+960) 443 147
Booking details: maldives@banyantree.com
Website: www.banyantree.com

Cast away on a secluded coral atoll in the heart of the Maldives archipelago, this branch of the Banyan Tree resorts exudes a magical, romantic and tranquil mood. You may as well take off your watch when you arrive, as time moves imperceptibly and your stomach and the position of the sun tends to determine your plan of action, or not, as the case may be.

Luxurious villas have spectacular ocean vistas, private terraces, open-air Jacuzzis and direct access to the white sandy beach, allowing you to wander down for morning or moonlit dips. The architecture of the intimate spa pavilions draws inspiration from local buildings and blends seamlessly with the beauty of the natural environment. You can enjoy a massage on the beach or right next to the azure sea on open-air *salas* (terraces). The attention to detail and to renewing your state of wellbeing is incredible. With this in mind they have devised what's called Time-Honoured Traditions, in which 30 minutes are automatically set aside within your spa session for you to unwind and enjoy a cooling mint footbath, refreshing herbal drink and exhilarating shower.

The ambience: Romantic and peaceful, with a charged atmosphere at night. Although a very exclusive resort, the only airs and graces come from nature.

Regular guests: Well-off, soft-heeled, immaculately pedicured travellers from all over the world. A favourite place for celebrities, although the resort won't reveal which ones. You're unlikely to see them anyway; like most of the other guests, they come here to keep a low, if not completely horizontal, profile.

Treatment menu: The traditional, all-natural, Asian treatments are oozing with local ingredients. The spa offers a diversity of experiences, from romantic couples' treatments to comprehensive one-day packages. Massage therapies embrace the most effective European and Asian techniques, including Swedish, Hawaiian lomi lomi, Indonesian and Thai strokes. Individually tailored spa programmes can also be devised.

House speciality: The Harmony Banyan is a massage conducted by two therapists, who work together to bring about a harmonious sense of wellbeing. The therapists perform a synchronized massage, and are chosen to complement one another perfectly in both physique and temperament. Maintaining balanced pressure, the strokes of their hands work each side of the body in unison. To ensure total equilibrium – from top to bottom – the head and the feet are then massaged at the same time, inducing a state of deep relaxation. The massage takes three hours and it might be wise to arrange an escort home. Every sense, including that of direction, will be sedated.

Cuisine: No calorie-controlled spa food, as such, is available, but you can binge on fresh, healthy food and swim off any excess calories in the sea. Delicious, eclectic Maldivian and international dishes are prepared and served in the resort's three informal dining rooms. Romantic couples can enjoy candle-lit barbecue dinners in the intimacy of their own villas, complete with private chef and waiter, or escape by speedboat to an isolated stretch of beach to sip champagne and dine on a sandbank with only the moon and torches lighting your feast.

Ideal for: Lovers. Everything is sprinkled with romance.

What to pack: A mini CD player so you can listen to your favourite music in your room or while watching the sun set.

Hilton Maldives Resort & Spa

✴✴✴

Address: Hilton Maldives Resort & Spa Rangali Island,
South Ari Atoll, PO Box 2034, Republic of Maldives
Telephone: (+960) 450 629
Booking details: reserved@maldiveshilton.com.mv
Website: www.maldives.hilton.com

This tropical paradise spans two islands, Ranglifinolhu and Rangali, connected by a bridge over the turquoise waters. There are two other uninhabited islands nearby and a deep, blue lagoon surrounded by a dramatic coral reef, creating a 'deserted island' kind of vibe. All of the residences are built and decorated with local, rustic materials so that they harmonize with the tropical environment, but at the same time they are equipped with high-tech home comforts and luxury extras. Both the 50 beach villas and the 50 deluxe beach villas are air-conditioned and surrounded by a pristine-white sandy beach. The eight deluxe water villas are incredibly indulgent, with a plasma TV and DVD player, as well as a freestanding ocean-view bathtub for two and a double sundeck complete with Jacuzzi and private pool. In addition, there are another 40 water villas. The two secluded sunset villas have a huge circular bed that rotates 180 degrees to follow the sunset. Sailing, scuba diving, fishing and other countless activities will keep you occupied when you tire of the beach.

The spa, managed by the Chiva-Som International Health Resorts group, is on Rangali Island and is built on stilts over the lagoon with four glass-floored treatment rooms, allowing you to watch the marine life below while being pampered. Although air-conditioned, the rooms have sliding windows that can be opened to let the sounds of the lagoon drift in. One room has a Japanese-style hot tub that brews up aromatic local herbs and spices to rejuvenate and relax, and another has an outdoor treatment room, which opens onto a deck so you can watch the long sunsets while you soak. This is where James Bond, complete with his latest Bond girl, would come after a particularly stressful assignment.

The ambience: Pure luxury meets pure paradise. The resort is relaxed but extremely stylish.

Regular guests: Honeymooners and couples getting married on the luxury yacht, *Goma*. Other customers include city traders wanting to swap dealing bonds for living like Bond, James Bond.

Treatment menu: Lots of facial and body treats of a relaxing, revitalizing nature – and more massages than anything else.

House speciality: Traditional Thai Herbal – a combination of Thai massage and aromatic heated herbal packs to help detoxify and alleviate muscular aches and pains.

Cuisine: Extensive. A handful of restaurants offer Mediterranean, Oriental and tandoori dishes, oak-fired pizzas, pasta and incredible local seafood. The locations are as stunning as the food. One restaurant is built 46 metres (50 feet) out in the ocean over a coral reef and another is on the edge of the azure lagoon. This is not a place for serious detoxers, as it has one of the Maldives' most comprehensively stocked wine cellars and the only in-house sommelier in the Indian Ocean.

Ideal for: A wedding, honeymoon or self-indulgent holiday.

What to pack: Your sexiest Ursula Andress-style bikini.

Nautilus Spa at the Coco Palm Resort & Spa

* * *

Address: Dunikolhu Island, Baa Atoll, Republic of Maldives
Telephone: +960 23 0011
Booking details: cocopalm@sunland.com.mv
Website: www.cocopalm-maldives.com

Located 30 minutes by seaplane from Malé, this tropical private island of pure white sand and swaying coconut palms, fringed by a sparkling turquoise lagoon, is the kind of deserted island you dream of being stranded on. It has all the luxury and privacy you would expect from a five-star resort, without a hint of commercialism. Protecting the natural beauty of the island and environment is paramount to all who live and work here. The diverse accommodation ranges from cute beach bungalows to exquisite ocean villas. Dotted amid coconut palms, or on stilts over the lagoon, they are luxurious without being over the top. White walls, dark, polished wood floors and four-poster beds draped in muslin set the scene. Some suites in the garden and over the lagoon have splash pools or sunken spa baths.

The stunning glass-roofed Nautilus Spa is distinctly Balinese, both in overall style and in its approach to beauty, and is ideal for men and women. Built in the shape of a nautilus shell, the spa stands at the end of a jetty on stilts over the lagoon, surrounded by palm trees gently swaying in the ocean breeze. All the treatment rooms offer sensational views of the ocean.

The ambience: A peaceful and serene haven in the middle of the Indian Ocean, enveloped in incredibly blue water.

Regular guests: Honeymooners and married couples whose last visit here was on their honeymoon. Lots of repeat guests – apparently, once is never enough.

Treatment menu: The menu features traditional Asian therapies and beauty rituals combined with classic European spa techniques. Various massage therapies, body treatments and facials are available. Deluxe spa packages have names like Rhapsody,

Baa Atoll, Maldives

Harmony and Ultimate Indulgence. The all-natural treatments make use of the local exotic spices, oils and flowers, and will leave you smelling absolutely heavenly.

House speciality: Just under two hours of unforgettable pampering, the Ultimate Indulgence consists of an aromatherapy footbath, lavender body wash, a choice of body scrub, Balinese massage, aromatherapy facial and reflexology.

Cuisine: The food ranges from international influences to more interesting fusions of flavours from the Maldives, Sri Lanka, India and Asia. Eating and drinking can take place almost anywhere, and outdoors is definitely the order of the day. Choose from in-villa dining, a seafood grill situated under a Banyan tree, and bars that you can wade into in your swimsuit; the spa isn't the only place where you'll be spoilt rotten.

Ideal for: Anyone after good spa facilities, gorgeous food and peace and quiet in a low-key, luxurious environment. This is also the perfect place to learn to scuba dive.

What to pack: A selection of brightly coloured sarongs.

The Island Spa

* * *

Address: Four Seasons Resort Maldives at Kuda Huraa,
North Malé Atoll, Republic of Maldives
Telephone: (+960) 444 888
Booking details: (+800) 6488 6488
Website: www.fourseasons.com

If a spa is about getting away from it all, then this is a spa and a half. It's the first spa in the world to be set on an island of its own – the Hura Fundhu – and the concept delivers an amazing experience. To get there, you are rowed across the turquoise waters in a *dhoni* – a traditional wooden boat – which is strewn with silk cushions. The moment you step into the boat you are on a journey to deep comfort and peace. A few minutes later you are greeted by a white-robed therapist who will accompany you to 'destination relaxation'.

Open-air treatment pavilions allow the gentle breezes from the ocean to waft through. There are also spa rooms that sit on stilts in the water, with glass windows in the floor that allow you to watch shoals of tiny fish swimming by while being massaged. Milk-white sandy beaches, crystal-clear sea, grass-thatched villas on the beach, water bungalows next to the lagoon, the Infinity Pool and attentive staff on call might all be of interest to you, too.

The ambience: Low-key luxury. A favourite with travel writers, thanks to its attention to detail and dedication to the feel-good factor.

Regular guests: Hollywood A-list, pop stars and ocean addicts (even the treatment rooms extend out over the water).

Treatment menu: A cross-section of treatments from India, Thailand and Indonesia are available, plus fabulous indigenous offerings using local herbs and spices. There's also a strong focus on the healing elements of the sea in many of the treatments. Prepare to have your mind and body restored to full health.

House speciality: Shirodhara is a mind-melting two-hour Ayurvedic treatment involving warm herbal oil drizzled onto the forehead and then massaged into the entire body. Also not to be missed is the Maldivian Monsoon Ritual, a native treatment for one or two people. With this one, you are scrubbed with ground sandalwood and rinsed in rosewater (you don't even need to stand up – seven showerheads are positioned above the bed and gently cascade down like a real monsoon rainstorm). Next, you are massaged with warm herbal oil, ever so gently warmed in a steam bath and then smoothed over with frankincense-infused body oil. Couples may need to give each other the kiss of life afterwards.

Cuisine: Three restaurants serve everything from fine international cuisine, gourmet Indian and Maldivian dishes (with lots of freshly caught, grilled fish) to lighter snacks and meals. Low-fat and low-calorie dishes are also in abundance.

Ideal for: Honeymooners (because it's the best wedding present a girl could have), potential proposers (no-one would say 'no' here) and divers (it offers some of the best scuba diving in the world).

What to pack: The ring, sunscreen, a snorkel, and something chic but simple to wear in the evenings.

Soneva Fushi Resort & Spa

★★★

Address: Kunfunadhoo Island, Baa Atoll,
Republic of Maldives
Telephone: (+960) 230 0304/0305
Booking details: sonresa@sonevafushi.com.mv
Website: www.six-senses.com/soneva-fushi

Hailed as a Robinson Crusoe-style hideaway on the uninhabited, tropical-paradise island of Kunfunadhoo, Soneva Fushi Resort & Spa has to be the most luxurious way of getting back in touch with nature there is. A real eco-luxury resort (as they are now called), the aim is to enjoy the natural world in its unadulterated form. You get around by bicycle, and getting lost down a sandy track in the middle of the jungle on the way to the spa adds to the sense of adventure.

No imposing hotel spoils the view here. Separate, private villas and rooms are hidden away in dense, lush vegetation leading out onto their own stretch of beach. The rooms are gorgeous in a rustic sort of way, with stripped wood and stone floors, beds draped with mosquito nets, sand gardens and open-air bathrooms (which make a trip to the bathroom in the middle of the night somewhat interesting). However, you're not left totally to your own devices; there are a few modern conveniences to ease your stay, such as air-conditioning, a mini-bar, a CD player, TV and video on request.

The spa experience is unique, too, with open-air treatment rooms on the beach. Here, you can check out the sea while the therapist checks out all those knots of tension. Alternatively, choose your own location and the therapist will put up a portable couch and do the treatment there.

The ambience: Tranquil, lazy and relaxed; the staff make you feel very at ease. Because the island is the resort, you feel secluded rather than isolated.

Regular guests: A very cosmopolitan crowd in terms of nationalities and people of all ages.

Treatment menu: The treatments are typical of tropical islands, with lots of massages for you and a partner under the sun or stars, next to the waves, with champagne or without. You can even book a sunset massage lesson where you both can learn basic techniques. Facials, massages, manicures and pedicures, plus many more look-good, feel-great treatments, are on offer. The spa does a great jet-lag package that involves a revitalizing massage.

House speciality: The Adam and Eve is perfect for a twosome. You both get a facial, scalp massage, manicure and pedicure (yes, him too), so you can look good on the beach.

Cuisine: Two restaurants offer delicious food, including plenty of local dishes and daily-caught fish. They do phenomenal barbecues and can even organize one just for you. All you have to do is point to the spot and they'll build the fire and cook the food. Your wish is their command here; you can eat just about whatever you want, wherever you want it – including on a neighbouring deserted island. For this dining experience, you are dropped off by boat with a picnic, candles and your only contact with the outside world: a walkie-talkie, which you use to let them know when you want to be picked up again.

Ideal for: Romance, so bring your partner, but also great for a group of friends who want a diving-based holiday.

What to pack: Very little. Gym shoes or simple footwear for biking, beachwear for the day and casual clothes for evenings. The 'no shoes' policy doesn't ban you from wearing shoes, but going barefoot, even for dinner, is wholeheartedly encouraged.

Veyoge Spa at the Kanuhura Resort

* * *

Address: Lhaviyani Atoll, Republic of Maldives
Telephone: (+960) 230 044
Booking details: reservations@kanuhura.com
Website: www.kanuhura.com

The Kanuhura really is a place unto itself. Not only does it have its own time zone, but it is also a self-contained, fully serviced island. Villas and beach suites, with muslin-draped four-poster beds, ensuite bathrooms and open-air but concealed courtyard showers, become home for the duration of your stay. Bathing is a whole new experience here, and the bathrooms almost count as spas themselves with their sunken, stone tubs that look as if they should be filled with petal-strewn water and relaxing bath oils. Considering that all the residences have their own verandahs overlooking the sea, it's a wonder anyone leaves their room. The two water villa suites even have their own personal Jacuzzis in private gardens. If you do want to venture further afield, the resort can book island-hopping excursions and watersports.

The Veyoge Spa, situated in the heart of the island, is a scaled-down version of a top-of-the-range health and beauty club. Complete with a gym, studio, locker rooms, open-air Jacuzzis, plunge pools and steam rooms, plus a shop, juice bar and café, it also offers yoga, aerobics and an extensive list of treatments. The design is funky but classic. Uplifting purple and checks imbue the spa with a motivating get-up-and-go feel, perfect for working out, while the stone carvings and burning incense sticks give it a serene atmosphere that is ideal for relaxation, before, during and post-massage.

If all that doing nothing during the day makes you feel like doing something at night, the Lava Lounge has karaoke on request and the Nashaa Club, located at the secluded end of the island under the stars, encourages partying well into the night.

The ambience: Unbelievably relaxed and chilled out, with a 'nothing's too much bother' vibe from the staff.

Regular guests: Well-off Europeans and lots of young families. Actress Juliette Binoche and singer Mel C from the Spice Girls have also stayed here.

Treatment menu: This nine-treatment-room spa is the largest in the Maldives and offers fabulous beauty treatments and bathing rituals based on holistic therapies from the East and West.

House speciality: They all are. Particularly recommended is the full-body, local-style Maldivian Theyo Demum massage, a 75-minute treatment that incorporates short, firm strokes and work on pressure points. The Coconut and Sandalwood Scrub, a gentle body scrub using real coconut, is another must-have. Can't decide? Book the Maldivian Loabi package, which includes both.

Cuisine: Three restaurants offer everything from grilled seafood and steaks, buffets and modern Mediterranean dishes to pizzas and homemade ice cream. The Veyoge Spa has a healthy-eating café, which will help you save up some calories to spend on dinner.

Ideal for: You and a partner, or you and a girlfriend. Anyone who enjoys pampering by day and partying at night.

What to pack: Bikini, snorkel and dancing shoes.

Dinarobin Hotel Golf & Spa

✦ ✦ ✦

Address: Le Morne Peninsula, Mauritius
Telephone: (+230) 401 4900
Booking details: dinarobin@bchot.com
Website: www.beachcomber-hotels.com

Dinarobin is part of the Mauritian Beachcomber group of hotels, which has eight resorts on the island: the Royal Palm on the north-west coast is their flagship facility, while Paradis on the southwest peninsula (next to Dinarobin) caters more for sports enthusiasts and families. Dinarobin is the most spa- and wellbeing-focused of their luxury cluster; love-struck honeymooners tend to stay at the other five. Some facilities, like golf and restaurants, are shared between Paradis and Dinarobin and, depending on your booking,

you can benefit from both resorts. It might be worth specifying what type of bed you'd like when you book, as twin beds are standard. Spa packages offered at Dinarobin include focused treatments spread over four or five days. A four-day anti-stress package combines massage, hydrotherapy and aromatherapy, while the five-day slimming programme will see you buffed, scrubbed, pummelled and eased into your teeniest bikini. Your entire holiday needn't be at a snail's pace, though. Waterskiing, surfing, sailing, tennis, sea-fishing and, of course, golf are on hand, but remember that these are extras and are often pricey.

The ambience: Elegant and essentially Mauritian. It's very quiet – the waves crashing off the barrier reef are about as wild as it gets.

Regular guests: Wealthy golfers, wealthy couples and those seeking more intimate accommodation.

Treatment menu: A comprehensive and luxurious range of treats and treatments, with an emphasis on the holistic, for every aspect of wellbeing. Balneotherapies, using seaweed, water and mud from the ocean, prepare you for chakra-balancing Ayurvedic massages with semi-precious stones and essential hot oils. These, in turn, complement cleansing hammam steams and detoxifying lymphatic drainage. Clarins facials, classic manicures and eyebrow shaping are available for those who want to look good at all costs.

House speciality: The Ayurvedic Shanti Massage is the best treatment to choose for the overwhelming sense of inner peace and serenity it brings. Imagine being enveloped in warm scented oils, and gentle hands massaging your body, easing away tension and regenerating your skin.

Cuisine: Borsalino is a small Italian restaurant, which tends to cater for guests on half-board. L'Harmonie is the main resort restaurant for breakfast, lunch and buffet dinners and overlooks the pool. La Ravanne is for romantic open-air dining under thatched canopies. Dishes on offer are English-, French- and Creole-influenced, with an emphasis on fish.

Ideal for: City dwellers and parents whose children have finally flown the nest.

What to pack: Playing cards and credit cards.

Givenchy Spa at Le Saint Géran

★ ★ ★

Address: Belle Mare, Mauritius
Telephone: (+230) 401 1688
Booking details: suncro@sunresort.com
Website: www.saintgeran.com

Being situated some 3,000 km (1,800 miles) off the east coast of Africa, just north of the tropic of Capricorn, makes Mauritius the perfect all-year-round destination and most beautiful backdrop for a truly inspiring spa and fitness resort. Nestled on the northeast coast of the island, Le Saint Géran hotel, spa and golf club is surrounded on one side by the turquoise waters of the Indian Ocean and on the other by a sheltered lagoon. The emphasis here is on first-rate service, relaxation, luxury and gastronomy, which, due to the four superb restaurants and world-class chefs, is a given.

A temple dedicated to beauty and wellbeing, the Givenchy Spa overlooks exotic flowers, tropical plants and a tranquil lagoon. Here, you can relax in the sauna and steam rooms or be pampered rotten in the treatment rooms. There is a hairdressing salon, so you can book in for a blow-dry after an afternoon spent burning off last night's dinner in the lap pool. If it'll take more than a few laps in a pool to burn off your intake of calories, head to the state-of-the-art Personal Training Centre set up by fitness expert Matt Roberts, or join the early morning 'wake-up' walk on the beach.

Experts and novices alike can enjoy a round of golf on the 9-hole golf course designed by South African golfer Gary Player. If you are still short of things to do, there's always tennis, watersports, and the casino for when the sun goes down.

The ambience: Considering that it is one of the chicest resorts in Mauritius, you might think it would be more stuffy and 'showy', but, in fact, Le Saint Géran is remarkably friendly and down to earth.

Regular guests: Attracts the rich and beautiful, like Tom Cruise and Elle Macpherson, who come here to sun and spa. But don't let

that put you off – judging by the treatments on offer, maybe it's coming here that makes them look so good. Prince William retreats to the mega-exclusive private villa that's hidden from prying eyes.

Treatment menu: The list includes everything from massage and facials to hydrotherapy and 'slimming' body wraps to prepare you for the beach.

House speciality: The three-stage Exclusive Givenchy combines a top-to-toe body scrub, a bath in regenerating Givenchy oils and a Swisscare Moisturizing Bath, which takes place on a massaging water bed. The results are softer skin and a gentler mood.

Cuisine: Four restaurants cater for all tastes and waists between them. There's a huge variety of salads, vegetarian dishes and buffets, so if you want to eat but not put on weight, you can. Calorie-controlled meals can be organized for serious dieters.

Ideal for: Those who want to fill their time – and their minds – with pleasure; and families – they've got a fantastic Sun Kids Club.

What to pack: Gym kit, swimsuit and something glamorous to slip into come the evening.

Guerlain Imperial Beauty Centre

✳ ✳ ✳

Address: Le Prince Maurice, Choisy Road,
Poste de Flacq, Mauritius
Telephone: (+230) 413 9100
Booking details: resa@princemaurice.com
Website: www.princemaurice.com

If you want turquoise sea and secluded beaches that look even better in real life than in the travel brochures, and would rather opt for a rustic but luxurious cottage than a traditional hotel, this is the place to come. The spa has a very natural feel with thatched-roof treatment rooms that have roll-up bamboo screens for indoor or outdoor treatments. Stunning but simple, the rooms contain little more than a comfy couch with a rich red mattress.

The ambience: Understated yet stylish, this place whispers wealth and attracts rich, unflashy types.

Regular guests: Wealthy Americans and Europeans over 40.

Treatment menu: Guerlain has teamed up with Prince Maurice to create a sensual experience for your body and mind (not to mention olfactory system). Treatments, mostly using Guerlain products, vary from facials through massages to more alternative remedies.

House speciality: The Issima Body Firming Treatment is an effective body-toner, or try the more exotic Four Hands Massage.

Cuisine: Though more concerned with the taste buds than the silhouette, superb French and international dishes fuse with local Mauritian flavours. Le Barachois restaurant is incredibly romantic and offers simpler choices of delicious seafood and grills.

Ideal for: People who want to be quiet and enjoy no-nonsense, natural surroundings. The sense of limitless space will help city dwellers feeling a little hemmed in by urban life.

What to pack: A water atomizer and bright, not brash swimwear.

Hilton Mauritius Resort & Spa

✳ ✳ ✳

Address: Wolmar, Flic-en-Flac, Mauritius
Telephone: (+230) 403 1000
Booking details: +800 444 58667
Website: www.hilton.com

The hotel, built mainly with local wood, marble and thatch, has first-class facilities but a slightly corporate feel, mainly because of the vastness of the place. The spa has delicate personal touches, like a decent choice of music, calming lighting and burning essential oils, which make the transition from massage bed back to beach lounger a trifle taxing. One special feature is the VIP *sala*, a raised pagoda with curtains, which caters for couples' massages. It's worth booking treatments in advance, as this quality spa doesn't offer exclusivity to hotel guests. Activities include swimming in the lagoon-like pool, tennis, waterskiing, windsurfing and diving.

The ambience: This peaceful, yet commercial hotel is beautifully located between lush vegetation and the white sandy beach.

Regular guests: Families, young professional couples and business executives attending hotshot conferences and tropical brainstorms.

Treatment menu: Seven treatment rooms offer many locally and naturally inspired wraps, rubs, scrubs, baths and soaks, and the products used draw their restorative powers from plants, aromatic herbs, essential oils, mineral mud and crushed salts.

House speciality: The Creole Package includes a reiki session, body scrub, ylang ylang wrap and hydrotherapy. Afterwards you'll be hard-pressed to take advantage of anything but the sun loungers.

Cuisine: The choice ranges from authentic Thai and Mediterranean-inspired menus to freshly made snacks, grills and salads.

Ideal for: An expensive, but worth it, family holiday in the sun.

What to pack: The kids, a Frisbee and a board game.

The Oberoi Mauritius

* * *

Address: Baie aux Tortues, Pointe aux Piments, Mauritius
Telephone: (+230) 204 3600
Booking details: reservations@oberoi.intnet.mu
Website: www.oberoihotels.com

The idyllic island of Mauritius, with its clear azure waters and white powdery beaches, is the perfect location for an Oberoi spa. Set in 8 hectares (20 acres) of meandering subtropical gardens, and bordered by coral reefs and the balmy Indian Ocean, the resort claims over 600 metres (2,000 feet) of oceanfront and golden beaches. If walking up and down the beach is your favourite way of 'exercising' and the only type of 'dips' you do involve wallowing in the sea, this could be just the place for you.

Accommodation comes in the form of terraced pavilions and private villas made of Indian slate and thatched roofs. No padding up long corridors in your towelling robe and slippers here – embroidered silk sarongs are the order of the day in this exotic resort. The spa has a very holistic approach and all the treatments aim to find 'peace within'. They include Ayurvedic, shiatsu and reflexology disciplines, among more usual techniques. You can relax in open-air Jacuzzis and rinse off in outdoor showers, or try the steam and sauna rooms. If you are looking for something to share exclusively with your partner, book one of the treatment suites for couples, where you can indulge in massages, body scrubs, facials and general out-and-out pampering together.

The ambience: Tranquil and calm, especially in the numerous beautiful gardens.

Regular guests: Holiday-makers and spa enthusiasts seeking the best of spa, sun, sea and sand.

Treatment menu: You'll leave feeling better from the inside out with the treatments on offer here. Choose from completely natural, fruity delights, like the detoxifying Ylang Ylang Purity treatment, which includes a salt scrub and full body wrap; hands-on healing therapies such as reiki; or more superficial 'surface' treatments like the Youth Bliss facial.

Point aux Piments, Mauritius

House speciality: The Paillasson Pure Indulgence begins with a gentle skin-brushing with coconut husk to stimulate the lymphatic system, followed by an exfoliation using freshly grated coconut to remove dead skin cells. After that, you are massaged with natural coconut extracts and vitamin E. And if all that doesn't leave you feeling heady with pleasure, the Indian head massage with sweet-smelling coconut oil will. The Spa Programmes are great, too. They're carefully selected, reflect the spa's holistic ethos and take the stress out of choosing treatments for yourself.

Cuisine: There are two restaurants, three bars, a tea pavilion and a pool bar that serves light meals. The Restaurant, an open-air fine-dining experience overlooking the ocean, offers a blend of Creole, Indian, Oriental and European cuisines. Sip cocktails, watch the sun set and listen to jazz at The Bar, or visit the Wine and Cigar Lounge for some wine-sampling.

Ideal for: A week of pure self-indulgence with minimal effort.

What to pack: Your camera and sunglasses.

Sanctuary Spa at The Residence

✳ ✳

Address: Costal Road, Belle Mare, Mauritius
Telephone: (+230) 401 8888
Booking details: hotel@theresidence.com
Website: www.theresidence.com

The moment you walk into The Residence it is very apparent that relaxation is the name of the game. From the oversized airy rooms that open onto tropical gardens, your own personal butler who is at your beck and call, and the ceramic diffusers sprinkled with drops of exotic-smelling ylang ylang oil that are placed over your bedside lamp at night to scent your room, this place is in a class of its own.

The sumptuous spa, decorated in calming shades of cream, caramel and beige, is situated in a luxury cabin in the middle of a tropical garden overlooking the lagoon. Gentle sea breezes keep you cool while one of the highly trained therapists carries out your treatment. The spa uses La Prairie products, the famous Swiss beauty skincare range that is well known for its luxurious but effective ingredients, and which specializes in everything from oily to ageing skin. By comparison, the impressive selection of watersports, fishing, glass-bottomed boat trips and horse-riding along the beach make lazing around in the spa seem almost immoral.

The ambience: Inspired by early twentieth-century plantation houses, The Residence and Sanctuary Spa smack of old money and style. The muted colour scheme of white and delicate shades of beige, coupled with natural woods and wrought iron, give the resort a casually sophisticated feel.

Regular guests: 'Epicureans searching for refinement and beauty,' according to the brochure. Put more plainly, well-travelled foodies who want to be pampered every step of the way.

Treatment menu: A good selection of skincare treatments, massages and custom-made packages are inspired by Asian techniques and philosophies. There's also a big focus on

alternative, holistic practices, including yoga, tai chi and meditation, which are positively encouraged and even woven into some of the more standard beauty treatment packages.

House speciality: Among the wonderful programmes that cater for inner and outer beauty, The Source is a particularly good package. It starts with a tai chi class that focuses on reflection and creating inner calm, followed by a short break over a cup of herbal tea, and completed with a luxurious La Prairie caviar body treatment. Self-indulgent? Oh yes ...

Cuisine: Three main restaurants: the Dining Room, the Verandah and the Plantation. Restaurants are sited in the grounds, in front of the ocean and at the poolside, serving everything from Western dishes to local Mauritian specialities using traditional herbs and spices. If you choose carefully you can eat like a king and not put on any weight; if you don't, it'll be worth every calorie.

Ideal for: Families. The Sanctuary Spa will take care of the adults and the Planters Kids Club will look after the children.

What to pack: White linen trousers and light-coloured floaty dresses. You'll want to look as elegant as you are comfortable.

Amanjena

* * *

Address: Route de Ouarzazate, km12, Marrakech, Morocco
Telephone: +212 44 403 353
Booking details: (+800) 2255 26 26 or
reservations@amanresorts.com
Website: www.amanresorts.com

When the Aman resorts group created this amazing spa, the location was their inspiration. Set behind pale-pink walls and surrounded by palm and olive groves in what once was royal land, it's the perfect site for a contemporary yet true-to-style Moroccan retreat. There are gazebos, reflecting pools and baths in each private garden of the 34 suites, and the seven *maisons* all have their own swimming pool and personal butler.

The style of Amanjena is typically Moorish and extremely – yet simply – lavish. With its ancient *bassin* centrepiece (an irrigation pool used to collect water from the Atlas Mountains), the Amanjena transports you back in time. Facilities include two hard-surface tennis courts that are floodlit at night, one 18-hole golf course situated right next door and a second, bigger, Royal Golf Course

less than a kilometre (²⁄₃ mile) away. The spa treatments are very cosseting and the aim is to enhance peace and discover the 'essence of being'. The treatment list is limited compared to some, but what is on offer is of the highest standard. The hammams alone, with separate whirlpools facing courtyard fountains, are a great way to unwind.

The ambience: Amanjena means 'peaceful paradise' and that's exactly what it is – a small luxurious oasis set in North Africa.

Regular guests: Bohemian couples, walkers wanting to get off the beaten track, and style-orientated climbers who also want to enjoy the height of luxury.

Treatment menu: From seaweed wraps to pedicures, all the treatments utilize wonderfully scented natural ingredients. In addition, there's a traditional Moroccan hammam which is free for all, whether you're indulging in a treatment or not. The traditional Moroccan hammam treatment involves the use of black soap, which is applied all over your body, followed by exfoliation using a special glove. The client is then covered with a smooth body mask containing lavender, rosewater and clay, which leaves the skin feeling soft and purified. The spa also offers some great day-spa and multiday packages, which incorporate a little bit of everything.

House speciality: The Maghreb offers a total body-care approach. It begins with a cleansing, natural body scrub of white algae and Dead Sea salt, followed by a bath of fragrant essential oils and Moroccan herbs, and then an hour-long massage that takes you into oblivion.

Cuisine: The Moroccan restaurant specializes in local delights and is only open for dinner. Breakfast, lunch and dinner is served in The Restaurant, which is slightly more informal and also does Western and Asian dishes.

Ideal for: Those wanting to mooch around colourful Marrakech (only 7 km/4¼ miles away), visit souks, mosques and palaces, and then get massaged back at base.

What to pack: A sun hat, sunscreen and suitable clothes; the temperatures soar to 38°C (100°F) in the summer.

Banyan Tree Seychelles

★ ★ ★

Address: Anse Intendance, Mahé,
Republic of Seychelles
Telephone: +248 383 500
Booking details: seychelles@banyantree.com
Website: www.banyantree.com

Nestled in Intendance Bay on Mahé Island, this Banyan Tree
resort lies on one of the most beautiful powder-fine beaches
in the world, with spectacular views of the Indian Ocean. Steep
mountains, hills carpeted with lush tropical vegetation and a
sweeping coastline fringed by swaying palm trees creates
a dreamy destination. The spa, set in lush greenery against the
backdrop of majestic granite mountains, embraces nature and
provides a sanctuary for the mind, body and soul. Here, urban
warriors can lay down their arms. If you should get bored of
being pampered, island-hopping is easily arranged.

In local Seychellois architectural style, its 36 stunning pool villas,
all with private swimming pools and Thai *salas* (terraces), combine
contemporary, colonial and 'plantation' decor. Ethnic, woven
textiles adorn rooms with high, sloping ceilings, airy verandahs
and louvered doors. Choose your villa according to its location.
Beachfront pool villas are accompanied by the sights and sounds
of the ocean. Hillside pool villas are situated higher up on a hill,
surrounded by rainforest, and have panoramic views of the Indian
Ocean. If you've got money to burn, the palatial Presidential villa
occupies its very own private cove by the water's edge, in a
'secret hideaway', and has two swimming pools, sundecks,
bedrooms with dressing rooms, a massage pavilion, an outdoor
Jacuzzi and shower, as well as a separate living-cum-dining
pavilion with pantry and bathroom.

The ambience: Being a Banyan Tree, the resort is relaxed and
shamelessly stylish, but this branch also has the added bonus
of that 'sand on your feet, sea breeze in your hair' beach-holiday
feeling, too.

Regular guests: Regular spa-goers wanting all four 'S's – sun,
sea, sand and spa.

Treatment menu: The extensive range of treatments uses a combination of Eastern and Western techniques and beliefs, from massages through holistic herbal remedies to more traditional beauty therapies.

House speciality: The Royal Banyan is the resort's long, drawn-out signature therapy. Originating from massage traditions used for centuries in the Royal Thai court, the treatment begins with an oil-free acupressure massage to improve blood circulation and alleviate muscle tension. Afterwards, Banyan herbal pouches, filled with lemongrass, cloves and coriander (cilantro), are used as sponges to apply warm sesame oil onto the body. The experience is finished with the Banyan Massage, which uses East-meets-West techniques to help balance the mind, body and soul.

Cuisine: A celebration of exotic cuisines, brimming with mouth-watering flavours and tantalizing fragrances, is the culinary focal point of the resort. Here, you can indulge in the succulent seafood creations, coconut dishes and curries that the Seychelles are famous for. Alternatively, sample some of the speciality dishes that mostly originate from Southeast Asia. Romantic outdoor barbecues on the beach, picnics and in-villa dining are also here for the taking. Calories can be carefully counted or blatantly ignored.

Ideal for: Holiday-makers who want to dip in and out of a spa as well as the sea and, when not massaging suntan lotion onto their own body, want to be massaged by somebody else.

What to pack: Sunscreen, after-sun lotion and a bit of get-up-and-go for exploring the numerous nearby islands.

High Rustenburg Health Hydro

*

Address: PO Box 3074, Matieland 7602,
Western Cape, South Africa
Telephone: +27 21 809 3800
Booking details: reservations@thehydro.co.za
Website: www.thehydro.co.za

The Hydro operates on five principles: dieting to cleanse; treatments to rejuvenate; exercise; relaxation; and lifestyle motivation. Their wellbeing ethos lies in education, via daily lectures on lifestyle, diet and naturopathy. Skincare is a strong point, with Alpha Peeling to help diminish age spots, pigmentation marks, fine wrinkles and superficial scarring, plus Affinoderm seaweed treatments to firm, slim and detoxify. If vanity is not your thing, Dancing for Health classes will get your heart beating in cha-cha, rumba, jive and samba rhythms, and could be a short-cut to long-term friends.

The ambience: A wholesome, friendly wellbeing centre.

Regular guests: Over-forties seeking to battle gravity, wrinkles and boredom. Wine fans lost on South Africa's picturesque Garden Route.

Treatment menu: As expected, the Hydro has many water-based facilities, such as saunas, steams and thalassotherapy, but draws on both medical and holistic practices. Manicures and pedicures are available, as well as reiki, shiatsu, reflexology and lymphatic drainage.

House speciality: The 10-day Classical Health regime includes a choice of detox, elimination or vegetarian diet, daily massages, hydrotherapy, supervised exercise, relaxation classes, lectures on nutrition and lifestyle, and a computerized body-composition analysis.

Cuisine: The emphasis is on detoxing diets and natural ingredients. Expect a choice of salads, grilled fish and meat, fruits and cereals.

Ideal for: Mature couples or singles with a zest for life.

What to pack: A beginner's guide to bridge.

Sérénité Wellness Centre

✳

Address: 16 Debaren Close, Constantia,
Cape Town, South Africa
Telephone: +27 21 713 1760
Booking details: info@serenite.co.za
Website: www.serenite.co.za

Sérénité Wellness Centre is situated in Cape Town's lush Constantia Valley, with spectacular views of the southern slopes of Table Mountain. Surrounded by vineyards and beaches, this is the place to kick back, relax and indulge in some 'me, me, me' time, whether you need a short pick-me-up or an intensive rest. It's a five-star, boutique hotel and spa with only 11 bedrooms, so you're not going to have to jostle too much for treatments or your own space.

The ambience: Small and discreet, relaxed and intimate. You can get close to nature without having to compromise on luxury.

Regular guests: Those wanting to experiment with different beauty treatments and try out yoga, tai chi and meditation. You may also see a guest or two wearing big, dark sunglasses at dinner — a dead giveaway of someone recovering from a bit of cosmetic surgery.

Treatment menu: Here, you will find a combination of ancient herbal remedies and the latest high-tech treatments. On one hand, there are pampering face and body treatments using well-known beauty products; on the other, there is pre- and post-operative plastic surgery care under medical supervision, and laser treatments.

House speciality: The Beauty Royal package, which features a medical check-up, nutritional advice and face and body boosters.

Cuisine: Qualified dieticians work closely with the chef to ensure that everything on offer is calorie-controlled, organic and delicious.

Ideal for: Ladies looking to recover (privately) from cosmetic surgery.

What to pack: Practical shoes to take you comfortably around the estate's wooded walkways and up and down the umpteen steps.

Ulpotha Sanctuary

**

Address: Ulpotha Village, Nr. Columbo, Sri Lanka
Booking details: info@ulpotha.com or
Neal's Yard Agency (+44) 0870 444 2702
Website: www.ulpotha.com

In 1994 three friends and some local villagers came up with the idea to transform Ulpotha, with its thousands of years of history, into an organic farming village using traditional practices. The work involved rehabilitating ancient irrigation systems, helping local reforestation and promoting traditional lifestyles in the surrounding communities. Ulpotha's guests are an 'organic' means of generating enough income for the village to support itself.

The Hilton this is not. Each *asana* - palm-thatched platform - sleeps two and has been built using traditional methods and materials (mainly clay, stone, wood and natural fabrics). There is no electricity, no hot water, no room service and you can forget about the mini-bar. Oil lamps, natural springs and Mother Nature will dictate your pace of life. For environmental reasons there is a strict limit on numbers and the duration of time that guests

can stay. There is an annual period in which village hospitality is provided, but the rest of the time Ulpotha is simply a tiny, ancient village. It should also be noted that 'service' is not something to expect; rather, a gracious, instinctive hospitality is evident. Uniquely, you are seen as a guest, not a client, and apart from treating yourself to a locally made sarong, there is no need for money once you are in Ulpotha. Be prepared for a culture shock, though; life in Ulpotha is very different and it might take you few days to adjust.

The ambience: A simple, organic sanctuary rooted in ancient unspoiled nature.

Regular guests: Travelling holistic practitioners, such as British hotelier Anoushka Hempel, and hardcore spiritual tourists.

Treatment menu: Ulpotha's spiritual emphasis attracts many travelling practitioners, with varied massage, healing and holistic experience. In keeping with the communal atmosphere, they are usually happy to practice on you. There are also Ayurvedic massages, yoga, hot-oil treatments and natural-spring steam baths.

House speciality: There isn't a speciality as such, as it depends on who is visiting at the time. The scheduling of treatments is very informal, involving a one-to-one discussion between you and the practitioner to work out a suitable time.

Cuisine: There are no restaurants, no bars, no brasseries and not a tofu bake in sight. Most eating is done in the pavilion of the main house. The villagers' diet is based on a vegetarian tradition, with the staple food being red rice. Meals, cooked in the indigenous style in clay pots over open fires, consist of curries, salads, buffalo-curd dishes and local delicacies using organically grown produce. Vegetables and melons fill the gardens, next to mature banana, papaya, mango and breadfruit trees. There is a Kadé, or teahouse hut, where you can breakfast on *gotukola kandhe*, a nutritious porridge-type drink, or enjoy tea and other (organic) snacks.

Ideal for: Singles and couples over 30 who are looking to alter their outlook on the modern world.

What to pack: A torch (flashlight), batteries, insect repellent and a bath towel (they're not supplied).

Thermes Marins de Carthage at The Residence

** **

Address: Les Côtes de Carthage, Boîte Postale 697,
2070 La Marsa, Tunisia
Telephone: (+216) 71 910 101
Booking details: sales.residence@gnet.tn
Website: www.theresidence-tunis.com

Set on the legendary site of Carthage, about 15 minutes from the airport, The Residence may be a luxury, lavish Tunisian hotel in itself, but the Thermes Marins de Carthage thalassotherapy spa is in a league of its own. The reason it is of such high quality may be because Tunisia is pushing a new kind of wellbeing tourism, so spa benefits and offerings are being taken very seriously.

The spa pumps water direct from the Mediterranean, 1,000 metres (1,100 yards) offshore, into the baths. The water is rich in sodium chloride and magnesium, minerals renowned for aiding relaxation of nerves and muscles. Similar to ancient Roman baths, the spa has majestic columns, patios, fountains, urns and lions' heads. The huge swimming pool is enhanced by waterfalls, massaging swan-neck taps (faucets), massage heads and Jacuzzis, and looks onto gardens and the sea. The 30 intimate and spacious treatment cabins are scattered around the flowered patios; with the fragrance of rose, jasmine and eucalyptus from the nearby wood carried on the fresh breeze, relaxation is even in the air.

There are about 170 rooms in the resort, including nine suites spread out over four levels, most with sea views and private terraces. A phenomenal number of activities are catered for, including watersports, sailing, line-fishing, horse-riding, golf, tennis, cross-country walking, hunting in the north, camel-riding in the Sahara and four-wheel-drive car rallies for the more adventurous. On starry summer nights, the *Khima* (a large Bedouin tent) is erected and the beach is lit by torches and campfire-style barbecues. Brightly coloured pouffes and cushions are arranged on the sand for lounging on. Veiled horsemen, traditional dancers and exotic music create a captivating scene.

The ambience: Even though this tranquil retreat may seem like an oasis of rest and relaxation, behind the scenes an army of experts are working hard on maintaining the feel-good factor.

Regular guests: Spa aficionados, tourists, heads of state, artists and a host of secret celebrities.

Treatment menu: The 20 treatments range from water therapies, through mesotherapy (injections to help shift cellulite) to massages. There are about 40 doctors, hydrotherapists, physiotherapists, physical education teachers and other specialists on site to provide all-encompassing, personally tailored consultations.

House speciality: Restoring Beauty Head to Toe is a good all-rounder. It combines thalassotherapy with a body scrub, lymphatic drainage, a facial, and manicure or pedicure.

Cuisine: The food here is outstanding. L'Olivier is a Mediterranean restaurant with a panoramic view from the terrace, while Li Bai serves authentic Chinese cuisine. There's also Café Flora, the spa restaurant; like L'Olivier and the poolside café, it prides itself on a healthy but nutritious 'bio-privilege' menu, where ingredients are cultivated with a minimum of chemical additives. The hotel's bakers use flours from freshly milled grains and combine traditional breadmaking techniques with natural yeast methods.

Ideal for: Those looking for a serious, luxurious getaway combined with authentic Tunisian culture and food.

What to pack: A list of your burning questions concerning health and beauty issues; the experts are here, so take advantage of them.

Glossary

ALGOTHERAPY
Algae and marine products like seaweed are applied to the body to detoxify, rebalance and relax.

AROMATHERAPY
An ancient art using essential oils from plants, leaves, bark, roots, seeds, resins and flowers. Used in pressure point massage, hydrotherapy and face and body treatments. Certain oils have therapeutic effects and work by being absorbed through the skin and inhalation, which in turn relaxes body and mind.

AYURVEDA
An ancient Indian medical science, which combines philosophy and folk medicine and uses herbs, aromatherapy, nutrition, massage and meditation to balance mind and body.

BALNEOTHERAPY
Water-based treatments using mineral hot springs or seawater to alleviate stresses and strains within the body. The healing power of water has been used for centuries to help improve circulation, boost the immune system and reduce stress.

BOREH
An age-old Indonesian tradition, originally used by rice farmers to ease aches and pains. After a Balinese massage, the patient is covered in a spicy-smelling, warm paste made from hand-ground ginger, turmeric and nutmeg.

CALDARIUM
A steam room that is infused with aromatic herbs.

COLD PLUNGE
A cold-water pool or spring usually used for plunging into following a heat treatment, such as a sauna, to rapidly cool the body and stimulate circulation.

COLONIC IRRIGATION
Intense water cleansing of the colon using an enema to detoxify and prevent the recycling of toxins into the bloodstream.

CRANIOSACRAL THERAPY
A treatment using gentle massage, pressure and holding techniques that centres on the head and neck, releasing tension and restoring equilibrium.

CRENOTHERAPY
Any treatment that combines the therapeutic use of mineral water, mud and steam.

CRYSTAL HEALING
Believed to promote physical and spiritual healing, crystals or gemstones are placed or worn on various parts of the body to draw out imbalanced energy.

DEAD SEA MUD THERAPY
Mineral rich mud from the Dead Sea is applied to the face and body to detoxify, cleanse pores, relax tight muscles and ease arthritic and rheumatic pain.

DEEP TISSUE MASSAGE
A deep muscle massage which remobilizes and realigns the body using a variety of occasionally painful massage techniques. This technique is great for relieving muscle tension and for treating sports injuries.

Glossary

DOSHAS
Ayurvedic practitioners believe that we have three governing forces called doshas working inside us, one or two of which are more dominant. These are called *vata* (air) *pitta* (fire) and *kapha* (earth), and must be kept in balance in order to maintain maximum health and wellbeing.

DRY FLOTATION BED
You are covered in a mud or an algae wrap then cocooned in a waterproof sheet and lowered via a sling into warm water stored within the customized bed.

DUO MASSAGE
Synchronized massage carried out by two therapists. This deeply relaxing treatment is also known as Four Hands Massage.

ENDERMOLOGIE
A French massage therapy that reduces the appearance of cellulite using a mechanical vacuum and rolling machine.

FLOTATION TANK
Clients float in a darkened tank, roughly the size of a double bed, filled with about 30 cm (1 foot) of mineral-enriched water and enough salt to keep you afloat and weightless. Often compared to the sensation of being in the womb, it induces deep relaxation.

HAMMAM
A Turkish or Middle Eastern communal bath house that means 'spreader of warmth' in Arabic. A hammam falls under 'sweat bathing' and is basically a type of steam room.

HERBAL WRAP
A detoxifying, softening and relaxing body treatment which involves being wrapped in herb-soaked hot linen sheets and then covered in blankets. A cool compress is usually applied to the forehead.

HOT SPRING
A natural, usually volcanic, spring of hot mineral water.

HYDROMASSAGE
An underwater massage that takes place in a deep bath tub using high-pressure jets and hand-held hoses. Helps to stimulate the blood and lymphatic system.

HYDROTHERAPY
A general term for the therapeutic use of water for healing and relaxation. Also known as water therapy, it includes underwater jet massage, jet sprays, showers and mineral baths.

KINESIOLOGY
A system of diagnosing weaknesses in the muscles caused by food allergies or vitamin and mineral deficiencies.

KNEIPP BATHS
Harnesses the healing power of herbal or mineral baths of varying temperatures. This treatment is combined with a diet and exercise plan as devised by Bavarian priest and hydrotherapist Father Sebastian Kneipp.

LACONIUM
A dry heat treatment room for resting and relaxing.

Glossary

LASTONE THERAPY
A massage technique using hot and cold stones on heavily oiled skin. Relaxes and recharges.

LOMI LOMI
Deep Hawaiian massage that uses rhythmical rocking and long stroking techniques.

LYMPHATIC DRAINAGE MASSAGE
A non-oily massage using a gentle pumping technique to reduce pockets of water retention. Lymph drainage can also be achieved through manual, hydro- or aromatherapy massage.

MANDI LULUR
Also known as Javanese Lulur, this time-honoured skin softener was originally a Royal bridal treatment used to prepare women for their wedding day (and night). A mask of flowers, herbs and spices is applied to the body, allowed to dry, and then buffed and rinsed off with yogurt. Usually applied after a massage and before soaking in a rose petal and jasmine bath.

OZONIZED BATHS
A tub of thermal water or seawater with underwater jets creating ozonized bubbles. Used for relaxation and to help stimulate circulation.

PHYTOTHERAPY
Therapeutic treatments using extracts from plants, herbs, aromatic essential oils and seaweed. Can be applied via massage, wraps, inhalation, steam therapies and herbal teas.

PILATES
A specialized exercise routine that combines stretching and strengthening the body with a series of synchronized breathing techniques.

RASUL BATH
A cleansing ceremony which takes place in a specially designed steam chamber. Four different types of mud are self-applied to the face, chest, back and thighs, and this is slowly absorbed as the heat increases and the body perspires. A tropical rain shower of warm droplets then washes the mud away.

REBIRTHING
A combination of meditation and Yogic breathing techniques that helps to clear the mind and promote total relaxation.

REFLEXOLOGY
An ancient Egyptian, Chinese and Indian technique designed to restore the natural energy flow around the body using finger-point pressure on the reflex zones on the soles of the feet (and sometimes the hands).

REIKI
A spiritually oriented, clothed treatment, which involves an 'attuned' therapist who gently lays her hands on – or hovers them over – specific points of the body to channel energy. Rebalances and restores mind, body and spirit and induces a deep sense of relaxation and nurturing. No oils or massage involved. Wear loose clothes.